ING ROOM

THE VINCE

TRIUMPH ENGINEERING CO. LTD.
COVENTRY.

T.D.C.-D.S.

T.D.C.-T.S.

Snap-on

LEANINGS

THE BEST OF **PETER EGAN** FROM ***CYCLE WORLD***® MAGAZINE

LEANINGS

THE BEST OF **PETER EGAN** FROM ***CYCLE WORLD*®** MAGAZINE

PETER EGAN

MOTORBOOKS

First published in 2002 by Motorbooks, an imprint of MBI Publishing Company, Galtier Plaza, Suite 200, 380 Jackson Street, St. Paul, MN 55101-3885 USA

Motorbooks titles are also available at discounts in bulk quantity for industrial or sales-promotional use. For details write to Special Sales Manager at MBI Publishing Company, Galtier Plaza, Suite 200, 380 Jackson Street, St. Paul, MN 55101-3885 USA

ISBN: 0-7603-1158-7

On the front cover: A collection of Peter Egan's favorite things, photographed in the den of his Wisconsin home. *Nick Cedar*

Endpapers: More Eganibilia. *Nick Cedar*

Eganibilia photography: *Nick Cedar*

Edited by Lee Klancher
Layout by Rebecca Pagel

Printed in China

DEDICATION

For my wife Barbara, who worked hard so I could type, and who has cheerfully ridden with me all over the world in wind, rain, sleet, and sunshine; for my friend and mentor, Allan Girdler, who changed my life by hiring me; and for David Edwards, who keeps it changing with new ideas and new roads to be ridden.

CONTENTS

SECTION I
THE FEATURES

SECTION II
THE COLUMNS

Foreword
THE NATURAL

by Allan Girdler

Begin with the fact that the reading public—no, make that the entire world—is in my debt. Too boldly put?

OK, begin again with how the world works:

Once upon a time, back in the previous century when people behaved just as they do now, I wrote the exact letter I needed to write, a letter that brought me to the attention of a man who needed help editing a magazine.

It came to pass, as they say in fables, that I became the editor of the magazine and got the credentials for the job, leading in turn to being hired at *Cycle World*, and then being dropped into that editorial chair.

At that point, quoting myself here, I had learned How To Do It. I knew that when you're a writer, you envy talent.

But when you're an editor, you hire it.

There I was at my desk, when in waltzed the managing editor with the day's submissions.

Oh yeah, that's jargon and inside stuff, but what it means is, editors get piles of articles and stories every day. Most of the stuff, to be charitable, doesn't, as the form rejection letters say, "meet our present needs."

Had I been asked to give an example of what doesn't work, I might have said, "Oh, a story about how a motorcycle trip ended in disaster." I mean, who needs an unhappy ending? And who cares what other kids did on their summer vacation?

But because I needed help, I made it a policy not to reject anything out of hand. I'd learned the hard way that the average editor believes he's earned the job, knows all the good people, and doesn't bother with anyone he doesn't already know.

So every morning I got a pile of stuff and checked it out.

In the morning's pile was an article from a sports car mechanic in the unlikely town of Madison, Wisconsin. He'd written an account of how he and his wife set out on their Norton and came home, so to speak, on their shields.

It was probably the best story I had read that year, rules or no.

I'll pause here, mostly because the actual story is part of this anthology, so you don't need me to tell you what's in it.

And you'll quickly understand why I read the piece and told the managing editor we *had* to buy it, and then wrote a note to the author, saying we'd buy the piece *and* I'd like to see anything and everything else he'd written.

And the rest, as we say when we've forgotten the details, is history.

Concluding my brag, and adding details Peter likely is too modest to mention, is that *Cycle World* wasn't the first publication he'd submitted stories to.

It was the first magazine that bought one.

Meaning, surely, I was the first editor who had bothered to read the submission, which returns us to my original point, that the average editor is too busy with meetings and lunches and swanking around to do the job right. That's why *Cycle World* is the biggest and best and the magazines that didn't read Peter Egan's stuff are now in history's dumpster. That's enough brag.

What I had had been lucky enough to find was, as they say in baseball and the movies, a Natural.

First off, Peter Egan has uncommon powers of observation. He's always aware of what's going on. Most of us pay less attention, so when he comments on what he's seen, we say "Oh, Yeah," and suddenly we're sharing the observations and the understanding.

Next, Peter doesn't have many themes, so to speak. He speaks of us, that is, he is one of those who buys more motorcycles than he needs and restores cars that might have been better off left in the wood lot. Judgement is being passed, all right, but it's judgement on us all, so there's never a hint of a put-down.

(Mark Twain took the same approach, by the way, and it didn't hurt him, either.)

But Peter Egan's main strength (and here I compare him with Jane Austen) is his voice.

His tone carries his creative and unique flavor. His turns of phrase form his observations and his affection for his subjects, unlike anything the rest of us could come up with even when we were there.

I've mentioned my good deed.

Wanna know my punishment?

Peter and I were at the racetrack one day, testing or practicing I forget which, and I made some comments to a spectator and dismissed the incident.

Peter didn't. He listened without saying much, but then he went back to his desk and wrote a column about my comments and what they meant to him.

Next thing I knew, I was getting letters and calls from people who wanted to thank me. Seems I'd told them what they needed to know, and I had improved their lives.

It was the best column I never wrote.

And now, it's time for the main event.

Section I
THE FEATURES

December 1977

DATELINE MISSOULA

When Cycle World *accepted this story, I had been trying for about 10 years to get something—anything—published, supporting myself as a rain gutter installer and British car mechanic while I wrote short stories, articles, and books that all came back rejected. My wife, Barbara, handed me the acceptance letter after work on a Friday evening, just as we were sitting down to a Mexican dinner with some friends. Many margaritas were drunk that night.*

This story is written exactly as it happened, with one point of obfuscation: the motorcycle we rode was not a 13-year-old British Twin, but was actually a 1975 Norton 850 Interstate, which I'd bought brand-new. The British motorcycle industry was teetering on the edge of extinction in the late 1970s, and I didn't want to provide another nail for the coffin by suggesting that a brand-new Norton would swallow a valve with only 3,000 miles on the odometer, which it did.

"I guess it's better to bend a valve in Missoula than to lose your mind in Bozeman," my wife said, patting my hand as if to console me. I winced and wondered if Phaedrus ever took the bus.

Our bus was rolling across the South Dakota night, late enough for all the reading lights to be out. Just across the aisle sat a nun beside a shrunken old man who reeked of some refreshment from a brown paper bag. The nun slept the sleep of the just—nearly upright, a ghost of a smile on her ivory face—while her companion snored in a kind of death rattle and was gradually toppling into the aisle. I feared that one of those wide ladies in polka dots would barge past on her way to the privy and break the poor fellow's neck.

We were riding back to Madison, Wisconsin, via Greyhound, returning to a city full of prophets honored in their own time. Everyone had told me not to ride my old British Twin to Seattle. Howard was the first.

An old friend and first-generation Honda mechanic, Howard had grown up among Super Hawks, Benlys, and Dreams, having little patience with things that leaked oil, blacked out, or had to be kicked. With just the lightest touch of derision, he had named my venerable motorcycle "the Manxton Contaminator Twin."

I told him, "Next month Barb and I are riding the bike out to Seattle." He looked at me exactly as my mother had when I told her I'd quit college to join the Army: wearily, quietly incredulous.

"Take a car," he said.

"What?"

"Take a car. Turn on the radio. Chew gum. Put one foot on the dash. You can steer with one finger and look around at the scenery. Write postcards while you drive. Read the *Wall Street Journal*, roll your windows up or roll them down—anything. But don't take your motorcycle."

"Why not?"

"Because on that bike, you can't get there from here."

Howard had a racer's bias against touring. He campaigned, sometimes successfully, a highly tuned Honda 350 Four against droves of "off-brand ring-dings" on Midwest road circuits. He thought touring a tedious penance for some unspecified sin committed in an earlier life. He also feared and distrusted venerable British Twins.

Howard's last word of advice was that I send a Honda Gold Wing to the post office in Council Bluffs, Iowa, and then pray that I made it that far, so I could change horses en route. No thanks, I said. I'd ridden a Gold Wing. Too easy. Like taking a tram up the Eiger, instead of climbing the face.

Anybody could get to Seattle on a Gold Wing. Farrah, for-God's-sake, Fawcett-Majors could get there on a Gold Wing. It was adventure I was after, not trip insurance.

The next day, I visited my friendly Suzuki-BMW dealer, who had the last shop in town with antique British parts moldering on its back shelves. On the side of the building the names of three extinct motorcycles had all but faded away, like those Mail Pouch Tobacco signs on old barns. It was a shop with a glorious past.

Yes, incredibly, they had both the throttle and clutch cables I wanted as spares. Jeff, the head BMW/ex-British Twin mechanic, stepped outside to look at my bike, wiping his hands on a rag. I told him about my trip and asked if there was anything special I should do, outside of regular maintenance, to prepare the bike for a 4,000-mile trip.

"If I were you," Jeff said, "I'd change my oil, adjust my chain, set the valves, and then, just before I left, I'd trade it in on a BMW."

Skeptics, heretics, and hooters were everywhere, like some chorus in a Greek tragedy, portending ill for their flawed and heedless hero. I finally quit telling people about the trip and made plans with my wife in the privacy of our own living room.

We would travel light and simply. No fairings, trailers, or saddlebags on the old bike. A strong luggage rack on the back, to hold an army duffel bagful of stuff, and a tank bag to hold the rest. For shelter from the storm we had Big Pink, a formerly red two-child Sears pup tent left over from my childhood (the replacement aluminum poles were too short, causing the tent, when erected, to look like a failed soufflé), and a double sleeping bag whose lining was printed with branding irons and cowboys. My wife had a modern fully enclosed helmet, while I clung to my cork-lined Everoak Clubman—a piece of Geoff Duke–era head gear that resembled a polo helmet—and my split-lens goggles. There was some rain gear, minimum clothes, and a carefully chosen tool kit. No compass, snakebite kit, or spare shoe laces. Traveling light on a motorcycle demands ruthless restraint, a fine sense of asceticism, and a big wad of colorful plastic credit cards. We left before sunup on a Saturday morning.

Two hours of ghostly pre-dawn gloom swirled past, and then at 7 A.M. the Twin delivered us to the crest of the palisades above the Mississippi River Valley. The air was cool, but the first rays of the sun warmed our backs and began to burn away the mist. Only the towers of the bridges below rose out of the fog. The hills on the opposite bank were golden green in the morning sun. "Not bad!" I shouted over my shoulder.

"What?" my wife replied. We were to have many such conversations in the miles ahead.

An hour later we were having breakfast in one of the famous "EAT" chains of fine restaurants on the edge of an Iowa farm town that was just opening for the morning, sipping coffee with the local merchants. They looked at us, and then at our motorcycle out in front of the café. Since we weren't dressed as pirates and were keeping a low profile, there was no hostility, just mild interest. It was OK. Talking and clatter resumed.

Iowa's rolling eastern hills stopped rolling, the trees dried up, and corn country arrived. The roads ran as straight as the crop rows, and the midsummer corn held down a hot blanket of humid air that defied even a 55 mile-per-hour chill factor. No breeze blew; the heat was stifling. Corn plants, I noted, breathe and perspire just as we do. Maybe more.

The Contaminator Twin loved it. The engine had not missed a beat crossing one-and-one-half states—nearly the length of, say, England. Gas station checks revealed no loose bolts or unnatural oil loss; the headlight still burned. I began to think that a little Loctite and silicone sealer might have changed the fate of British motorcycling.

As Iowa is firmly Middle West, South Dakota, for me, is the beginning of the West. The True West, of course, begins at the Missouri River Valley, which comes upon you as a startling strip of bluish-green washes and shorn, rounded hills. The road is wonderful, a quintessential cyclist's road of smooth, sweeping curves through a fantasy landscape of dwarfed trees on billiard-cloth hillsides—a land that might have nurtured tiny horses and reptilian birds. Like the Badlands, it has that quiet, dawn-of-time feel. "Lovely," I said to myself, making an expansive sweep of my arm over the view. My wife repeated the motion, knowing what I meant. One of the 10 great gestures of motorcycle wind language, that sweep of the arm.

By evening we were in Winner, South Dakota, camped just outside of town. After a truck stop dinner, we rode into town to see what there was to see. There are two theaters in Winner—the Pix and the Ritz, and they face each other on the main street. The Pix was closed, and the Ritz was showing "Flesh Gordon," the Buster Crabbe-goes-hedonist remake. The popcorn stand was closed, the glass-covered poster case was empty, and nine people sat through the film. We emerged, not feeling terribly uplifted, onto a main street lined with pickup trucks and flashing bar signs. There was not a soul on the sidewalks. A wind had come up, and a lot of dust was blowing through the streets. "When I was a kid," Barb said as we climbed on the bike, "going to the movies was—different . . ." We rode back to the campground and a stormy night in Big Pink, The Two-Child Tent, which affords about as much rain protection as a tree with quite a few leaves. In the morning we were awakened by a rooster that actually said, "Cock-a-doodle-do," as if reading the word.

My dislike of Interstates and love of secondary roads found us the following day on a clay and gravel goat path south of the Badlands. The road wound through some butte and gully country with dozens of pastel shades of rock and dust muting the strong sunlight. The dust, in fact, was worrisome. We were trailing a wide plume of the stuff, and I wondered what deleterious effects it was having on Manxton chain, bearings, and cylinder walls. I hoped the air filters were keeping the inside of the engine cleaner than the outside. The Twin was never intended for Baja. After a few hours, I began to feel like a courier in the Afrika Korps, and decided it would be best to avoid dotted-line roads and stick to the red ones in the future.

We rose over a ridge, where the road dropped straight across a wide sunken plain. Far on the horizon we saw a second cloud of dust, pushing a small dot along the road. Another motorcycle. I decided to pursue. The other bike was wasting no time, and it took us an hour to reel him in. Though the Contaminator is capable of quite respectable speeds, I was loath to push its 13-year-old engine to its limits for any distance, being no stranger to the Last Straw Theory of engine failure.

The other motorcycle stopped with us at a highway intersection. The bike was a Honda 550 carrying Tom, a friendly, slightly overheated-looking 18-year-old who happened to be from our home state. He looked at the Contaminator Twin with amazement. His 550 was clean and dry, while our Twin was covered with a thick layer of chalky dust that clung to all the oil that had sweated through the bike's mated surfaces. It looked like the ghost motorcycle of the Plains. "You guys are a long way from home with that thing," he said. I didn't much care for the awe in his voice. It made me nervous.

We rode and camped with Tom for the next two days. He had left Wisconsin with $65, two weeks of vacation, and absolutely no plans except to go "out West." It was nice to ride with another bike, and the two machines made an interesting pair. The 550 whirred along silken and revvy, while the Twin sort of pulsed, and at a much lower note. The Twin had gearing left over from the age of 70 mile-per-hour freeways, and turned less than 4,000 rpm at that speed (in theory, of course), producing all kinds of torque right down to the 2,000 rpm shudder barrier. Critics of British Twins have complained much about their vibration, yet that problem has never bothered me since the vibration is more of a throbbing phenomenon than the sort of hectic, buzzing condition that drives feet off footpegs and hands from handlebars. With tall gearing, it is a one-pulse-every-telephone-pole vibration that merely assures the rider he is on a motorcycle and that his engine is still running.

On what was to be, it turned out, the last night of our cycle trip, we were turned back from Yellowstone Park by a "Yellowstone Full" sign on the entrance gate (now that folks can drive their houses out West, camping is more popular than ever), so we back-tracked to a very pleasant campground in the Shoshone National Forest. Just before sundown, a group of chopper aficionados with mamas rode into camp, set up tents, then raced off to nearby Pahaska Teepee Lodge Bar. They returned at closing time, cycles blazing. After riding around their own tents until a couple of their bikes tipped over, they settled down to about 15 minutes of shouting "Yahoo!" and "Krrriii!" and punching each other in the shoulder, before building a five billion BTU log and tree-stump fire. Someone got out a guitar and they all sang "Dead Skunk in the Middle of the Road" until passing out at 3 A.M.

"That's pretty good," Barb said at one point during the party, "listen to them sing. They all know the words. When was the last time you heard 20 people who all knew the words to the same song, singing together like that?"

"Church?" I suggested "Or maybe the Army . . ."

She listened for a while, then shook her head. "No, that's not the same."

The Twin started hard (i.e., not at all) in the morning. The weather was cool, and the 50-weight oil about as viscous as three quarts of Smuckers topping. Each time I jumped on the kick starter, the engine went "tufff" and moved through half a stroke. Our friend Tom turned on his gas, set the choke, hit the starter button, and then walked away to brush his teeth while the Honda quietly purred and warmed itself up. Something was not right with the Contaminator. Usually two kicks, no matter how slow, were enough to make it fire. That morning, we finally pushed it downhill while I popped the clutch. It started reluctantly and ran less smoothly.

"Bad gas," I said. "It's that dishwater they're selling as premium now."

Tom said goodbye and turned south toward the Tetons, while we pushed north into Montana. If ever a license plate blurb carried a grain of truth, it is Montana's "Big Sky Country." There is no other place in the world where you are eternally surrounded by mountains that are forever 50 miles away. We rode up the Madison River Valley into the first rainstorm of the trip, invincible in our rubber rain suits. By noon, a cool wind dried the pavement and we were on the dreaded Interstate—our only choice—near Butte, headed for a night with some friends in Moscow, Idaho. After 1,400 miles and five days on the road, the Manxton Contaminator Twin still lived, running better than it had any right to. I began to suspect that we would not only reach Seattle, but possibly even make it home again. I felt guilty, however, pushing this old sporting machine over endless miles of Interstate, even for one afternoon. It was like some interminable torture test, with the engine hovering at one constant, dull, unvarying pitch. Finally, the Twin decided it had endured enough.

About 25 miles from Missoula, the engine gave out a raucous mechanical clatter and stopped running on one cylinder. We pulled over, removed the rocker covers, and found three hundred thousandths of rocker clearance on the right-hand exhaust valve. It was not returning all the way. Bent, as it were. The right cylinder had just enough compression to blow one very faint smoke ring. I adjusted the tappet to cut down some of the clatter and tried to restart the bike. Oddly enough, it started and ran. We were on our way, albeit not too swiftly or silently. For 25 miles, the (now) Contaminator Single pulled us across the country, up- and downhill, at 45 miles per hour.

I listened to the engine for sounds of further disaster, waiting for the worst. The bike kept on, lugging its 300 pound burden of passengers and gear on one tired cylinder. My emotions vacillated wildly; I couldn't decide whether to heap abuse or praise on the machine. But it was a painful ride for us, like forcing a crippled horse to run. We were exhausted from tension by the time we reached the first motel Missoula had.

Some quick telephones calls confirmed the worst. No shop in town had parts for, or could fix, the old Manxton. No one knew where to get parts, or anyone who even had such a bike. Someone at a Yamaha shop said one guy in town might be able to fix it if he had the parts, which he didn't, but he was on vacation.

The next morning, on Missoula's Annual Hottest Day of the Year, we pushed the Twin two miles across town to a Bekins freight office. The proud Manxton, which had conquered the Bighorns with impunity, now had me trembling at the sight of Missoula's manhole covers. As we pushed, swarms of children on banana-seat bicycles encircled us and asked clever questions or made witty remarks. Why, I asked myself, aren't these children working in coal mines or textile mills where they belong? By the time we finished pushing I'd made a mental note to refrain from having any children, and had, at the same time, found new respect for the latent energy in a cup of gasoline. We filled out all the forms and mailed the bike home.

The trip to Moscow, Idaho, and then to Seattle, was made by bus and train. We took the Greyhound home.

Riding in the bus, I thought about the trip and about the motorcycle. When the Twin arrived home, I would fix the valve, clean the engine, polish the chrome, and keep the bike for special occasions like Sunday rides, the way one uses an MG TC or a Piper Cub. It deserves care, rest, and respect, as do all things that carry their age with grace. I had, unfairly, asked too much of the motorcycle. My fault.

Everyone had warned me what might, or surely would, happen. My own instincts had warned me. I knew the trip to be an undertaking whose outcome was uncertain. There was plenty of good advice to that effect. On any of a dozen other motorcycles our finishing the trip would have been a foregone conclusion. Maybe, in the end, that was why we took a 13-year-old British Twin. It's not so terrible, just two weeks out of the year, to not know what's going to happen next.

As the South Dakota night slipped by, I looked out the bus window and fell to aimless reverie. Could a Honda 50, I found myself wondering, make it all the way from Madison to Mexico City . . .

March 1978

BECAUSE IT'S SMALL

With its Faithful 10-Speed Companion, Stella, a 50cc Step-Through Honda Tackles Pike's Peak (Well, No, Not *That* Pike's Peak)

Re-reading this story today, I am still amazed at the phenomenal mileage we recorded with the little Honda 50. When people tell me we need more fuel-efficient personal transportation, I often say, "Honda's already done it, 40 years ago." This assumes, of course, that people want to cruise at 30 miles per hour...

After a decade in California, Barb and I moved back to Wisconsin. We now live in the country, only a few miles from the route John Oakey and I took in this story, so these roads have become a regular part of my Sunday morning rides. I often pass the places we stopped to rest or camp and reflect fondly on the trip, and on John's cheerful endurance. He still lives in Madison, riding his bike to work.

Like so many good things, the trip began over drinks in an air-conditioned bar. My friend John was drinking unusually large amounts of Tequila Sunrise, not only because it "doesn't taste like booze," but because his Madison City League slow-pitch softball team, the Stupor Starz, had just taken a dreadful 28–3 drubbing from the West Side Opthamology Assistants. I was drinking along in sympathy.

"I've decided to take a motorcycle trip," I said, after a decent change-of-subject silence.

"Another one?"

"This is different. I'm taking my Honda 50."

John eyed me warily. "You serious?"

"Sure, why not? I've been riding the 50 to work all summer and it runs perfectly. Now I have a hankering to hit the open road. It would be sort of a low-key 35 mile-per-hour odyssey. Something to soothe the mind, instead of another mad dash across the continent. All I lack is a destination.

It's not enough merely to ride, I need a goal, a Mecca, a terminus worthy of the inherent rigors . . ."

John furrowed his brows and concentrated on the problem as best he could. I sat watching an idle Pong game construct mindless labyrinthine patterns on a gray TV screen, apparently entertaining itself. I loved my Honda 50. It was a 1964 step-through, C100, two-tone blue, with 6,000 miles on the odometer. I bought it from a doctor who was cleaning his garage and wasn't sure if anyone would want the little thing, but took a chance on throwing an ad in the paper. His doubts were understandable. Who, after all, would want a used $75 machine that takes almost no maintenance, is reliable as a stone (though slightly faster), and takes the owner to work and back all week for 37¢? The day I drove out to look at the machine it was sitting in the doctor's driveway, and even as I drove up I could see that the bike was in mint condition. It nearly brought tears to my eyes. My Volkswagen was still dieseling as I wrote out the check.

A year later, the 50 still ran flawlessly, though I sensed it needed a good road run; something to blow out the cobwebs and decarbonize the head. In short, the bike needed a good tour. I knew the 50 could go the distance. After all, my old college roommate had a friend who heard about a guy whose brother rode a step-through from Wisconsin to Los Angeles and back . . . twice. But L.A. was a little more distance than I could handle in the few days of vacation I had available.

"I've got it," John said suddenly, halting his glass in mid-arc. "Pike's Peak!"

I let out a low whistle. "Boy, I don't know. Colorado and back is a long way to go in less than a week."

"Not Pike's Peak, Colorado, dummy. Pike's Peak, IOWA!"

"Never heard of it."

"It's a state park, just across the border, about 150 miles from here. I camped there once with my girlfriend on a geology field trip. Fine place. Excellent." He took a sip of his Sunrise. "Best place I ever camped. Lord, it was great . . ."

I entertained the notion for a few moments. The more I thought about it, the better I liked it. It wasn't terribly far. The country between Madison and the Iowa border is green and hilly, full of curving secondary roads. And as destinations went, the place had a nice ring to it. I grinned at John. "Sort of a 50cc Pike's Peak, right?"

"Exactly."

Later that evening, John confessed to a nostalgic attachment to the peak, and asked if he could come along with me on his bicycle. Sure, I said. What the hell. John is an accomplished bicycle racer and has arms and legs that look like those bundles of steel cable that support the Golden Gate Bridge—certainly a match for the little Honda and its film-canister piston. It might be fun, a bicycle and a 50, though I wondered if John would have to wait for me at the bottoms of hills. Or at the tops.

That very week, I prepared the Honda for touring. Cycle shops, I discovered, don't carry a lot of Honda 50 accessories any more. The beardless young salesman blinked and looked at me oddly when I asked about a luggage rack for a 50. I might as well have asked if he knew any Ray Charles tunes. Honda can still find you any part for the bike in just a few days, he said, through their computerized central supply system, but the aftermarket goodies have all but dried up. Unavailability being the mother of invention, I managed to adapt an old Bridgestone 50 rack I've been hoarding in a box of keepsakes these many years. With a few tweaks and bends, I made it fit.

A trip to the Army Surplus store yielded a matched combo of touring luggage—all olive drab. I found a pair of genuine U.S. Cavalry saddlebags (circa Pancho Villa) with the legend "1909, Cambridge Armory" stamped on the backs, and a small rucksack for camera equipment, which I planned to hang over the handlebars. In addition, I had an old Army duffel bag I'd used on other trips. Strapped to the bike, it all fit together perfectly, giving the 50 the vague aura of a frontier supply mule, clashing a bit oddly with that mid-Sixties Petula Clark perkiness the Honda exudes so well.

For advice on mechanical preparation, I contacted my old friend Howard, the aging Honda mechanic. "What should I do to get this thing ready for a 300-mile tour?" I asked.

"Nothing," he said, savoring the word. "Well, almost nothing. Just make sure the oil is clean and your valves are adjusted. You can check your points and the plug if you want to, but there won't be anything wrong with them. Oil the chain and check the tire pressure. That's it. You won't have any problems. I know a guy who rode his 50 to the coast and back, twice. After the second trip he lapped his valves, just out of guilt, but the bike was running fine."

I nodded and wondered if this was the same guy I'd heard about.

I changed my oil—"Above 15 deg. C. (60 deg. F.) SAE #30," as it said on the crankcase—and oiled and adjusted my drive chain. My Honda 50 owner's manual said to adjust the valves to .002 for normal use and .004 "heard running" (Japanese translations into English have come a long way since 1964). I checked the plugs, points, and timing and Howard was right; they were fine. The tires got 31 and 28 lb., respectively, for heavy load conditions.

The load was quite heavy. John declined to compromise the purity of his Stella/Campagnolo racing bicycle by having it laden with earthly goods, so the Honda took it all: sleeping bags, clothes, tools, rain gear, cameras, pharmaceuticals, and Big Pink, my touring tent (originally red) since childhood, a piece of equipment so lacking in both size and water repellency that it builds incredible character on every trip. The whole load weighed 65 pounds. That, added to my 175, I surmised, would keep those 50 ccs hopping during the final assault on Pike's Peak. In all fairness, John did carry the maps, his warm-up jacket, and one wrench, in a small handlebar pack. Big deal.

Labor Day weekend was chosen for the trip, more for its length than out of love for the other five billion people who would be on the road for the holiday. We both managed to wriggle out of work on Friday, giving us a four-day weekend.

Friday morning was dark and threatening rain as we escaped the city through Madison's beautiful Arboretum Drive. With all of our planning, John and I had not once tried riding the bicycle and the Honda side by side to see how compatibly they would tour. Many bets had been made regarding the ability of the Honda to speed up- and downhill and of the bicycle to hold its pace on the level. ("Level," John claims, "is a mythical state. It does not exist.") It all worked out quite well. On moderate terrain John could cruise at about 22 miles per hour, which put the Honda just above lugging speed in top gear. On mild hills, second gear for the Honda was matched by comfortable work for the bicycle, and killer hills demanded low gear from both, leaving engine and rider sucking wind.

Only two flaws reared their ugly heads. The main one was John's choice of gears. He'd elected to use his road racing rear cluster, rather than his lower-range touring set. These gears were fine in the morning, but by afternoon his legs were aching for sprockets with more teeth; revs, rather than raw torque, were needed. The only other problem, and a very small one, was the Honda's gaping hole between first and second gears, complicated by a neutral slot in the middle. The bike almost rolled backward when downshifting on steep hills, and all but stopped rolling forward on upshifts. The engine had to be wound into a screaming frenzy in first, followed by two clubby upshifts to reach second, which, by then, would not pull the bike. So back into first. And so on. The only answer, I discovered, was to be At One with very, very, slow speeds; to enjoy the birds and the trees and the sky as the Honda churned along in first gear, a tiny mechanical Juggernaut devouring hills as inexorably and relentlessly as a glacier.

Our route was lifted straight off the dotted red lines of a bicycle touring map of southwestern Wisconsin, and the roads were well chosen. Even on Labor Day, traffic was virtually non-existent except when we chanced into larger towns or when one of our country roads crossed a major highway. At the main artery crossroads, we were treated to a vision of vacationing Americans acting out some sort of lemming nightmare, crawling along bumper-to-bumper with their boats and motor homes and trailers. And yes, there were even some motorcycles in there, poor devils, all going . . . somewhere. But minutes later we would be back on the country roads with curves and fields, farms and old stone houses. No cars.

A few hours into the trip we rolled into a small glen that sheltered a cluster of buildings called Postville; a general store with gas pumps, a real blacksmith shop across the street, five houses, and a mobile home. On the corner, right in front of the blacksmith shop, stood an old Triumph Bonneville. The bike was that rarest of aged Bonnies, the complete, original, unchopped, and fairly clean variety (these defenseless motorcycles seem to attract more than their share of vandal-owners). It was parked at the corner of the lot in such a way as to suggest it might be for sale. I looked for a fallen sign, but found none. The blacksmith shop was closed. The general store was closed. The gas pumps were locked. Not one thing moved in the village. I knocked at all five houses and the mobile home to ask about the bike, but no one answered. Wind chimes on someone's porch made brittle, random music in the light breeze. It was all quite eerie, and I found myself humming the theme from "On the Beach" and scanning the village for Rod Serling. I took a last, longing look at the beautiful, restorable old Bonneville. Restoring vehicles is a disease with me, and this one cried to be taken home and made to run again (the plug wires were missing). Then we got on our bikes and left.

By evening we were in Mineral Point, an old Cornish lead-mining town with many of its old stone miners' cottages restored to landmark condition. John and I dined at the Red Rooster Café on Cornish Pastys (sic), a delicious sort of meat and vegetable pie. After dinner, we decided to get our nightmares over early and see *Exorcist II* at the local theater. I can't resist movies in small-town theaters when I'm touring, and I'll go to see anything the industry can throw at me—as John discovered to his dismay. We came out onto a late-night square full of prowling muscle cars and chubby girls who shouted things at them from the street corners. We rode just out of town to our campground-by-the-highway, where we were lulled to sleep by the music of many semis upshifting their way past our tent and off into the night.

I awoke before John in the morning and crawled out of the tent to find that the last two feet of his sleeping bag were sticking out of Big Pink like a blue tongue (John is 6'4" and the tent is 4'x4'), and that a brief night shower had soaked the end of his bag. Not only that, a huge orange cat had nested in a pocket of sodden goose down between his feet. Nothing disturbs the sleep of the touring bicyclist. On our trip John slept so hard that he actually frowned from the effort.

My first gas stop, on the second morning, revealed that the Honda had guzzled no less than half a gallon during the 80 miles we'd covered the previous day, at a cost of 32¢. That was 160 miles per gallon. John was numb. "Thirty-two cents? That's crazy! Hell, I spent over a dollar on granola bars yesterday, just so I'd have enough energy to pedal this bike." He stared at the Honda with a troubled frown, as if trying to grasp some searing new truth. "That's plain madness. You can't make a gas tank *leak* that slowly, much less run a vehicle . . ."

That same day, we hit our highest mutual speed of the trip while racing down a long hill (one of those inclines so evil that a sign at the top says HILL, and shows a truck perched on a steep triangle). We reached 46 miles per hour, wheel to wheel, just as the road bottomed onto a one-lane bridge whose ramp-like apron nearly tossed us off our bikes. We got into the low 40s a few times after that, but never again broke the magic 46. Uphills were less speedy that day, when a strong wind shifted into our faces. The Honda was unbothered by the wind at low speeds, but the bicycle's progress took a quantum leap downward and John appeared to be pedaling in a slow-motion bionic frenzy.

We had a late lunch at a small café in Lancaster, a small city whose skyline is dominated by two landmarks: an intricate green glass dome on the Grant County Courthouse, and one of those space age water towers that look like giant turquoise golf balls. "Some day," I told John as we rode into town, "God, with his enraged sense of aesthetics, will descend from heaven with a giant fiery Gary Player–autographed driver and tee off on all those water towers and then we won't have to see them any more." John nodded grimly, sweat running off his nose. He loved to joke while pedaling into the wind.

We ate at Bud's, where the waitress, seeing our bikes outside, asked if we were in some kind of contest. John looked up suddenly and in a hoarse, distracted voice said, "Huh?" Proof that fatigue was setting in. Normally, he would have said something like, "Yeah, we're trying to see who can leave the smallest tip at restaurants," card that he is.

Toward evening we were blessed by the long descent into the Mississippi River Valley at Prairie du Chien. The town was crawling with Labor Day tourists and our hopes of finding a motel (and a shower for John, who was beginning to smell like the Chicago Bears), were soon dashed. We ended up at a commercial campground right next to the river. As we were about to register, the manager asked if we had a pup tent. We nodded. He closed the registration book and pointed to a sign that said "No Pup Tents."

"Can't allow them any more," he said sadly. "Last year a motor home backed over a pup tent with two campers in it, and now the insurance company won't allow any tent that isn't tall enough to be seen in truck mirrors." John and I turned to each other, incredulous. A campground that doesn't allow pup tents? Crazy. I looked around at the gleaming row of campers, trailers, and motor homes. I suddenly felt like I'd drifted into camp from another era, some kind of Dust Bowl Okie, with my miserable little canvas tent and only a sleeping bag to put in it. John looked so forlorn at the prospect of more pedaling and searching that the camp manager was moved. "I'll tell you what. I've got a Jeep camper by the house. You can sleep in that." We gladly accepted. He apologized for the rules several times. He didn't like it any more than we did, but it was the insurance.

Living well being the best revenge, we got even for our lack of motel that night by eating steak and lobster at the Blue Heaven Supper Club, a place with tiny blinking lights embedded in the blue ceiling, and cherubs on the walls. Later, we saw *Joyride* at the theater on Main Street. John's resistance to the nightly movie was building, I sensed. When we came out the street was almost violently alive with drunks, more muscle cars, big motorcycles, shouting youth, cruising squad cars, and roving bands of cowboys in town for a rodeo. Sundown on Labor Day. By the time we returned to the campground, it seemed like a very good place. It was soothingly peaceful; dotted with campfires, Japanese lanterns, and murmuring circles of friends. John went right to sleep in the truck and I walked down to the willows at the edge of the river and sat on the shore, enjoying the quiet and smoking a corncob pipe I'd bought off a cardboard display at a café—something I'd wanted to do ever since I read *Tom Sawyer* at the age of 10. The Mississippi, when you sit next to it at night, is a dark and powerful thing.

Prairie du Chien was our final camp in the assault on Pike's Peak. On a bright Sunday morning we rolled across the Mississippi bridge into Iowa and began the climb out of the town of McGregor. It was strictly low gear for Honda and Stella, but after a 15-minute ascent we wheezed into Pike's Peak State Park. We had a man take our picture at the gate, then went directly to the highest spot on the Peak (which is really a bluff overlooking the Mississippi) and planted a tiny Wisconsin State Flag to commemorate our conquest. We savored the magnificent view of the junction of the

Wisconsin and Mississippi Rivers in the valley far below, and read a tourist leaflet explaining that Zebulon Pike had picked this spot for a U.S. fort during an exploration trip in 1805, but that the government, always seeking the lower ground, had eventually built the fort next to the river, in Prairie du Chien.

At the park concession stand, we bought postcards, T-shirts, ice cream, and a corncob pipe with "Pike's Peak" burned into the stem. Mailing all those cards telling people we'd made it was a glorious moment.

We coasted back across the river into Wisconsin, and turned up the Wisconsin River Valley to head for home. That night we finally found indoor lodging. An ancient hotel in Muscoda (pronounced Mus-kah-day) took us in for $11. The place had beautiful old woodwork, a lobby with a potted fern, spotlessly clean rooms that looked like something from "Gunsmoke," and, best of all, a bathroom with a shower at the end of the hall. John returned from the shower reborn. We dined on catfish at the Blackhawk Supper Club to celebrate his cleanliness. After dinner, John refused to take in *Sinbad and the Eye of the Tiger* at the local Bijou, so we went to the hotel bar and I called my wife, who was much relieved to hear that we still existed. That night, John and I discovered the Muscoda was the world's highest per capita population of Harley-Davidsons with straight pipes. All of them patronize the bar across the street from our hotel window, taking turns doing demonstration burnouts on Main Street for a throng of cheering drag fans.

In the morning we had breakfast at the Chieftain's Teepee, feeling a little out of place as the only customers not wearing Muscoda Gun Club jackets. We loaded our bikes with gear in front of the hotel and met two other guests, a couple in their fifties who were touring by bicycle. They wore safety-orange vests, safety bike helmets, safety flags on fiberglass poles, safety reflector stripes on their packs, pedals, and spokes, and little rear-view mirrors attached to their helmets. Nice folks, but a little too safe for my tastes.

A few hours up the river we found Taliesin, the beautiful home of the Frank Lloyd Wright foundation, just outside of Spring Green. We stopped to visit Bill Logue, an old friend of mine who works for the foundation, and he gave us a tour of the buildings and grounds, showing us some of the new architectural works-in-progress, the most spectacular being a mountain-top home for the daughter of the Shah of Iran. We had lunch at the Spring Green, a Wright-designed restaurant overlooking the Wisconsin River, then left on our last leg of the trip, the 30 miles home to Madison. We were home just at sundown.

We cleaned up and went out for a celebratory pizza, rehashing our trip and doing some calculations. The ride had been exactly 303 miles long, over four days. The Honda used 1.8 gallons of leaded regular or premium, depending on what was available, which is 168.3 miles per gallon, at a cost of $1.13. With over 6,000 miles on the original engine, the Honda used no discernible amount of oil—the dipstick level was constant throughout the trip. John ate about $4 worth of granola bars while riding, plus a peach and three apples. There were no malfunctions of any kind on either machine.

In 15 years of riding and touring on all kinds of bikes, this was my favorite trip. It was a microcosm tour, measured in time rather than distance. Two days from home, the Mississippi River felt as far away from home as Denver or Montreal had on other trips with faster motorcycles. The pace was slow and enjoyable, largely over roads and through towns we had never seen before, though all were within a one-day drive by car. The natives spoke English, or some dialect thereof, and our currency was accepted everywhere. Best of all, we beat our postcards home, thus receiving news of our progress while it was still fresh and exciting.

April 1979

THE FRENCH QUARTER CONNECTION

A Sense of Adventure, a Honda 400, and a Search for Cheap Chicory Coffee

While this trip was ostensibly made to find some cheap French-roast coffee in New Orleans, the real reason for taking it was my fanatical interest in Blues music and the Mississippi Delta. I had to go there.

I am happy to report that I reprised this trip a few years ago (in a 1963 Cadillac this time) and found Hannibal, Missouri, much cleaned up and restored, and the famous Beale Street in Memphis rebuilt, refurbished, and thriving with Blues clubs and live music. The 1970s were not a good decade for America's pride in its own past.

I stared at the top of the coffee can in disbelief. "Five sixty-nine for a pound of Louisiana French Roast Coffee? That's ridiculous!" I exclaimed to my wife, who agreed. "Three months ago it was two ninety-five." I couldn't believe it. My favorite blend of chicory coffee—which everyone tells me tastes like kerosene—had nearly doubled in price. I put the can back on the shelf. "I won't pay it!" I said, loudly enough to be overheard by the assistant manager of the supermarket, who was hovering nearby with a clipboard and a matching shirt and tie. "In fact," I added, "I think I'll run down to New Orleans to buy my coffee."

It was a pretty flimsy excuse for a 3,000 mile motorcycle odyssey that would take me the full length of the Mississippi, all the way to the Gulf and back to Wisconsin, but it was just what I was looking for.

Ever since I was a kid I'd wanted to take a raft trip down the Mississippi; maybe start in Minnesota near the headwaters and drift down to New Orleans, watching the famous old river towns and the green shoreline slip past while I sat back on a pile of provisions and smoked a pipe.

Then one summer I worked on a Burlington Railroad section crew along the Mississippi and I saw the river in action. Whole oak trees floated by, only to disappear in sudden, mysterious undercurrents; hydroelectric towers and dams swallowed millions of gallons of water from greenish whirlpools of their own making; and tugs pushed half a mile of unwieldy barges around blind river bends. It was all a far cry from Huck Finn's sleepy river, and no place for a novice—especially a novice with an unnatural fear of Indifferent Nature, as manifested in the force of fast-moving water.

It suddenly dawned on me that a motorcycle trip down the Great River Road might be a pleasant, relatively non-lethal, alternative to rafting. I could still visit those famous cities and towns and keep an eye on the river itself. "And," I asked myself, "what Twentieth Century vehicle lives more in the spirit of Huck Finn's raft than a motorcycle?"

"Why, none," I answered.

The prospect of a river trip, together with a chance to score a can of cheap French Roast coffee was too much. I opened the attic closet and got out My Things.

My Things, it turned out, were all wrong for the trip. I realized that nearly all of my cycle gear is intended for cold or cool weather riding, which is the rule rather than the exception in Wisconsin. Since I was heading south in the middle of August, I would have to leave it all behind—my leather jacket, my Belstaff suit, gauntlet-style gloves, down bag, and riding boots. It was strictly tennis shoe and T-shirt weather. I took a denim jacket for early morning and late evening riding, an old Army blanket to sleep on rather than in, half a gallon of Cutter's mosquito repellent, and Big Pink—a faded red pup tent from childhood, so shopworn that I can gaze at stars through the fabric at night.

The motorcycle would be my latest pride and joy, a 1975 fire-engine red Honda 400F Super Sport. There are those who would (and several who did) point out that the 400F is a rather precise instrument to use in the bludgeoning of 3,000 miles of open highway; a waste, in effect, of a machine whose forte is 410 Production racing or the Sunday morning ride on twisty blacktop. They are right, of course. It was for that kind of sport that I bought the bike. Even as it sat in my garage, the 400 was on the brink of being converted into a 410 Production racer. All of the racing parts were laid out in neat array on my workbench. I had a set of Konis, some flashy orange S&W 70-110 progressive springs, two new K-81s, three plastic number panels, a set of Racer-1 clubman bars, four quarts of Castrol G.P. 50-weight, and a roll of safety wire. But my first race was five weeks away, and I was up for a good road trip.

And, purist considerations aside, the 400 does make a fine road bike. It is utterly reliable, handles legal and extra-legal highway speeds easily, is not awkward to maneuver in tight places (no embarrassing assumption of the beached whale position while a whole campground looks on), and it looks and sounds good. Also, I prefer the short, straight bars so I can lean into the wind while I ride, as opposed to the more popular dumping-a-wheel-barrow-full-of-concrete riding style. With a light luggage load—I took only an Eclipse tank bag and a duffel bag on the rear seat—the bike handles almost as well as the unladen item, and makes riding on curving roads a genuine pleasure. Nothing is more annoying than to be stuck with half a ton of mechanical corpulence when the riding gets fun.

At seven o'clock on a Friday morning I kissed my wife goodbye, patted our three cats on the head, and rode off into a hot and gloriously sunny morning. Just outside of town I stopped to install some earplugs I'd bought to ward off total deafness on the long trip. After five minutes, I had to stop and take them out. They worked too well; I couldn't hear a thing. They made riding surreal and eerily quiet. For all I knew, my exhaust header had fallen off and a broken rod was hammering my block to pieces. I began to fantasize engine and chassis noises, much the way someone wearing stereo headphones constantly imagines that the phone and doorbell are ringing. Like those early airline pilots who objected to enclosed cockpits, I preferred to hear the wind in the wires and ignore the instruments.

The first leg of my trip did not take me south toward New Orleans, but 500 miles north to the Minnesota resort town of Brainerd. I wanted to make a proper river trip out of it, and start near the headwaters of the Mississippi. The true source of the river is Lake Itasca, northwest of Brainerd, from which the river flows in none-too-impressive volume through Bemidji and southward through many small lakes, gathering strength. I went to Brainerd because I have good friends, Tom and Lynn Dettman, who have a farm and cabin near the town. I also wanted to scout around Brainerd International Raceway for an upcoming road race—and another chance to unleash Lola the Vicious Underdog, my battlescarred and outdated Formula Ford racing car. (Lively, these little towns in the North Woods.)

I rode into Brainerd after 10 hours on the bike and after dark, equipped with a copy of a copy of a hand-drawn map purporting to show the way to the Dettmans' cabin, some 20 miles from town. Three hours later, on a mosquito-clouded back road in the dark forest, I gave up searching for the imaginary landmarks on my map, switched my tank to reserve, and prayed I'd make it back to town. I rolled into a gas station and café in Brainerd at one in the morning, my engine sputtering.

"Is there anyplace around here I can lie down and sleep?" I asked the waitress over a cup of coffee in the restaurant. "I must have sleep. I've been on my motorcycle for thirteen hours."

"There's some old railroad cars down by the river. You could sleep in those," she offered.

"Perfect," I said. As I left the café, the cook at the grill shouted, "You bed down in one of them railroad cars and you just might wake up in North Dakota!" She cackled and flipped a hamburger. I didn't care. I had to lie down.

In the morning I awoke on a bench in a vandalized caboose car and found myself lying in a bed of cigarette butts, crushed Dixie Cups, and spent lime vodka bottles; all features I'd overlooked while stumbling in from the night fog. I brushed myself off and looked out the train window. I was still in Minnesota—or what the mosquitos had left of me was still in Minnesota. The mosquitos in that state are so large that they lack the usual high-pitched whine, and drum their wings at a much lower frequency, like quail taking off from a thicket.

With the aid of sunlight and friendly natives I managed to find the Dettmans' place, a remote cabin on a beautiful lake, which they share only with a Bible camp. Tom showed me around the town and the racetrack. We spent the evening visiting, and my second night on the road, sleeping in their cabin on the lake, was considerably more pleasant than the first—though Tom persisted in addressing me as "Boxcar Egan." They fixed me a good breakfast for a sendoff down the river.

South of Brainerd, the Mississippi develops into a solid, respectable little river that winds easily through flat Minnesota farm land, widening here and there to water the marshlands of wild rice and cattails. It passes through Little Falls, where Charles Lindbergh lived before he had the good sense to move to Madison, Wisconsin—where he attended the University before he had the good sense to quit school and take up flying. South of St. Cloud, the river gets lost in the fast-growing suburbs and the downtown(s) of the Twin Cities. The Falls of St. Anthony, once a landmark and barrier to upper river navigation, are now caught between two dams and circumvented by a lock system. Modern cities have a way of overwhelming the physical features that once determined their locations, until those features are lost and unimportant. I spent part of my youth in St. Paul and never heard anyone mention the Falls, nor did I ever see them.

At Prescott, Wisconsin, the St. Croix River joins its crystal clear waters to the already Muddy, if not very Big, Mississippi. I decided to follow Highway 61 down the Minnesota side, having seen too much of the Wisconsin side when I worked on the railroad and literally shoveled my way from Prescott to Bluff Siding.

Highway 61, from Hastings to LaCrosse, Wisconsin, is one of the nicest cycle rides on the Mississippi; four lanes, smooth and uncrowded, undulate along the river bank high enough to afford a constant panorama of the river and its islands. I discovered at this stage of the ride that every gas station, no matter where you go, employs one high school student who either owns or is about to own a motorcycle, and can discuss motorcycles with incredible expertise, usually quoting cycle magazines verbatim. A station attendant in Red Wing told me that my 400F had "an engine that lives just to bury the tach needle." I nodded my agreement, suppressing a shiver of déjà vu and wondering where I'd read those words.

At La Crosse, I shifted to the more scenic Wisconsin river bank and cruised through a dozen small river towns until I reached Wyalusing State Park. The park sits high on the bluffs at the junction of the Wisconsin and

Mississippi, and offers a splendid view of both rivers. I erected Big Pink near the campsite of a young couple who had a trailer and two curious children. The father seemed determined that the kids stay clear of me and my motorcycle and shouted at them roughly whenever they ventured too close. Feeling rather untouchable (perhaps it was the dead insects pasted to my chin), I sat alone on the bluffs, watching a huge red sun set over Iowa and sipping a little Cabin Still from a brown paper bag I'd brought along.

The day was already calm and breathlessly hot at seven in the morning when I broke camp and rode down to Galena, Illinois, for breakfast. Galena was a prosperous old river town that fell upon hard times and was nearly abandoned, until a later generation recognized the value and charm of the beautiful old homes and shops in the city. Galena is now a tourist attraction, with hundreds of nicely restored buildings and a remarkable collection of brick storefronts along its main street. It is a town that must have the highest ratio of antique shops to population in the entire country. On the edge of town, I visited the home of Ulysses S. Grant, which is filled with photographs of the General and his family, Grant always looking a bit rough-hewn and out of place amid the lavish parlor trappings of that era. In my own heat-distorted mind I began to pity the people in the photographs for their lack of shorts and sandals because it was about 100 degrees in Grant's house. It was good to get back on the Honda.

In Fulton, Illinois, farther down the river, I sat at a lunch counter with two young men who told me that St. Louis was a tough town, and I should steer around it. "You go through St. Louis on that shiny red motorcycle and, sure as hell, someone'll drag you right off that bike and take all your stuff away. I heard about it." His friend concurred grimly, then ordered a turkey sandwich with gravy. As he ate the sandwich, he leaned over to his buddy and said, "Bird Dog can eat six of these."

"Hail."

"I seen 'im."

I walked out onto the street, keeping a sharp eye out for the legendary Bird Dog and wondering if I dared go through St. Louis on my shiny red bike. I tossed caution to the wind and headed south.

I followed the Great River Road (always marked with a green sign that bears a giant steamboat wheel) and cruised through the Moline and Rock

Island half of the Quad Cities—factory towns that are incredibly clean and modern-looking for a traditional industrial area. The John Deere plant is so gleaming and up-to-date it looks almost Japanese.

Just north of Nauvoo, Illinois, I ran across another touring motorcyclist. At a four-way stop in the middle of nowhere we got off our bikes to have a cigarette and talk. He was Roy Perkins, from Roanoke, Virginia, and he was touring on a Kawasaki 400 triple. "I wouldn't ride anything but a Kawasaki two-stroke," he told me. "I've never had a lick of trouble with 'em. And I wouldn't ride anything bigger than a 400—you don't need any more than that." Roy was traveling even lighter than I was; he had nothing but a backrest with a pack strapped to it and a tent roll across his rear seat. "I'm going to Seattle, down to Mexico, then back home around the Gulf coast and Florida," he said. "The main thing I like to see is Indian mounds. I've seen every Indian mound between here and Virginia, and I plan to see them all along my trip." I thought of Kawasaki's "We know why you ride" advertising slogan, and I wondered if they knew about Roy Perkins and his Indian mounds. Before we parted, he warned me to stay out of Mississippi. I asked why. He kick-started his bike and lifted his face shield for a moment. "Trouble," he said. He flipped his shield down and rode away, waving.

Before sundown I was in Nauvoo State Park, staking down my tent. As soon as my cycle stopped moving, I realized that the only factor preventing me from melting into a smouldering, shapeless lump of steaming flesh was the air that moved past me and the Honda all day. By the time my tent was in place I was a sweaty wreck, so I rode into town and had five beers for dinner at an air-conditioned bar, where I watched an entire Pirates vs. Reds baseball game on TV, even though I was not a dedicated fan of either team, being from Brewers country. When the bar closed, I was forced back to my tent for a long night of involuntary weight loss.

In the morning I toured Historic Nauvoo, the last home of the Mormons before they were forced by persecution to move west to Utah, led by Brigham Young. A Mormon restoration corporation is buying up and rebuilding the old brick settlement, and the restoration they have already done is first-class. Four acres surround each home and shop in an idyllic setting whose beauty imparts some of the sorrow those settlers must have felt in leaving what they'd built. Before I left town, I bought a bottle of Old

Nauvoo Brand Burgundy Wine, a modern legacy of the French Icarians who moved in to plant vineyards when the Mormons left. (The wine was excellent when I got home, even after five days in my tank bag; truly a Burgundy that travels well.)

At Keokuk, I paid 30 cents to cross the Mississippi on a steel-mesh bridge—the kind of surface that sends motorcycle tires into a frenzy of squirming indecision—and was greeted by a sign that said "Welcome to Keokuk, Iowa. Sailors have more fun!" (Okay, sure. But in Keokuk, Iowa?) I turned south on 61 toward Hannibal, Missouri, home of Mark Twain.

In *Tom Sawyer*, Twain described his home town as a "poor little shabby village." It's not so little any more, but the river town that surrounds the block of old houses claiming to be Tom Sawyer's neighborhood has taken on a modern shabbiness to disillusion romantics and young readers. A giant rotating fried chicken barrel looms just beyond Tom's house, and trucks rumble across the busy highway bridge behind it. A few blocks away, a scrap metal yard lines the river bank. There are many small towns, up and down the river, much closer in spirit and form to the village Twain immortalized than Hannibal is today.

I had lunch at Huck Finn's Hideaway, seated beneath woodcarvings of the Big Three (Elvis, Jesus, and John F. Kennedy), bought a copy of *Tom Sawyer* at Becky Thatcher's Book Store, and rode on toward St. Louis.

Highway 79 from Hannibal to St. Louis is another one of those roads where it's good to have a 400F, setbacks, six speeds, a pair of K-81s, and an engine that lives to bury the tach. It is 50 miles of road that goes up- and downhill through the trees, winding up valleys, and bursting into hilltop clearings with observation vistas on the river below. Euphoric and glassy-eyed from the ride, I came snarling and downshifting into Wentzville, like Hailwood pulling into the pits at Douglas, on the Isle of Man. Wentzville, Missouri, just west of St. Louis, is the home of Chuck Berry, a living legend of Rock 'n' Roll.

A group of giggling 13-year-old girls on Main Street told me where Berry lived. "Just follow that road out of town. It's called Berry Park. You'll see it. He should be home. He was in town with his Cadillac this morning, and I saw him shopping." More giggling. "He's not too popular around here anymore."

"No? Why is that?"

"Well, you know . . . he's kind of old and everything. He's just not . . . too cool."

They all blushed and giggled, and I thanked them for the directions. Not too cool? Granted, I thought, he's not Shaun Cassidy, but still . . .

Berry's house was right where they said it would be, about five miles out of town; a fenced-in country estate with a duck pond and some houses and buildings hidden back in the willows. The gate was open, so I walked up the driveway and talked to a young woman who told me that Chuck was playing in St. Louis that night, at the Rainbow Bar. As I walked back down the drive, a bronze Cadillac rolled in with none other than the Brown-Eyed Handsome Man himself at the wheel. He smiled and waved, if a little thinly, doubtless underawed at the novelty of another camera-carrying stranger stalking his grounds.

I found the Rainbow Bar and checked into a nearby motel. Berry was a knockout that night, playing to a cheering crowd of about 300 who'd jammed into the little roadside club. He led off with "Roll Over Beethoven" (tell Cha-kosky da news!), "Johnny B. Goode," and "Sweet Little Sixteen," cranking out guitar riffs that are copied by every rock musician in the world, doing his famous duckwalk and leering happily at the crowd over his earthiest lyrics.

Unfortunately, Berry is not too cool, so at two in the morning, after three frenzied encores, and despite the objections of the wildly applauding crowd, he quit playing and everyone went home.

In the bleary morning light, I rode past the awesome St. Louis Arch and somehow managed to sneak out of the city without being dragged off my bike by local toughs. I turned south on Highway 3, through the lower tip of Illinois. (Illinois is, subjectively, the longest state in the Union.) I crossed the river at Cairo, where the Ohio joins the Mississippi, and it is here that the river begins to Mean Business. The Ohio actually dumps in twice as much water as the Mississippi, much to the embarrassment of Mississippi fans.

I pushed south toward Memphis, where the police were on strike, the National Guard was in control, an 8 P.M. curfew was being enforced, and thousands of people were flocking into town for the First Anniversary of Elvis' Death; a truly irresistible combination. I camped outside the city, part of an army preparing for a dawn invasion.

I got into town early and searched out Beale Street in downtown Memphis. Once the lively bar and nightclub Mecca of Mississippi Delta musicians heading north, the famous Beale Street is now a victim of urban renewal. Only two blocks of the old street remain, and they are rundown, vacant, and boarded up. The rest is parking lots. After a moment of silence for the vanished street, I rode out to Graceland, home and final resting place of Elvis.

One year and one day after his death, a large but respectful crowd rummaged through the shopping center of Elvis memorabilia and then crossed Elvis Presley Boulevard to file up the lawn of the Graceland Mansion to see his grave. Elvis is buried next to his mother in a little alcove near the swimming pool. The grounds and grave were decorated with hundreds of floral tributes, variously shaped like gold records, hearts, hound dogs, and teddy bears. At the gate, a man was trying to sell a Harley XLCH that he claimed was one of Elvis' stable. I shuffled past the bronze tombstone, following a family of four who had driven 2,200 miles straight through from Nova Scotia, just to be there on the anniversary of his death. They were a day late. "It's still worth every mile of the drive," the man told me. "Being here is something we'll never forget as long as we live."

Dizzy and dehydrated from standing in line for two hours, I was glad to get back on the 400F and enjoy the luxury of moving air. I crossed into the flat, hot cotton country that is Mississippi's Yazoo Delta, and is—to a Blues fan and record collector—Holy Ground.

For reasons that are unclear (something in the water, perhaps), this northwestern corner of Mississippi produced nearly every great American bluesman in the twentieth century. Son House, Robert Johnson, Howling Wolf, Muddy Waters, John Lee Hooker, and Charlie Patton, to name just a few, all came from a small area around Clarksdale, Mississippi. And, as if that were not enough, William Faulkner's home at Oxford—the center of this mythical Yoknapatawpha County—lies just to the east. Never was such a small area of the earth graced with so much genius.

I stopped at a music store in Clarksdale and bought a couple of magic Fender guitar picks, one for me and one for my friend David Rhodes, who already plays guitar quite well and doesn't need a magic pick as badly as I do. The people at the music store said that not much is left of the old music, since all the bluesmen went north in the forties. Clarksdale was not the somnolent little cotton town I'd expected. It is a bustling go-into-town-and-shop farm community, indistinguishable from a thriving county seat in Wisconsin. It has a McDonald's and a small, but significant, suburbia.

I threw the guitar picks in my tank bag, downed three glasses of iced tea at a little air-conditioned restaurant, and rode out of Clarksdale. Highway 61 is not exactly Racer Road as it runs through the Delta. The pavement is straight and flat, and towns appear on the highway as islands of buildings and trees in the sprawling cotton fields. The most visible sign of life between towns is the large number of colorful crop dusters that sweep back and forth over the road. The landscape everywhere is dotted with rusted tin roofs of old sharecroppers' houses, many of which are abandoned, relics now on the big corporate plantations. As you ride, the air has a distinctive fuel oil smell left by the crop dusters.

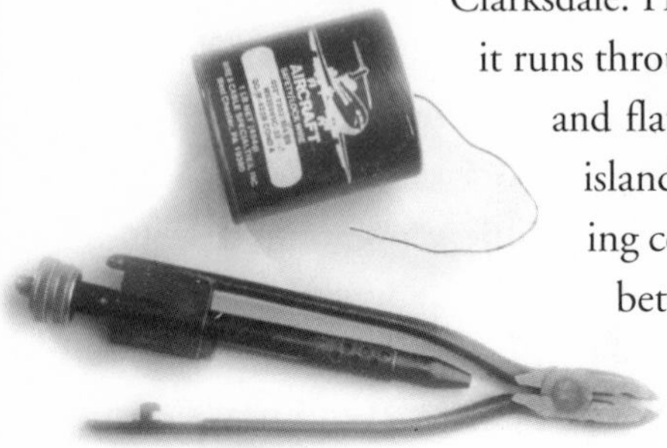

By evening I found myself in Arkansas on a river-made peninsula that is Chicot State Park. I was rather a mess, having ridden late in the day through a plague of four-winged, dragonfly-looking insects called snake doctors by the local people. These things burst on your knuckles and chin like small pigeons' eggs. Miraculously, the park had hot showers and a laundromat. I showered, left my clothes to test the competence of the washing machine, and examined my faithful Honda. Other than lubing the chain and checking the engine oil, I hadn't touched the bike. The oil level was unchanged since I'd left home, but the chain was sagging a bit, so I tightened it. The rear K-81, never intended as a touring tire, had vaporized about 40 percent of its tread somewhere on the Great River Road, which left me 60 percent to make it to New Orleans and home—or about the right amount.

Before leaving home, I'd installed plugs two ranges colder than stock, thinking of long fast rides in the hot sun. This was a mistake, since on a trip of this kind I did much more duffing and bogging around towns and parks than I would do on my home turf. But the plugs looked okay, and they still worked. I adjusted my valves and cam chain and revved the engine; the 400 sounded like the same competent, enraged little sewing machine with whom I'd left home.

With clean clothes and an adjusted bike, I cruised down Highway 61 into Rolling Fork, Mississippi, the birthplace of Muddy Waters. "Yes, yes," said one of the old men on the park bench in the town square, "I knew McKinley Morganfield (a.k.a. Muddy Waters). He was here in a big black Cadillac six years ago when his mother died. His brother Robert and his sister-in-law Frankie live in that yellow house down the street."

I stopped at the house and talked to Frankie Morganfield. I said that Muddy had a lot of fans up in Wisconsin and she said, "Yes, he told me a lot of you white folks like that music up there." I laughed. "Yes, we sure do." She thanked me for stopping and said she'd give my best to Muddy. I rode away confident that I'd done my share of tiresome meddling for the day.

At the hilltop city of Vicksburg, I finally got high enough above the levees to see the river again. I rode out to the military park and cemetery, and toured the 16 miles of road that wind through the battleground. When Grant took Vicksburg, the Mississippi was opened to the Union and the war was over for the South, though the Confederacy struggled on for another two years. The graves at Vicksburg go on and on, as far as you can see; antique artillery pieces are poised at each ridge and hilltop beside bronze plaques of explanation. The battleground is one of those places where the historian could spend a year, and the passing tourist just long enough to realize how little he understands from what he sees.

The same is true of Natchez, an old, old city with a colorful and varied history, and a collection of beautiful antebellum homes. It is the terminus of the Natchez Trace, the canyon-like ancient trail, now paved, that cuts cross-country nearly to Nashville. I wandered around Natchez in the evening looking for a motel room, and found that everything was filled because the Corps of Engineers was in town (the Corps has built most of the levees that keep lower Mississippi towns from floating into the Gulf each spring). I rode south to Woodville where, I was told, I could find a motel.

The road to Woodville ran through dark and hilly pine tree country, with lots of traffic coming the other way. I began to assemble reasons for why I hate riding at night. I decided that they included: (1) drunks, (2) deer, (3) bright headlights that force you to ride blind down a lane that may be littered with hay bales, dead possums, or kegs of nails fallen from trucks, and (4) insects. By the time I got to Woodville, half of the flying insects in Mississippi had made a graveyard of my shirt and face shield. I found a road-side motel with vacancy and cleaned up for my early morning sweep into New Orleans. My room was hot, so I cranked the air-conditioner up to full and went to bed.

In the morning, I woke up dreaming I'd died and gone to Alaska. The room was freezing. Feeling very refreshed, I stepped out into the steamy-hot morning at about six o'clock and rode off into the mist and dawn light into West Feliciana Parish, Louisiana. This stretch of Highway 61 passes more Southern mansions than I thought existed in all the South. With huge oaks hung with Spanish moss shading their pillared facades, like something out of *Gone With the Wind*, they pass by with names like The Catalpas, The Oaks, or The Cottage (yes, some cottage, you are supposed to think). The homes along the road became newer and less grand as I entered Baton Rouge, city of smoking oil refineries and Huey Long's tower building. I stayed on 61 and rode along the south shore of Lake Pontchartrain to New Orleans.

I took the Vieux Carre exit, down Orleans Avenue and Toulouse Street into the heart of the French Quarter. Anxious to get off my bike and look around, I found a room at the Cornstalk Hotel on Royal Street, changed my shirt, and walked out on the town. The French Quarter, which surrounds St. Louis Cathedral and Jackson Square, is old, beautiful, and much larger in area than I expected. The Quarter is a labyrinth of narrow streets, old hotels, fine restaurants, topless/bottomless joints, night clubs, cool dark bars, souvenir shops, oyster bars, book stores, coffee houses, and expensive antique shops, all thrown together in wonderful unzoned anarchy. Music is everywhere; the great jazz clubs are open to the street. You can stand in the street, listening and watching, or sit down with a $1.50 beer and relax at the bar or a table. The music is good; not some contrived Dixieland Muzak for tourists, but genuinely well-played jazz.

I sat in Maison Bourbon, listening to the Robert Jefferson Jazz Band for a while, lunched nearby on oysters and gumbo, and then wandered down to the river, where I stumbled upon the French Market and its open-air stalls of fruits and vegetables. At the edge of the marketplace was a sight for sore and weary eyes—the French Market Café. I had café au lait, chicory-style of course, and an order of beignets—a sort of square donut, all brought by waiters in ties and black coats. Reminded of my original goal, I looked through the nearby shops for some French roast chicory coffee and immediately found a one-pound can for $2.85. Suddenly the whole trip was worth it. I took the can back to the hotel, locked my door, and carefully packed the coffee away in my tank bag. All that remained was to get it home.

I counted my money, found that I had $32 left, and suddenly realized that my trip home was going to be, of necessity, a straight shot of dreaded Interstate, with few food and rest stops. I had just enough money for gas and a couple of Big Macs.

On an early Sunday New Orleans morning, with the streets nearly vacant, I rolled out of the Vieux Carre, turned North onto I-55, snicked the 400 into sixth gear, and opened all four throttles. I was all buzzed up and ready to ride, speeding on four cups of black coffee. I rode and filled my tank, rode and filled my tank, stopped for a Big Mac, and rode and filled my tank until it was too dark and cold to ride. Just south of St. Louis, after 14 hours on the bike, I pulled off the I-road, rolled up in my tent behind an abandoned gas station, and slept. I got back on the bike at 5:30 A.M., filled my tank, drank more coffee, rode my bike, ate a Big Mac, and rode like an express train.

Thirty-four hours after leaving New Orleans, I entered Wisconsin with $5 in my pocket and the 400 still running like a champ. I patted the side of the tank with my sunburned hand and said, "This is a very, very good motorcycle." The odometer showed just over 11,000 miles, or 3,000 more than I'd left with. I was burned-out, punch-drunk, and traveling in a senseless state of tunnel-vision from the long ride, but as I crossed the border I still managed to grin. My bike was running perfectly, I hadn't been issued a single traffic ticket, my bald rear tire was still holding air, I'd not met even one unpleasant person on the entire trip, despite vague and shadowy warnings to the contrary, and there had been, incredibly, no rain in seven days on the road. But, best of all, I knew that buried deep in my tank bag was a $2.85 pound of Louisiana French roast chicory coffee, with a Wisconsin street value of nearly $6.

May 1979

'SNOW PLACE FOR A MOTORCYCLE

Should a Norton Come Out of Hibernation at Winter's First Thaw?

I was doing a lot of rock climbing and backpacking at the time I wrote this story, and wanted to capture some of the nutty essence of adventure, as well as the essence of freezing half to death on a motorcycle, a common occurrence here in the North.

Just as a postscript to this story, Jim Wargula and I are still good friends. He lives nearby and we play guitars together in the same garage-quality blues band. Last weekend we took a mid-November ride together on our Ducatis and got ourselves well chilled. Again.

There are certain regions clearly delimited by Nature as off-limits to humans. They are places you shouldn't go, even on a bet, and most people are fairly adept at spotting them. A short list of examples might include: the north face of Everest during the monsoons, the Lake of the Woods in blackfly season, the Colorado River in spring flood, and for the motorcyclist, Wisconsin highways in winter. You can go to those places if you wish, but only with the understanding that you go in harm's way, and that there are perfectly good reasons why nobody will be there when you arrive. Uninhabited zones, like pinnacles of success, tend to be lonely simply because everyone is off somewhere else having a good time.

These notions weighed heavily on my mind as I sped down the road on my 850 Commando, dodging knife-edged drifts on the plowed highway and watching angry snow clouds scud in from the northwest, a solid, fast-moving bank of leaden gray and purple. There were no other motorcycles on the road, and very few cars. It was hardly noon and yet the streetlights, with their photo-cells sensitive to the growing darkness, were switching themselves on in the small towns. In the country, farmyard lights were blinking on. I wasn't sure whether it was the absence of light or of heat that set them glowing. The temperature had dropped about one degree per mile, as though synchronized with my odometer. It was growing dark and cold.

I knew, dumb frozen beast that I was, that as soon as my brain thawed out I would blame Wargula for this whole fiasco. It was Jim Wargula, an old college roommate, who had phoned me at eight o'clock on a Saturday morning in March to see if I wanted to do some country roadracing. Jim lives 100 miles away, in Oshkosh—the city with the name that gets laughs in Catskill nightclubs.

"Get up, Egan," he said. "It's beautiful outside. I just went out to feed the dogs and discovered that a warm front is upon us. It must be 50 degrees out there. Spring is here! What do you say we blow the cosmoline out of the Nortons?"

Jim and I had both bought Norton 850s, his red and mine black, in the last days of the Empire when Norton was trying to recoup some capital by selling Commandos for a song. We had reunions several times a year in which we met at some chosen place and then frightened ourselves all day on twisty back roads, dodging bullchips and farm dogs. Most of these rides took place in the summer, that magical time of year when you can see the ground.

Jim waited on the phone while I climbed out of bed and raised a window shade. As soon as I recovered from the sudden searing pain in my eyes, I could see that it was a bright, beautiful morning. The streets were wet with melting snow and there was the sort of vaporous white haze in the air you see only on winter mornings that are unusually warm.

"Okay," I said. "I'll go for a ride. Where do you want to meet?"

"How about the A & W in Columbus," Jim suggested. "It's halfway between here and there and it has an indoor restaurant. We can eat lunch and then go for a ride."

I made some coffee and then went downstairs into the dungeon that is our garage and basement to have a look at the Norton. It was in the corner, covered with a white sheet, like the furniture of the rich when they have left for the South of France. I bought the sheet, then couldn't afford the vacation. The battery was out; the gas tank drained. I'm not prepared on short notice to ride in winter anymore. I've had too many close brushes with death-by-shivering. As a student, I spent most of one winter commuting to class on a Honda CB-160, and that experience taught me a lot of valuable lessons. I learned, for instance, that if you corner a motorcycle with bald tires fast enough on new-fallen snow, it is possible to narrowly miss a skidding city bus and knock over three garbage cans filled exclusively with egg shells and grapefruit rinds while sustaining no injury more serious than a sprained thumb and a term paper on Kierkegaard ruined by slush. On a more metaphysical level, I discovered that hot tea is inherently Good, while cold wind represents a sort of Evil.

When I couldn't stand it anymore, I sold my 160 and bought a sports car—a 1959 Triumph TR-3 with no side curtains and a hole the size of a cannonball in the otherwise opaque rear window of the convertible top. The Triumph, of course, was no warmer than the Honda, but since it never ran more than three minutes at a time I never had a chance to get really cold. Also, when you tapped the horn button the steering wheel began to smolder and melt, which added a touch of comfort in cold weather. The wiring harness finally burned up and I sold the car for a tremendous profit and bought myself another bike; a 305 Superhawk. By that time it was summer. I was done with winter riding for good.

I took the sheet off the Norton, dumped in a gallon of stale lawnmower gas, strapped its trickle-charged battery back under the seat, and went upstairs to dress. I put on all the clothes I owned and then went down to the garage to get my waxed-cotton Belstaff jacket. My wife won't let me keep it in the regular coat closet because she says it smells like creosote. I wrapped a scarf around my face and buckled my helmet. The Norton's anemic electric starter went "dit," so I started the bike with just enough kicks to steam up my face shield with hot panting breath.

The streets in town were wet, but out on the highway the pavement was dry and clean, bleached bone-white from three months of salting by the county road crews. I stopped at a gas station to fill my tank. "Beautiful day for a ride," the attendant said. "I heard we were supposed to get some snow, but it sure doesn't look like it now."

I agreed, a little uneasily, and remarked that I'd put on too many layers of clothes and actually felt too warm riding through town—unheard of in early March. I pulled out on the highway feeling good about the weather and happy to be back on my bike and going somewhere. The sun shone down on the fields and woods, and the birds sang brightly on the telephone wires—or so I imagined, in the whistling isolation of my Star 120.

Then 10 miles down the road, a small shiver passed over my body. Not an actual, visible shudder, but the kind of shiver that is more psychic than physical. The sun had gone behind a cloud. I turned and looked over my shoulder. Wrong. The sun had gone behind a lot of clouds. It had disappeared behind a textbook vision of the rolling cold front. A mass of dark winter clouds moved across the sky from the northwest like a giant focal-plane shutter. I shrugged; the air was still nice and warm. About 10 minutes later I plunged into one of those zones of sudden cold that are as vivid to a motorcyclist as a brick wall, or a border on a colored map. From red to blue, faster than you can say "brass monkey." I felt as though I'd dived into Lake Superior. In 15 minutes the day had gone from benign to angry. I tucked my chin a little tighter into my collar and pressed on.

By the time I'd made the 50-mile trip to the A & W in Columbus, it was dark and cold. The sky was a uniform turbulent nasty gray, and the lights from the restaurant had a warm orange glow. I walked in stiffly, knocking small icicles off my beard, and ordered a very large coffee. The waitress asked cheerfully, "Is that for here or to go?" I was too cold to be kind. I just looked at her and said, "You must be joking." I took the coffee back to a window table and waited for Wargula.

Motorcyclists in cold weather are always in a quandary over their speed. Should they ride fast and get it over with, enduring the ravages of high-speed wind, or should they ride slowly, prolonging a slightly less terrible agony?

Jim had chosen Slow Death. Coming down the highway, his bike looked like one of those lone cavalry horses returning to the fort with a dead rider full of arrows slumped in its saddle, stopping here and there to nibble on sagebrush. I'd never seen Jim ride so slowly, or so stiffly. And I'd never seen a motorcycle turn a corner without leaning, but Jim did it as he pulled into the parking lot. He pulled to a stop and sat on his bike; just sat, not bothering to shut the engine off, as though he expected some kind of emergency ground crew to run out of the restaurant and lift him off his Commando. No help arrived, so he slowly reached for the key and turned it off. A minute later he tilted his head downward and began to look for the kickstand. A stiff robot leg caught the edge of the stand and kicked it out.

He swung his other leg over the bike, stood up, looked around to see where he was, and then walked toward the restaurant door with a ponderous I'm-so-cold-now-there's-no-need-to-hurry dignity.

He walked right past my table without looking at me and went to the counter. "Coffee," he said. The waitress started to ask if that was for here or to go, but something in his voice made her think the better of it. She quickly set out a large white Styrofoam cup with a plastic lid. Jim paid and walked over to my table. He sat down heavily, without speaking, and peeled the lid from his cup with a hand like a claw. He took a drink and looked darkly into the cup. I feared for a moment that he might dump the stuff over his head, or at least pour it down his boot. But he just warmed his hands over the steaming cup and looked at me, raising one eyebrow in a sudden show of levity.

"Been here long?" he asked.

"I can't tell yet."

Jim looked out the window. "Lovely weather. It looks like midnight."

"It's supposed to snow."

Jim nodded. "We better warm up and head for home. I don't want to spend the winter in this place." He looked around. "Even if it is warm."

It took us about two hours to warm up. We'd both quit smoking but we bought a pack of Lucky Strikes out of the cigarette machine, just for old times, and smoked one after the other. (When you are cold enough, there is something ineffably charming about a glowing cigarette and great clouds of smoke.) Then we had some hamburgers and more coffee. We talked about motorcycles and summer and what it must be like to live in California and then had some more coffee. Snow flurries began to blow against the window. My watch said it was two in the afternoon, but the darkness of the sky made it much later. A light dusting of snow settled into the quilting pattern on our cycle seats and formed a wind-blown vee on the pavement around our tires. It was time to go, so we smoked another half a pack of cigarettes, drank some more coffee, and sloshed out the front door reeling from an overdose of caffeine and nicotine. Jim brushed off the seat, started his cycle with one kick—aided slightly by the electric starter—and closed his face shield. He waited until my bike was running, then held up his hand in a gesture disturbingly similar to a Papal benediction. We put the bikes in gear and split off at the highway in opposite directions.

All of the cars had their headlights on and left swirling wakes of dry, hard snow that worked its way down the back of my neck and melted. I discovered in a very short time that I'd worn too many layers of clothes in the restaurant; I was a little on the warm and sweaty side. The wind made short work of the heat I'd brought with me, and soon I began to shake. I shook mildly at first with a sort of high-pitched tuning fork resonance, and then more heavily, my uncontrolled shuddering moving down the scale to roughly an open E, played on a bass guitar with a badly wound fourth string. It went from there to the kind of all-out jerking and twitching usually associated with wind-up toy monkeys that hop and play the cymbals at the same time. The rhythm began to feed into my handlebars, sending the bike into those deadly vibrations that warn of an upcoming tank-slapper. I slowed down, got a grip on myself, and several miles down the road pulled into a roadside tavern. There I had a plastic cup of evil brown acidic fluid which the bartender jokingly referred to as "coffee." I asked if I could have the remains of yesterday's *Milwaukee Journal*, which lay on the bar, and then retired to the men's room. I stuffed the want-ad and comic sections, respectively, down the pantlegs that covered my left and right thighs; two more pages went up around my calves and tucked into my boots, and the entire front page was spread across my chest, tucked into my belt, and buttoned into my shirt. I emerged from the men's room and crinkled my way stiffly out of the bar, to the momentary distraction of a row of bored farmers who were watching the halftime show of a Texas football game—broadcast from a mythical land where the grass is green, the sun shines, and the cheerleaders wear neither Belstaff jackets, nor, as far as I could tell, newspapers stuffed in their undergarments.

I stepped out into the frozen North, mounted the bike carefully so as not to disturb my armor, and motored down the road. The snow, I noted, had taken a turn for the worse. The flakes grew steadily larger and began to stick to the road instead of blowing across it. My headlight shone into a billowing cloud of whiteness where the snow came at me in perfectly horizontal flight, parallel to the road, rather than falling from the sky. Headlights loomed in my mirror and a semi roared past and disappeared, heading into its own swirling snowstorm, leaving me blinded to the exact location of the highway. I slowed down to about 35 and then realized that my Norton and I would make a fine hood ornament for the next Peterbilt to catch us from the rear. I cranked it back up to 50, fishtailing slightly on the slippery road. On a long sweeping curve the bike began a slow drift to the outside, dangerously close to the berm of the snow. I pulled in some opposite lock and stuck my foot out in a clumsy, half-speed parody of Dick Mann at the San Jose Mile. This move caused me to break out in perhaps the world's coldest sweat, so I slowed down again.

When the road straightened out I began to grin, as best I could, inside my scarf and helmet. It was the same self-deprecating grin I might use if I discovered that a con artist had tricked me out of my life's savings and stolen my car, taking my wife along as a willing hostage. Tricked again. Had. Lured from my snug house by the shabby promise of a warm day in winter; the flip side of a cold day in hell. I must have been crazy. I'd broken all my own rules; I'd gone to a place where I don't belong.

Going where you don't belong, I decided a long time ago, is the root of all misery and the soul of all adventure. For instance, if you jump out of an airplane and find that your parachute doesn't open, you realize very quickly that your problem is much more basic than a malfunctioning silk canopy; the real problem is that you are 5,000 feet off the ground and falling through space. That is, you are in a place where you don't belong. Or, if you are a Formula One driver and you hit some oil in a very high-speed curve, say in the Karussel at Nurburgring, the problem is not so much that you've hit oil; the problem is that you are in a very fragile machine going 120 miles per hour. You are—you guessed it—in a Place Where You Don't Belong. If you hadn't gone there, you'd be home now. Everything would be all right. There are hundreds of other places where people don't belong; mountainsides in the Himalayas, foxholes in foreign countries, 13-foot sailboats in the mid-Atlantic, bars full of drunks, spying in the Kremlin, whorehouses, New York, milking rattlesnakes, hang-gliding off El Capitan, shrieking down Bray Hill on an OW-1, dodging bulls in Pamplona, consorting with minors, and so on. All wonderful adventures, but fraught with some degree of peril because you really shouldn't be there. You are more or less asking for it. And if you get it, not much sympathy will be forthcoming. You've gone by your own device to a place without mercy. Sometimes a motorcycle is a place where you don't belong. Like in the winter, when the first good blizzard of the year blows out of the northwest and clogs the road with drifts of blinding snow. Sometimes you find yourself in a place where you don't belong not because you are adventurous, but because you haven't got the sense God gave a chipmunk. Because you are, in the words of my third-grade teacher, a silly goose. And, yes, because you are dumb as a stump.

A four-wheel-drive Bronco sped easily past me. Two children in the back watched me wide-eyed and then waved. I waved back by cautiously lifting a couple of my fingers from the grips. The children suddenly turned away and made animated gestures of conversation with their father, who was driving. I couldn't hear the conversation, but I knew what they were saying. (Daddy, what does "cretin" mean?)

The road was ridiculous. A solid layer of snow now blanketed the pavement, except where the strongest wind swept across it. Drifts were forming at a diagonal to the centerline. My front tire began to turn more slowly than the rear; it was only a matter of time until the front fender jammed with ice and snow and set technology back ten thousand years by turning my wheel into a skid—or a runner. A restaurant billboard told me that I was still five miles from town, and I suddenly had to ask myself, "Is it possible to go any farther?"

"No," said a voice that I barely recognized as my own, but was nevertheless glad to hear. "Dump this two-wheeled deathtrap somewhere and thumb it home."

Just then, like a mirage in a frozen Sahara, there appeared a lighted building on the roadside. It was a turquoise steel building in the middle of nowhere (i.e., just west of Sun Prairie, Wisconsin) with big display windows across the front and a giant yellow Yamaha sign shining like a star in the east out of the snowy darkness. "Thank God for tin buildings and giant international corporations," I mumbled to myself, punching my left turn signal switch with a remote, frozen appendage I recognized as my left thumb.

When I walked inside, two men and a boy in fluorescent orange deer-hunting hats and open galoshes were trying to trade in a purple snowmobile with a leopard-skin seat, bargaining with a salesman in a camouflaged duck-hunting hat and open galoshes. Each of the four had one foot on the snowmobile in question. The salesman smiled and said, "Hell of a day for bikes!

We're supposed to get fifteen inches tonight. I suppose you come in here to buy a set of chains for that thing!"

"Snow tires, probly," one of the men said and we all had a good laugh. Then I asked if they had winter storage space for motorcycles.

"You bet. Five bucks a month. Pay when you pick it up. Bring it around back."

I pushed the Norton around to the rear of the building while the salesman opened an electric overhead garage door. It was a dark, cold warehouse-style room with maybe 100 bikes jammed in tank-to-tank. A winter tomb for the two-wheeled undead; consecrated earth in a Dracula's castle of slumbering bikes who only come out when it's warm. The salesman looked over the sea of mirrors and handlebars and finally found an open space. I shut off the fuel, wiped the bike down with a rag, and eased the Norton into a slot between a Honda 305 Dream with a duct-tape seat and a full-dress Yamaha 200 Electric Start with ape-hangers and a backrest that somehow reminded me of the monogrammed aluminum screen door on my neighbor's house. The Norton looked lost in the vast stygian chaos of bikes, and I felt a tinge of regret when the lights went out and the garage door came down; it was like leaving my dog at the kennels. But blizzards were Nature's way of telling you to park your bike.

I told the salesman I'd be back on the first warm day of spring, then trudged out to the highway to hitch a ride. It was snowing harder and the flakes were coming down the size of small paper plates. The wind was really blowing now. The headlights of passing cars were nothing but soft globes of whiteness in the swirling snow. The third car to pass suddenly locked up his tires and stopped just down the road. I ran up and got in. A young man was driving. He had hangers in the back window and looked like a college student.

"Terrible time to be out hitchhiking," he said. "How did you ever end up way out here?"

"I rode my motorcycle," I said.

The smile froze on his face and he cast a sidelong glance at my clothes and the helmet in my lap. He laughed, a little uneasily. It was the same reaction you get if you tell people you've just arrived from the planet Mongo. With a more subdued and cautious voice he asked, "Where are you headed?"

"Home," I said, savoring the word and thinking about a steaming hot shower, "where I belong."

April 1980

THE FLASHBACK EXPRESS

You Can't Go Home Again, But You Can Enjoy the Ride with a Honda Benly 150 Touring

Can't go home again? As Bob Dylan says, "Of course you can." For those of us who paid attention to them when we were young, the mechanical details of motorcycles can be a sort of visual time machine, powerful touchstones to an earlier era, just like a visit to your home town. I still ride there at least once every summer to consider the passage of time and other deep matters, but mostly for lunch at the Elroy Café.

When the Sunday paper arrived that morning, I glanced at the front page where American statesmen were saying thoughtful things about countries that have a lot of oil, then I cast it aside. Digging through the center section I zeroed in on the heart of the paper, the motorcycle classifieds. I was in the market for a good cheap utility bike for running around town and the occasional jaunt into the countryside. My 400F was decked out as a production racer with no sidestand and had to be leaned on a tree wherever I went. Also, I'd grown weary of warming up four quarts of genuine Blackstrap 40-weight Racing Oil every time I had to run to the 7-Eleven for some nacho bean dip and a throw-away razor. I had a vague longing for an easygoing duffer of a motorcycle, a mechanical respite from the hectic, urgent quality of the 400 Four.

I opened the paper wide, set my coffee cup on it, and started down the column of used bikes. There were two BSAs, one chopped and one partly chopped—but with much chrome—followed by a "loaded" BMW R100 that cost $119 less than I made last year. "A nice bike, and money left over for gas," I mused. Skimming over a Can-Am that was only raced four seasons, I worked my way down the long list of H-bikes, where I suddenly stumbled over the following item:

For Sale: 1962 Honda 150 Benly Touring. Can be made to run again. $50.

An alarm went off somewhere deep in the fiasco-defense portion of my brain, but I drowned it out with some quick scoffing. "Of course it can be made to run again," I mumbled to myself. "The bloody Hindenburg can be made to run again, if you've got money to burn. Hell, raise the Titanic!"

I let it pass and continued scanning the column, stopping by force of habit at those missing letters of the alphabet where various British and European Singles and Twins used to appear—and occasionally still do. Nothing there. No hundred-dollar Metrallas; not a single AJS 7-R offered for a fraction of its worth by an unsuspecting widow with her mortgage in arrears; not even a faded Desmo being tossed out of the garage by a confused couple whose son is in the Air Force in Turkey and never writes. A dull day for the classifieds.

I returned to the Honda and frowned. Good grief . . . a 150 Benly. Little brother to the Dream. I hadn't seen one in years. I thought they'd all been patched up and run into oblivion by beatniks. That, or died of exposure chained to the front bumper of some camper with mallard decals all over it. Fifty bucks was not much money, even for a 150, if it could really be made to run. At that price you never knew what to expect; it might be scattered around in six peach crates, or have nothing worse than burned points. Anything could happen to a motorcycle in 17 years. Old bikes survived from one decade to the next on odd twists of fate and the whims of a succession of owners, like the horses and dogs in children's stories—generally the victims of some casual human vice. You couldn't always get there in time to save them.

Before calling the number I dragged out my Castrol box of old motorcycle sales literature and sifted through for some hard information on the Benly. I finally found a 1964 folder, gleaned from the sales rack of a Honda-and-fishing-tackle shop where I used to hang around. The folder opened up four ways into a poster that showed every big road bike that Honda made that year, from the 305 Superhawk down to the Super 90. There was a nice picture of the 150, all in scarlet and chrome, with big fat whitewall tires. Beneath the photo the legend read:

Here's one of the best all-around motorcycles ever built, with an enviable engine performance record. The Advanced Honda engine is a two-cylinder, four-stroke power plant designed to use a high compression ratio of 7.5:1. The overhead camshaft eliminates unnecessary reciprocating weight for peak efficiency. The Honda CA-95 produces 16.0 hp at 10,000 rpm. Electric starter of course.

Of course.

Thinking back as hard as I might, I honestly couldn't remember anybody who envied the performance of the 150, except maybe those of us who rode 50s—and even we knew they weren't Japan's answer to the Vincent Black Shadow. A friend of mine used to call the Benlys "retro rockets." They were famous, in fact, for being quite slow at a time when other Hondas raised eyebrows by going so fast. Still, they were reliable, and in 1962 reliability was one aspect of performance you could truly envy, especially in an engine that held together at 10,000 rpm, didn't leak oil, and consumed almost no gasoline.

A close check of the Honda spec sheet further revealed that the bike had a 49 x 41mm bore and stroke, weighed 246 pounds, had a four-speed forward constant mesh transmission, and was supposed to deliver "approx." 75 miles per hour and 141 (not a mere 140) miles per gallon. A perfect bike for the age of windfall profits.

That night I drove out to look at the 150. It belonged to a man who had taken it to work every day until the right-side cam bearing housing fell off onto the road and was lost. Since the bike had bad mufflers and a slipping clutch, he reasoned it wasn't worth fixing and parked it in the back of the garage, just behind the Weber grill and the cluster of 10-speeds. It sat just so for three years, until a better job beckoned the family to Houston and the Honda was found to be worth less per pound than the cost of its shipping by Mayflower. So the owner, working on the one-born-every-minute principle, ran an ad in the paper. Twenty-four hours later I was standing at his doorstep.

When we pushed the Honda out into the center of the garage it looked a little rough, even under the dangling 40-watt light bulb. The seat was torn; the unsupported end of the camshaft wobbled luridly when the engine was kicked over (yes, Virginia . . .), and the raw, rusted-off ends of the mufflers stuck out like a pair of blown howitzers. The paint was faded from the original factory Light Scarlet to a sort of Allis-Chalmers orange, and the engine was flocked with that curious mixture of brown oil and kitty-litter that seems drawn to the cooling fins of forgotten bikes.

As I stood back and looked at the Honda, words other than "prime" and "cherry" crossed my mind. The 150 was in pretty sad shape; a quintessential $50 motorcycle suffering its last chance to be owned. Yet beneath all that disarray—I told myself—there lurked a certain camp, period-piece beauty. And except for the cam cover and a few pounds of truant muffler material all the parts were there.

Normally I would have fled from a cycle in this condition, counting myself rich and prudent for all the money I hadn't spent. But this one I had to have. I knew even before I drove out to look at the thing that I would probably weaken and buy it. The bike, for me, was more than just an old crock. A 150 Benly Touring, Light Scarlet in color, was the first Japanese motorcycle to penetrate the great barrier of rolling farmland that surrounded my home town. It was the first Honda I ever saw.

I wrote out a check for $50 and the owner and his sons loaded the bike into their Chevy van and delivered it to my house. When it arrived I rolled the 150 into the middle of my garage, turned on all the lights, opened a beer, and pulled up a lawn chair. It was a nice summer night full of crickets, so I left the garage doors open. I was in the mood for a long look, a chance just to sit and study the bike. There are times when a motorcycle is just like an old song or a forgotten photograph. You run across one from the past and it floods you with memories, conjuring up all kinds of forgotten details from another era. You see a certain bike or hear it run and suddenly you can remember exactly what you were doing when it was around. Brain cells you'd given up as long lost to all that Southern Comfort and lime vodka in your formative years somehow regenerate and send clear and perfect messages. For me, the Benly was that kind of machine. It brought back things I hadn't thought of for a long time. I sipped on my beer, looked at the bike, and let myself drift.

It was 1962 when I first saw one. I was 14 years old and living in a primitive civilization without shopping malls. We had stores then, and Muzak hadn't yet been perfected. My parents drove a 1956 Buick Special three-tone (blue, white, and blue) with a plush rope across the back seat in case you wanted to hang on to something, since there were no seatbelts.

When we drove into the city, the parking meters accepted pennies and you could buy hamburgers as big as quarters for 19 cents. Words like Emission Control were used, discreetly, only by doctors and nurses. Elvis was out of the Army, and Saigon was a place called the Paris of the Orient. My nine-transistor radio, permanently tuned to a distant WLS in Chicago, was blasting Duke of Earl and Telstar from its pathetic tin speaker. There were no sound systems then, so I made do with a record player. Henry Gregor Felsen novels were checked out of a library rather than an Instructional Materials Center. Von Trips was dead. Phil Hill was reining World Champion, and on the screen Peter O'Toole had just put a thrilling end to the Cinemascope life of T. E. Lawrence by crashing a JAP-engined Brough Superior on an English country lane. In 1962 Ernie Kovacs died, and my shop teacher bought a new Corvair Monza. It was the year a 21-pound chunk of Sputnik Four landed on a street corner in Manitowoc, Wisconsin.

Just 100 miles inland from that little-known non-disaster, I was spending the weekend on the farm of a friend of mine from school. We'd both just graduated from eighth grade and we were playing badminton with his three brothers on the lawn of the farmhouse. Suddenly we heard a high-revving motor, accompanied by the country sound of gravel plinking off the insides of metal fenders. We turned to see a young woman in helmet, goggles, and a jacket with a map of Korea on the back riding up the driveway on a bright red motorcycle. It was my friend's older sister. She was 19 years old, with dark eyes and long brown hair, and I thought she was beautiful. A Bohemian at heart and one of the original free spirits of the decade, she had the previous summer motored all over the West on a beat-up Indian V-Twin.

She removed her helmet, shook out her hair, and told us the bike was a brand-new Honda 150 and she'd sold her Indian to buy it. She said you could rev the Honda to 10,000 rpm and it didn't leak oil, so you could keep it right in your house if you wanted to. We all let out a low whistle of approval. The mother of the family brought out some iced tea and we all sat on the lawn to admire the bike. Even then I thought it was sort of funny looking—and a poor trade for an Indian V-Twin—but I didn't say anything.

The Honda didn't have that bare-bones hard mechanical look that motorcycles were supposed to have. It was all sculptured and full of sheet metal, like a Vespa or a Talbot-Lago with fender skirts. Everything was enclosed: battery, chain, air filter, electrics, and cables were all hidden beneath covers, tunnels, and overlapping shrouds. The fenders looked like Roman gladiators' helmets, and the rear shocks were square. (Were there square springs and shock seals beneath those covers?) The styling was pure cream puff, full of flowing, swoopy lines that managed to appear squared-off at their edges. There was a new message of cleanliness and civility in the machine, and I wasn't so sure I liked the message. Honda was trying to tell you that you didn't have to know how a motorcycle worked in order to own one, any more than Sophia Loren had to be a Lambretta mechanic to ride around Rome.

Back then I judged every motorcycle by how much it looked like a Triumph (a habit not entirely lost) and I immediately dismissed the Benly as cushy and decadent. Always a callow youth, I failed to appreciate many of the good points buried in the design. How, at 14, could I know that the pressed-steel frame, swing arm, and front forks with their swinging-link suspension were not merely a compromise with cheap mass-production, but an effort to incorporate the best features of the light and modern NSU racing bikes, so much admired by Honda? Or that the odd-looking, very tall cylinder head enclosed a chain-driven overhead cam, and that all those little clacking and whirring bits and pieces turned over at speeds normally seen only on racing bikes that had to be rebuilt every half hour? Or that the electrical system, hidden deep in the frame, might still be working, untouched, after 17 years—electric starter and all?

And looking at the bike as it sat in my garage that night, I was struck by something else—a view from the era of one-liter-plus superbikes. Honda had taken 150ccs of displacement and stuck it into a real motorcycle; not a downsized mini-chopper or a pit bike for kids, but a cycle with the aura and proportions of a full-sized road machine. A remarkable, lost concept lived in the Benly—it was a 246-pound luxury touring bike, a plush cruiser with the displacement of two Dixie cups. I wondered if you could really tour with the Benly Touring. The word was right in the official title, but would a 150 really carry two people and some luggage in any kind of comfort? Or was the designation a misnomer, like the word scrambler applied to certain high-pipe road bikes of the 1960s? I vowed that if the Benly could be got running I'd take it for a short but proper tour.

Maybe my wife, Barbara, could be persuaded to come along. We could go north into the country and journey back to the farm where I saw that first Honda. We could take our tent and camp. A bike was no touring machine, after all, if you couldn't go two-up and camp.

It took a little time and money to get the 150 right. Fifty-dollar motorcycles are like blackmail or a drug habit—they keep costing more and more, but you're in too deep to quit. Before I was done, I'd lavished many hours and $150 on the Honda, right up to the magic buck-a-cc limit. I cleaned the bike thoroughly, polished the chrome, and rubbed out the faded paint. Then it got new mufflers, battery, clutch, air cleaner, side-cover knobs, plugs, points, oil (0.8 qt.), and a right-side cam bearing. All the parts were available on order from Honda and took about two weeks to arrive. Only the baffle inserts for the mufflers were out of stock. No problem. Back in high school removing baffles was the ultimate demon tweak of the backyard tuner. The Benly would have to go on the street sounding a little louder than stock. I just hoped I was up to handling all that extra power.

With all the parts in place, I cranked the engine over. The electric starter worked fine and the engine fired almost immediately. Great clouds of smoke, smelling like old lawnmower gas and flaming cobwebs, billowed from the mufflers, but it soon settled down to a clean, steady idle. It had a throaty, mellow note that sounded much more like a large British Twin than like the cammy little whizzer I'd expected. I clunked it into first, extinguishing the red neutral light (still working after all these years, in the square headlight nacelle just behind the built-in speedometer), and motored down the driveway.

Out on the street the Honda performed just the way it sounded—all low-end torque and thunder. You could ride and shift it just like a big British Twin, and with the baffles gone the effect was fairly convincing. The only difference was that when you were done shifting and flat-out in fourth, the Honda was going about 55 instead of 110. It rode and sounded like an honest-to-God big bike, except that everything happened at a 50 percent increment of the normal range.

Top end of the Benly was just a wild guess, of course, based on the progress of the other traffic. The speedometer needle wagged and vacillated crazily, like an admonishing finger telling you to slow down. It reminded me of a floating cork-and-needle compass I once made in Scouts. Curious about the true speed of the bike, I had Barb follow me out onto the highway and clock it against our Nash station wagon, that world standard of precision. The Nash speedo had me flat out at 57 miles per hour, once it caught up. Then, with the help of neighbor Lee Heggelund (a track coach and no slouch with a stopwatch), we marked off a quarter mile at the famous K-Mart Parking Lot Drag Strip and I took a few runs at it. On my third and best try I got down to a scintillating 24.66 seconds, trap speed unknown. "Maybe some bleach on the rear tire . . ." Lee suggested. A new 150 may have gone "75 approx. mph" back in 1962 with a bantam-weight jockey strapped to the tank and a friendly wind sweeping off the slopes of Mt. Fuji, but there was no way in 1979—not with a 165-pound pizza-eating American in the saddle and 13,000 on the odometer.

Unenviable track performance aside, the 150 worked just fine on the street and was perfect for riding around town. Its tires were the only remaining problem. The rear was an ancient K-70 Dunlop, and the front carried no identification at all except the single word, "Riken," which I took to be either a brand name or a misspelled assessment of the tire's road-holding qualities. Both tires were worn perfectly square across the bottom, leaving a heeled-over footprint about the thickness of a dime. The mildest lean caused the bike to handle very oddly, cornering in swoops and dips, like a playful otter chasing trout. Also, the rear tire tried to slide a quick 180 into every turn, which was no fun at all. So I went down to the cycle shop and bought a pair of Universal tires, legendary for their low price and for cutting down on sparks and noise by keeping your rims off the pavement. They were a vast improvement.

Universal shod, I rode off into town to show people my new bike. The Benly drew mixed reviews that first day. Everyone had an opinion; no one was neutral. A friend of mine said it was "a bike only a pimp could love," and a man at a stoplight told me it was the "best damned bike I ever had." The child across the street, who just recently learned to talk, described it as "a funny motorcycle." People who knew absolutely nothing about motorcycles thought it was "very pretty," or even "beautiful." Those more acquainted with the breed rolled their eyes back in their heads and snorted, or merely chuckled quietly. Then, when they settled down to examine the old bike, their eyes took on a vague, faraway look and I knew that they too were being transported back to something or someplace.

In the end, the 150 brought out the best in people. Two friends contributed accessories to the Benly. One was a handlebar-mounted windshield with a green panel at the bottom. I normally don't care much for windshields, but this one fit the essence of the bike perfectly and gave it that hard-core touring look. The other donation, from a retired Honda mechanic, was the crowning touch—a genuine Benly fender ornament with a flying wing. Vibration, he explained, used to cause a fatigue crack in the leading edge of the front fender, so Honda came up with a factory fix to hold it all together—a fender emblem. He also informed me that when the Benly first came out, a certain Italian fashion designer was so taken with the lines of the bike that he created an entire wardrobe to be worn while riding. (When I looked at the Benly, the only wardrobe that came to mind was some sort of Dobie Gillis outfit—chinos, bleeding madras shirt, and penny loafers.)

With the windscreen and flying wing in place, the Honda was ready to head into the country. We loaded it down with a tank bag, two sleeping bags, and Big Pink—a faded pup tent from my youth, originally designed to hold a pile of comic books and two nine-year-olds with a flashlight. It was waterproofed on the assumption you could run into the house if it rained. I filled a backpacker's plastic fuel container with gasoline and stuffed it into my tank bag, just in case the gas stations were closed for the weekend. I noted with effortless irony the unfairness of having to haul extra gas on a motorcycle simply because so many people drove grotesquely overweight automobiles.

We got underway early on a Saturday morning, heading north out of Madison toward a town called Sauk City. The first 15 miles of highway were crowded and busy. The 150 felt smooth and crisp in the cool morning air, but just couldn't push two people and a windscreen through the air at anything over 50 miles per hour. We got passed by everything on the road; funeral processions, farm implements, three nuns in a station wagon—everything but a homecoming float and the Tijuana Marching Guitar Band. Most people seemed to sense we were working with some kind of power deficit and gave us waves of encouragement.

We relaxed over a big breakfast at the Jailhouse Café in Sauk City, then rode off into the welcome quiet and emptiness of the county roads that would take us all the way to Elroy, Wisconsin, my erstwhile hometown. Out of faster traffic the 150 was in its element, cruising along serenely and easily at about 45 miles per hour. Climbing hills, the big twin ran out of clout very quickly, but a downshift to third handled all but the steepest grades. I kept looking down at the engine, trying to figure out where all the torque was coming from. On long, flat stretches it reminded me of a 36-horse Volkswagen I once had. You'd shift into fourth and then reach for another gear that wasn't there, not so much to go faster as to muffle that Spad-climbing-into-the-dawn engine roar. The machine was telling you it was time to back off and be content. Only when you had to use the brakes or swerve to avoid a rabid farm dog did the bike's built-in moderation make sense. The suspension and brakes simply weren't built to handle any more speed. If Mr. Honda had intended for Man to fly on a Benly he'd have changed the design slightly, raised the price, and called it a 305 Dream.

Fifty miles from home we stopped at a roadside cheese factory and picked up some two-year-old cheddar and a bottle of much younger Mountain Red for lunch. The stop was a welcome one. After a few hours on the Benly we both had that numb, end-of-the-cattle-drive feeling. The handlebars, footpegs, and seat were laid out in roomy, comfortable fashion for a relatively small bike (even the American Longhorn handlebars weren't too bad, since there was no stiff wind to lean on), but the seat began to feel hard and narrow as the miles wore on. We soon found ourselves taking turns standing on the footpegs; the bike handled strangely with both of us standing at once, so Barb had to wait in line.

We took our wine and cheese up the road to the farm of David and Lucy Rhodes, a pair of reformed cosmopolitans who for reasons of their own prefer to live without alternate-side-street parking. David, who once owned a BSA Gold Star, among other fine machines, had nothing but praise for the Honda.

"That's certainly an interesting bike," he said.

We had lunch and then headed for my home town. I was anxious to see the old place. My parents had long since moved away and I hadn't been back for years. Elroy is a nice farm community that was once a booming railroad center. It was the C&NW's halfway point between Chicago and the Twin Cities. When I was a kid, there were two giant roundhouses working around the clock and you could hardly cross town for all the trains. The railroad is all but gone now; the ticket office is being renovated as an historical landmark and the main rail line has become a state bicycle trail. The town is built against a large hill with streets that are steep beyond belief—a sort of San Francisco of the Midwest with 1,500 people and no harbor. Strictly first gear stuff for the 150. We spent an hour chugging up and down hills while I bored Barbara to tears by pointing out meaningless landmarks and recounting stories from my childhood—all shouted over my shoulder.

With that out of my system, we rode out to the city fairgrounds and set up Big Pink next to the empty 4-H cattle barns. Then we went into town for dinner at the Elroy Café, took in *The China Syndrome* at the Elroy Theater, and later stopped at Mr. Ed's Bar, where we ran into some old high school friends and polished off a few Heinekens before returning to camp. It didn't rain that night and we escaped sleeping in the cattle barns. We packed up early, had breakfast at the Elroy Café, and headed for home.

Ten miles from town I had one last stop to make. I wanted to visit the farmhouse where I saw my first Honda, that harbinger of the Japanese Invasion. We turned off County WW into a deep valley where the winding gravel road followed a creek. I missed the driveway at first and had to go back and look for it.

My visions of reunion with old friends faded as soon as we pulled up to the mailbox. The big white farmhouse where I'd stayed was empty and unpainted. Most of the windows were broken, or dark and curtainless. A back wing of the house had black streaks on the wall, as though damaged by fire. In the front yard, where we once sat drinking iced tea and admiring a shiny new motorcycle, was a mobile home surrounded by a clump of flowers. A 1966 Mustang with oversized tires and a raised rear end sat in the driveway, and a limping collie dog came out from beneath the car and barked at us from a safe distance. A young woman came to the door of the mobile home. She shouted something at the dog and then waved to us, tentatively. We waved back. She was no one I'd ever seen before. Different people lived here now; everything was gone, changed. We turned around and rode up the valley toward the county highway.

We took the long way home, winding down the Kickapoo River Valley, then joining up with the Wisconsin and heading east along the sandy floodplane. The sun was at our backs, setting a deep gold in both my mirrors, and the early evening air had a nice warmth left over from the afternoon. We crossed a bridge to the less-traveled southern bank of the river and motored along the water's edge, nearly alone on the highway. The Benly was running strong and clear, its exhaust note a steady, faultless drone muffled by the wind. It couldn't have run any better, even in 1962. Cars were turning their lights on as we entered the city. It was almost dark when we got home.

As always after a long ride, it felt good to be back in a cool, quiet house. I called to have a pizza delivered, then opened a beer and sat down on the front porch. The wind noise was still in my ears, like the sound of two seashells, slowly fading away. I sipped on my beer and looked at the Benly out in the driveway.

Touring on a 150 was good fun, I decided, providing you chose your highways carefully. A bike like the Benly wasn't cut out to mingle with traffic on Interstates or major highways, but those roads were not much fun on any motorcycle. The 150 encouraged you to pick pleasant, low-pressure routes across the countryside and then to ride at speeds that allowed you to enjoy the scenery. It was a good device for watching the country slip by. It got excellent gas mileage (90 miles per gallon with two people, luggage, and a windshield), ran well, and all its pieces continued to do what they were supposed to, mile after mile. While there were other bikes for other moods and purposes, this one was just right for a tenth-and-a-half liter tour.

But in 1979, the Benly did more than carry you efficiently down the road. It brought back, if you were lucky, visions of a big farmhouse where a nice family lived, of someone's pretty older sister who one summer rode all over the West, of gas for 24.9, and a small town with a busy train station. As a private indulgence, the 150 was a nice thing to have around. For $150 you could afford to keep it as part of a small collection, taking it out for a ride or looking at it every so often, like an old photograph. Well-maintained, a motorcycle was a thing that stayed fixed in time. It didn't change or move away, but always stood by, waiting at any time to become animated and to continue from where it left off. All you had to do was park it in your garage and keep it ready. Which was exactly what I intended to do with the Benly. If you couldn't go home again, you could at least enjoy the ride.

I picked up the Sunday paper, still wedged in the screen door, and carried it back to my chair. I slid the want ads out of the middle and tossed the other 40 pounds of newsprint on the floor. I read over the list of motorcycles a few times and then went back to the one that caught my eye. It was a 1968 Triumph T100C, a Tiger Competition 500. The very bike I was about to buy when I got drafted. Good Lord . . . a 1968 Tiger. I could almost see the sculptured aquamarine tank and the high double pipes and stainless steel fenders, smell the hot oil around the valve caps and hear the chuffing exhaust note at tickover. It would look nice in the garage, sitting right next to the Benly. The price in the paper was ridiculously low; the Triumph probably needed a lot of work. I circled the ad with a pen and went to the phone.

"Who are you calling?" Barb asked as she walked into the room.

"Oh, no one," I said whistling to myself and listening to the phone ring on the other end. I checked my watch and wondered if it would be too late after the pizza came to take an evening ride on the Benly and look at an old bike.

November 1980

DOWN THE ROAD AGAIN

Life Can't Pass You by as Long as There Are Triumphs

On a cold and snowy December evening in 1979, I came home from my job as a service manager at a Volkswagen repair shop in Madison, Wisconsin. My wife, Barbara, had made a wonderful dinner, but I told her I had to take two Excedrin and lie down for a while. I'd had arguments with two impossible customers at the service desk and my head was splitting. So I went upstairs and lay in the dark, still with my workboots and workshirt on, and put a cold cloth over my eyes, listening to the winter wind howl around the chimney of our house.

A few minutes later, the phone rang in the dark room. I fumbled for it and found myself speaking with Allan Girdler, Editor of Cycle World. *He asked if I would like to come to California and work full-time for the magazine.*

My headache was suddenly gone, and we had a wonderful dinner.

This is a story I brought with me when we moved to California, just completed as a freelance submission. I think it's still my favorite piece of work, probably because old Triumphs remain my favorite motorcycles for the reasons described here.

The rain came down in solid sheets, like one of those B-movie monsoons where you suspect they're dumping a watering can in front of the lens. It was the kind of downpour a friend of mine from Texas calls a toadstrangler. Barb and I were waiting it out in an abandoned barn along the road, standing one foot back from the door, perfectly dry. We'd seen the storm coming. Our motorcycle was parked behind us, still making hard plinking sounds as it cooled. The barn smelled like pigeons and burlap dust.

The sky didn't promise any sudden change, so we sat down in a corner of the barn and leaned back against the wall. I took a cigarette from the bent, crumbling pack that stays in my Barbour suit for just such occasions and settled back for a long gaze at the motorcycle. I didn't care if it rained all day; I never got tired of looking at the bike.

It was a 1967 Triumph Bonneville, burgundy in color, on its maiden post-restoration voyage. We were traveling to a Country-Blues festival in a little Wisconsin town called Arena. Muddy Waters, Luther Allison, and the Ozark Mountain Daredevils were supposed to be there. The radio had been plugging the concert for weeks. Mass quantities of beer and bratwurst were promised. It all sounded good, but for me the trip was more than just a chance to sit on a grassy hillside, snacking and listening to music. It was the fulfillment of a half-forgotten, leftover dream. And, in some twisted sense, a small private revenge on the likes of Melvin Laird, and a couple of ex-presidents to boot.

Just ten years late, a mere decade out of sync with the mainstream of American culture, I was finally going to a music festival on a Triumph motorcycle. It had been, in the immortal words of David Crosby, a long time coming.

It started in the late 1960s, when I was languishing in college. Back in those days I thought that the three finest things in the world were a Nikon camera, a Martin guitar, and a Triumph motorcycle. (I was trying hard to shun materialism, but hadn't quite got the hang of it.) I was certain that if you could latch onto those three items, your earthly needs would be forever complete. Sure, you might need some clothes, a place to sleep, an occasional meal, and a few Jack Kerouac novels—but those were all minor, secondary considerations.

In this simple material hierarchy, the Triumph was important above everything. It allowed you to go to all the right places where you could take pictures with the Nikon and play your Martin guitar, and to properly punctuate those arrivals and exits with a certain romantic flair. It was also important just because it was a Triumph, the best-handling, good-looking all-around motorcycle an enthusiast could buy. The machine was a cultural legend.

Everyone who knew anything seemed to have a Triumph. Dylan appeared on the cover of *Highway 61* wearing a Triumph T-shirt and was reputed in whispers of the Rock grapevine to have been riding a Triumph 500 at the time of his reportedly terrible, possibly disfiguring accident near Woodstock that may or may not have nearly killed him and ended his career. Arlo Guthrie sat astride a Triumph on the cover of *Running Down the Road*, and everyone knew that when Arlo said he didn't want a pickle but just wanted to ride his motorsickle, he was talking about his big Twin. Steve McQueen made the national magazines desert-sledding his 650, and even on the screen he chose a thinly disguised Wehrmacht-grey Triumph for his Great Escape (you could hardly expect him to jump a 10-foot fence into Switzerland riding a BMW and sidecar with armor plate).

In the real world of competition and road riding, Triumphs were the universal motorcycles of the 1960s. They were expected to go everywhere and do everything well, just as today's roadburners are not. They won at desert races, flat tracks, endures, TTs, Bonneville, and Daytona. The great names—Nixon, Elmore, Romero, Castro, and dozens of others—all wore leathers emblazoned with that swooping Triumph emblem.

With minor changes in pipes, handlebars, carbs, and gearing, the 500s and 650s could be set up for any purpose. An ordinary, everyday owner expected to be able to use his bike for touring, cowtrailing, stoplight drags, or suddenly peeling off a country road to tear across some farmer's field of new-mown hay. Triumphs were not generally transported in pickup trucks; riding started from your garage.

If you had a garage. Or a Triumph. Which I did not.

I had a Honda CB160. I didn't have a Nikon or a Martin, either. Just a secondhand twin-lens reflex camera and a $50 Harmony guitar. I was attending the university and sharing a student-dive apartment with three roommates who did their dishes once a week with a can of Raid. Those were wonderful times. We all lived in a world of gray underwear because we didn't sort colors from whites at the laundromat, and we thought chivalry was hiding old pizza cartons under the sofa when someone's girlfriend came for the weekend. Every night about nine the police cruised by and shot a teargas canister onto the front porch, just as a warning.

Next to the typewriter on my desk was a coffee can with a slot in the top, marked "Triumph Fund." I was working nights unloading trucks at the Coca-Cola bottling plant and setting aside a share of those earnings for a new cycle. Any Triumph would have been acceptable, but I had settled on a Competition Tiger 500, not only because it was the cheapest of the line, but because it looked like the most versatile. It had a single carb and E.T. ignition, which I imagined would make it easier to tune, and a 500 seemed like a sensible step between my 160 and the ultimate purchase, a Bonneville.

But even a 500 cost over a thousand dollars, which represented a lot of truckloads of Coke bottles in those pioneer days of inflation, and somehow the Triumph fund never grew large enough for even a respectable down payment. It was always being robbed for tuition or going to see *Blow-Up* for the fifth time. One of my roommates was also working at the Coke plant and saving for a Triumph, with about the same success. The idea was that we would buy a pair of them, at some tremendous volume discount, and then take the Ideal Trip to some Rock festival or other celebration against doom. We worked and saved, unloaded bottles and calculated profits, but never seemed to gain much financial ground.

Then one day my roommate got lucky. He showed up in the driveway on a nice blue and white T100R—a Daytona. He'd got an absolutely incredible deal on the bike. He bought it from a fraternity boy who had flunked out and was selling off all his luxuries—cowboy boots, Head skis, Four Tops albums, stolen beer steins, etc.—in that timeless ritual of prodigal sons everywhere who return home dishonored and humble. My roommate paid the poor guy just enough for some sackcloth and ashes and a bus ticket east.

The Daytona was put to hard use. In the months that followed, it made dozens of flat-out runs between Madison and Chicago. My roommate, after a heated phone call with his sometime-girlfriend, would slam down the receiver, hop on his bike, and dash off to Chicago in the middle of the night. When he got there he'd pound on her apartment door and have a terrible fight in the hallway, then ride back home at high speed, arriving at our apartment in the early hours of the morning, completely worn out and looking like frozen Death. Then he'd crash into bed, still wearing his boots and leather jacket, and sleep for about two days.

Nothing quite so dramatic was possible on my Honda 160. You could get to Chicago and back with no problem, but the 160 was missing an element of passion and fire-breathing style that only a raucous British Twin could deliver. The Triumph was good theater; it was made for the dashing arrival and the bellowing, angry departure. When you left on one, people were supposed to watch you shift off into the distance and think, "That guy's out there somewhere on a Triumph now. I hope he's all right . . ." If you rode a 160 they just assumed you were fine, which was no fun at all.

The money never fell together for a Triumph. School ended and a slightly desiccated lady at the draft board branded me U.S. Choice. Most of the next two years were spent perspiring, carrying a radio around on my back, and driving a Jeep down tropical roads clogged with Honda 50s and 90s. We all went on a lot of neat hikes and cookouts. It was fascinating, but we missed things that were happening at home and had to enjoy them vicariously through letters and movies. *Woodstock* and *Alice's Restaurant* came to camp and were projected on the side of a reinforced concrete latrine with a sandbag roof. (Odd concept, the rocket-proof latrine; even odder when you're in one and Hendrix is playing his unearthly version of the Star-Spangled Banner on the other side of the wall.)

My ex-roommate kept in touch with letters and told exotic tales of dry socks, air conditioning, and riding his Triumph on country roads—and going to Chicago. He also sent along a color brochure of the new Trophy 650 for 1970, a nice green bike with high double pipes. The brochure was carried around until it finally broke in half from being folded and re-folded. Whenever I got the chance, I'd sit down to look at the Triumph picture and reflect on the merits of being out of the Army. It was during those idle moments that the vision gradually formed; a single enduring image that seemed to embrace everything good about civilian life. It came as a recurring dream. It was a scenario in which I was on a motorcycle trip, going it-didn't-matter-where, dressed in clean civilian clothes of my own choosing and seated at a roadside restaurant, drinking coffee and looking out the window at a Triumph motorcycle. That was it; nothing more than a simple daydream. An American still life waiting to happen.

But it was winter when I got home, so I bought a car with a heater and snow tires and went back to school. By the time there was money for another cycle, the Triumph plant was closed with labor and management problems, British bikes had been eclipsed by new Japanese offerings, and I was lured away by a fast, reliable machine with a lot of cylinders and exhaust pipes. There was no more Triumph fund, and the notion of owning one was allowed to simmer on a back burner. I'd bought a Nikon camera by then, but still didn't own a Martin guitar because you have to play well to deserve one. The Harmless Seventies slipped by, various bikes were bought and sold, and Triumphs became something admired from afar and regarded wistfully when seen on the street.

Then last summer I took a weekend motorcycle trip. While passing through a little unmapped bar-and-gas-pump village, I spotted an old and very ratty Bonneville leaning on the wall of a defunct garage. I inquired after the bike at some nearby houses, but no one was home. The bar and gas station were closed. I left reluctantly and continued the trip, but all through the next winter visions of that neglected, weatherbeaten Bonneville caused me to toss in my sleep, eat poorly, and lose weight. There were troubled dreams of an old garage with a giant snow drift blown up against the wall and nothing sticking out of it but a chromed clutch lever.

In spring I returned to the village. The bike was still there, though it appeared to have been used—the carbs dripped gas and the chaincase was streaked with fresh oil. An old woman was in her yard nearby, watering some flowers clumped around a little windmill. The windmill had a crank and rod arrangement that caused a small wooden lumberjack to drag a saw back and forth over a log. She directed me to the farm of the Bonnneville owner, some two miles away, and said the man ran a sawmill. Sawing wood was a big industry in the village.

I found the man ripping through some logs at his mill. He shut down the saw to talk to me. Yes, he was interested in selling the bike. Property taxes were coming up. He wanted a lot of money for the Triumph and was not interested in taking less; the bike was worth it, he said. He was right, of course. You don't find country folks anymore who have old vehicles and don't know their value—if you ever did. On the contrary, there are farmers who think a Studebaker Lark is worth money. But the myth of the $50 Henderson covered with hay bales is right up there with Babe the Blue Ox.

We went back to the village and I took the Triumph for a test ride. Everything was loose, but the bike ran fine. So, after a moment of silence for my life's savings, I swallowed hard and wrote out a check. We were only 25 miles from the city, so I decided to live dangerously and ride the Bonneville home. Barb drove our Volkswagen. "Follow me, but keep your distance," I advised. "Watch for falling parts and blink your lights if you run over anything."

The trip home was my first ride on a Bonneville. As I motored along those country roads, the bike struck me as a great bundle of conflict and paradox. It vibrated and surged annoyingly through town in lower gears, but you could drop it into fourth and rumble along on the idle circuit with no commotion at all. And at full chat (a foreign term peculiar to the sound and feel of British bikes), it smoothed out into a rushing, headlong resonance no more disturbing than the clicking of rails on a fast passenger train. The brakes were terrible, but every time I dived into a corner at unchecked, suicidal speed I discovered there was no cause for alarm; the Triumph heeled over into an easy arc and came out of the corner without flinching. The hand and foot controls felt crude and antique after the velvet-and-Teflon smoothness of those on my Japanese Four, yet the performance of the bike was anything but antique. The speedometer needle touched a surprisingly easy 105 miles per hour as I moved out to put some distance on a gravel-tossing milk tanker. The Bonneville tracked down the road with an uncanny, almost gyroscopic stability at that speed, encouraging you to go faster than 12-year-old maladjusted engines full of dirty old oil ought to go. I got a firm grip on my enthusiasm, slowed down, and made it home without blowing the thing up.

Most modern Triumph dealers now handle another line of bikes and sell new models and parts on an order-only basis. But in our small city, I found no fewer than four repair shops who welcomed Triumph work and stocked bins of new and used parts. In a few trips I dug up the appropriate tank emblems (missing on mine), primary and drive chains, gaskets, fork seals, gaitors, cables, tune-up parts, and miscellaneous Whitworth nuts and bolts whose standard of measure is the instep of some dead king or the distance between two alehouses; I can't remember which. The rear tire was replaced with a K-81 Dunlop I had lying around, but it didn't look right. Only the original K-70 had the necessary bulk to fill that roomy fender well, so I bought a new one. The front got a new 19-inch ribbed Continental because it looked nearly authentic and someone gave it to me.

Original tank kneepads were unavailable and long gone everywhere I checked. ("If you find any, let me know where you got 'em.") No one had a paint code for a 1967 Bonneville or knew where I might find one. A magazine out of my 1967 archives showed a dark burgundy tank, a color described as "Aubergine," with white and gold trim, and I finally found a very close match with (Gott in Himmel) a Mercedes Medium Red. The tank looked good in a solid color, so I decided not to spoil it by trying my hand at white accent lines and gold pinstripe to match the old photos.

Stripping the tank and sidecovers for painting rivaled the labors of Schliemann unearthing the layered ruins of Troy. The paint revealed a varied past. Beneath the outer coat of flat black primer was a thick layer of metalflake blue, and under that was white metalflake with the understated elegance of a sequined bowling shirt. Then came a Kalifornia Kandy-apple red overlaid with green pinstripe patterns of trapezoids and triangles with the artist's initials, "J.R.," at the bottom. ("That's Joe Rembrandt," my friend Wargula pronounced without hesitation, "Sam Picasso's cousin.")

And on the bottom coat, painted into the original lacquer at the corner of each sidecover, was a small white peace emblem.

In three weeks of weekend and late-night fanaticism the Triumph was ready to roll. With the mechanicals refurbished and the paint nearly dry, we rolled down the driveway and turned west, in the general direction of the Country-Blues festival. The trip was to be a 300-mile meandering back-country ride that would allow us to visit some friends on a farm, hit the festival, and then circle home. The tank was too wet for a tank bag and a luggage rack was aesthetically out of the question, so we left with our pockets bulging and clanking. Just to be safe, we took enough tools and spares to do a major roadside overhaul; everything but a frame jig and crankshaft lathe.

We made it to the end of the block before the Triumph stopped running. The tach cable had pushed the hot wire off the ignition switch. No problem. I rerouted the wire, plugged it in, and we were on our way.

Just out of town, I smelled gasoline and pulled off the road. We were suffering from that dreaded British ailment, Petcock Failure. The brass flare nut was cracked and fuel was hissing onto the hot exhaust. I pulled a tube of silicone sealer and a 7/16 Whitworth from my coat pocket, made an instant O-ring, and everything was fine.

There were no other problems on the rest of the trip. The big Twin thundered serenely along twisting valleys, up and down hills, and across bridges without missing a beat. And at one point, it absolutely blew the doors off a rally-equipped Scirocco when the driver foolishly tried to race with us, apparently believing that a pathetic 90 miles per hour would keep us in his dust. "So long, pal," I said, tossing off a Lafayette Escadrille wave as the car became a dancing speck in our mirrors. "This bike had your name on it."

The Triumph was made for fast, winding country roads. At right around 70 miles per hour it came into its own and maintained the pace easily, backing down from only the worst curves. I didn't know if it was any faster than my Multi, but it certainly had more grace under pressure. We reached our friends' farm in two euphoric hours—record time. We had a nice evening on the farm, eating, drinking, playing guitars, patting dogs on the head, and examining horses.

The sky was threatening rain when we left early in the morning and headed south for the music festival. Around 10 o'clock the air became suddenly cool and the wind dropped off to a deathly stillness that could be sensed even on a motorcycle. We got to the old barn just before the storm landed.

The old Bonneville was a pleasant object to contemplate on a rainy day—or any other time. It provoked a bad case of XKE Syndrome; impossible to park and walk away from without looking back over your shoulder. It was a simple, clean design with all its elements in harmony. I never looked at it and thought, "Nice bike, except for the gas tank," or "I'd buy one if I could throw the seat and mufflers away." I couldn't find an offensive piece or a jarring transition of line anywhere on the motorcycle. It seemed, like the DC-3 or the Winchester saddle gun, to be the final product and distillation of everything learned about balance and proportion in the era that preceeded it. Its lines were, as Saint-Exuperay once said of a favorite aircraft, not invented but simply discovered.

Owners of more modern bikes often commented that you could "see through" the Triumph, or "see what all the parts are for." The starkness and simplicity fostering that impression translate into a unique road feel. At 363 pounds, the Bonneville is light for a 650 and carries its weight low in the frame, so that the roll axis of the bike feels to be between your ankles rather than sloshing and lost somewhere in the gas tank. It gives you the odd, anachronistic sensation you are riding a motorbike—a genuine motorized bicycle, a Schwinn paper-boy special with a big hairy engine bolted into the frame—rather than a two-wheeled transportation module. Perhaps the heart of the Triumph's appeal lies in the subconscious feeling of eternal wonderment that you are hurtling down the road without having to pedal.

The 1967 Bonneville's big advantage, of course, is that it was built just before unelected public servants got into vehicle design. So the Triumph has a front fork unburdened by turn signals, beepers, reflectors, timers, dashboards, and idiot lights, which makes the steering light and precise. The tail light, though visible at night, is smaller than a breadbox, and the shift lever is on the right because, by God, that's where the transmission is. The muffler muffles without strangling (silencer, the British term, is an exaggeration) and the engine has no emission controls to help motorcyclists atone for the past sins of Eldorado owners.

But, like all machines of character, the Triumph had a few spanners designed into its venerable works. By modern standards, it is not a perfect motorcycle. If suffers from medieval wiring (though at least repairable by anyone with a basic waterpipe concept of electrical flow), an engine with all the well-documented vibratory failings of the vertical Twin, and brakes that make reversing the props on the Queen Mary or recalling the Three Hundred from the Valley of Death seem quick and positive. The clutch plates like to stick together on cool (below 80 degrees) mornings, though they can be freed by bumping the bike or jabbing the kick starter with the clutch out. The carbs are sensitive to lean angle and engine heat, and they wear out from their own jittering. (To compensate for carb problems, however, the factory always listed thousands of needle and jet options to help in your personal search for the rhythmic tickover and the light-chocolate electrode.)

The rear wheel is installed so that suicide seems a rational alternative to changing a road-side flat (improved, like most of these problems, on later models). And then, of course, the carbs, petcocks, and gaskets tend to seep, further reinforcing a popular belief that the British should never have been allowed to handle any fluid less viscous than chilled window putty.

But I knew all these things when I bought the bike. I didn't expect mechanical perfection. If I wanted that, there were plenty of other motorcycles to choose from; machines like Interstate highways—much better than the old roads, but not always as interesting. The Triumph was no four-lane Interstate. It was a twisting country lane with potholes, loose gravel, one-lane bridges, and switchbacks. And old barns.

The rain ended just before noon. The clouds parted and a shaft of sunlight streamed through the open barn door onto the motorcycle, like some heavenly message from a Charlton Heston epic. The Triumph started, as always, halfway through the first kick, and we were on the road again.

The first band had just begun to play when we arrived at the festival. I parked the Triumph under a tree, between a KZ1300 and a GS1000, and we found a comfortable spot to sit on the hillside not far from the stage. We got something to eat and drink, and sat back in the sun.

Festivals haven't changed so much in 10 or 12 years, I decided. True, Ken Kesey and the Hog Farm didn't show, Canned Heat was gone forever, and the Airplane was off somewhere being a Starship. But there was a dog wearing a red bandana and catching Frisbees in mid-air; a band of jugglers juggling non-stop all afternoon and evening; a pioneer couple whose blond children ran naked around a VW bus; a smattering of outlaws; a girl wearing a rose in her hat and blowing soap bubbles that floated away in the wind; a lone flute player oblivious to the music coming from the stage; a tanned, aging man with a ponytail doing yoga beneath a tree; and a girl in a long dress dancing near the stage by spinning around and around with her arms floating outward until she fell down. We sat next to a man with a wispy satyr beard who smoked a small brass pipe and offered it to everyone who passed, or sat next to him.

With the last rays of the sun slanting through the low cloud of blue smoke and dust that only a crowd of several thousand can raise, Luther Allison offered his last song to the memory of Jimi Hendrix and played a half-hour low-down version of "Little Red Rooster."

We headed home at dusk and rode into darkness. A fog settled on the river valley, and droplets of water formed on my face shield and gloves and blew to the side. The headlights of cars were yellow and vague in the mist, a nice touch at the end of a day in bright sunlight. Halfway home, we stopped at a roadside restaurant for a late dinner. We sat at a window booth where I could look out at the Triumph and sip coffee.

We sat in silence for a while, and then Barb asked, "What are you thinking?"

"I was just thinking," I said, "That riding well is the best revenge."

A lady in the next booth overheard me and snickered, then began to cough and choke on her Bacon-Burger Deluxe. When that was over, she turned in her seat for a look at the person who had uttered this wonderful truth. I stared back and she returned to her dinner. She'd get no apologies from me. I was dead serious.

When we got home I picked up my guitar and started to plunk around on it, running through my cheating, half-the-hard-stuff-missing version of "Little Red Rooster." In the end, I sat up half the night practicing. I figured maybe if I got good enough, I'd finally deserve a Martin guitar. Then I'd have everything I needed.

May 1981

LOST HIGHWAY: IN SEARCH OF OLD 66

Like Beale St. in Memphis, Route 66 was almost a forgotten idea when Barb and I took this trip in 1980, and most people had no idea where the old highway had gone. Now there are whole books on the subject, and the route is sprinkled with gift shops full of souvenir Route 66 key fobs, coffee mugs, signs, and posters. Once again, we seem to have caught our past just before it slipped away.

"You are going to be mighty disappointed," our friend John told us. "There is no such thing as Route 66. Not anymore. I've been out to California and back twice, and 66 is gone. Nonexistent. Finished. It is an ex-highway. It's called Interstate 40 now. Four big lanes nearly all the way from Chicago to L.A."

"Gone?" I rolled one fearful, suspicious eye in John's direction, doing my best impression of Jack Elam acting incredulous.

"How in thunder can 2,500 miles of the most famous road in America be gone?"

"Okay. Maybe there are still a couple of places in Arizona or New Mexico where I-40 bypasses part of the old road, but the rest is pretty much paved over."

I was stunned. Route 66 gone? Paved over and renamed? It was like planning a raft trip down the Mississippi and being told the river was all dried up. Nothing but a dusty riverbed full of catfish skeletons and old tires. Impossible. I'd wanted to take a motorcycle trip on Route 66 to California ever since my budding passion for bikes had collided head-on with a TV program named after the highway. Two guys named Todd and Buzz started it all.

They appeared one evening two decades ago on the black and white snowstorm of my parents' 12-inch TV screen. It was a new program with an unusual premise. It seemed these two single guys had bought a Corvette and set out to work their way across the country. They were searching for something but didn't know what. Every time they cruised into some dusty little town they found jobs driving forklifts at the plant or erecting oil rigs. They inevitably got tangled up with some menacing local types who were dragging their knuckles around and looking for trouble, and usually there was a wistful young (but aging fast) woman who worked at the diner, waiting for someone to take her away from it all. In the end, Todd and Buzz always left town a little wiser but still searching, alone in their Corvette on Route 66.

Stirling Siliphant wrote most of the fine, hard-hitting scripts, and the music by Nelson Riddle had a jazzy, spirit-of-the-open-road kind of sound. The Corvette, the lost women, the music, the freedom . . . it was a heady combination to a 12-year-old who was, at any given moment, in hot water with his parents for not raking the lawn or painting the other half of the garage door.

A few years later, when I got so I could read without moving my lips, I discovered John Steinbeck and read *The Grapes of Wrath.* This story traced the misadventures of the Joad family, a clan of dust bowl farmers, from their ruined Oklahoma homestead to a supposedly better life in California. They suffered every setback a long journey can dish out to folks without enough money. Route 66 in the 1930s was the setting, and Steinbeck described the two-lane road and its towns, car lots, and roadside camps so well, the Joad family and the highway itself became American institutions.

By 1965 I'd become an R & B fan, listening to Chuck Berry and the Rolling Stones belt out their own versions of Bobby Troup's much recorded song, "Route 66." "Well it winds from Chicago to L.A., more than two thousand miles all the way . . . well get your kicks on Route Sixty-Six . . ." That was enough for me. I'd seen the TV program, read the book, and now my record player was driving the message home. It was clear no self-respecting person could call himself an American if he hadn't checked out this fabled highway. Route 66, the pipeline to California, path to the Promised Land, was a fixture in the American consciousness as surely as the

Mississippi River, the Natchez Trace, Pennsylvania Avenue, Main Street, and the Sunset Strip.

It was the kind of trip that, sooner or later, you have to make. Especially if you are a motorcyclist and always looking for a good reason to travel. Or in my case, even a fairly mediocre reason of practically no discernable consequence or socially redeeming value.

The opportunity came last summer. Editor Girdler dispatched a Suzuki GS1000 to cover the Winston Pro races at Elkhart Lake in my home state of Wisconsin and asked if I would ride the bike. My wife, Barbara, could go along for the ride. The plan was this: Take the most direct northerly Interstate east, making all due speed with a Gypsy Scout radar detector scanning for cops, cover the races, and then make a more leisurely return trip on Route 66.

Borrowing from our stock of items to evaluate, we outfitted the GS with a Silhouette Fairing, a Lockhart luggage rack, a clip-on Tourmaster rack bag, my old eclipse tank bag, and a nice set of low Superbike bars I carry around and bolt on to every bike I ride. The GS1000, with 3,000 miles on the odometer, got an oil change and plugs. We made it to Wisconsin in three days on the Interstate and got one speeding ticket, $50 worth, at a speed trap near Denver. It was a visual speed trap—no radar—where they time your progress between two stationary objects. They said we were making too much progress.

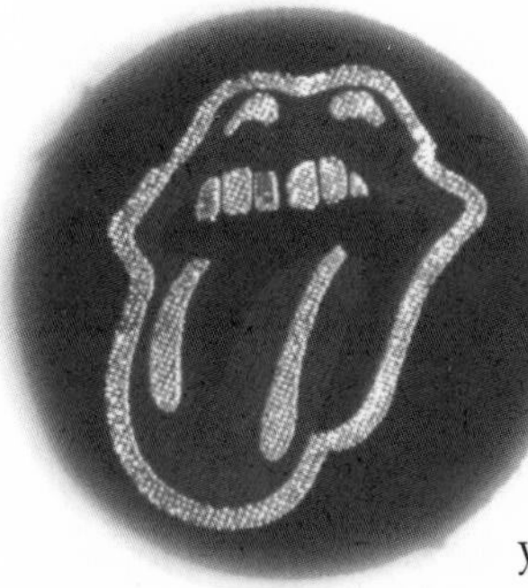

We averaged 85 miles per hour for the trip. The radar detector saved us from at least a dozen other tickets in Iowa alone, which was literally crawling with police, all throwing out enough radar beams to fry an egg or raise your voice one octave. The GS1000 got 40 miles per gallon and used one quart of oil and a small can of chain lube.

It was in Madison, Wisconsin, after the Elkhart races, that our old friend John Oakey cast his rather large, hulking shadow on our return trip. "Dull," he pronounced. "Nothing but freeway and desert. I don't envy you."

The map indeed showed only a few small portions of road marked US 66. There were a few miles in Oklahoma parallel to I-40 west of Tulsa, a patch of incomplete I-road near Tucumcari, and a stretch that followed the Rio Grande south of Albuquerque. Arizona was most promising, with a big northern loop of old 66 bypassing the freeway from Ash Fork to Kingman.

There had to be more; maybe some small traces of the old road going through the small towns. There must be old motels, gas stations, and restaurants still intact near the four-lane. It couldn't all be torn down, hauled away, and gone. America covers its architectural tracks fast, but not that fast. The time was clearly ripe for another of those field trips in Contemporary Archaeology and the Study of Modern Antiquities, those same quasi-academic disciplines that search out and preserve Gene Vincent albums, 1959 Cadillac Coupes de Ville, unfiltered Camels, and juke boxes that look like neon cathedrals.

We left Madison on a blistering hot Wednesday morning in June and headed down Highway 51 to pick up I-55 (aka US 66) at Bloomington, Illinois. We hit the Interstate just in time to join an accordion of cars following a black and white sedan from the Illinois State Patrol at 55 miles per hour. Exactly 55 miles per hour. We shifted down a gear and waited. There's something fairly pathetic about 10 or 20 adults backed up and crawling along in orderly procession behind a squad car. It reminds me of following my fourth grade teacher down the street on a class trip to the fire station. The patrol car finally eased itself down an exit ramp and the tail pipe of every trailing car coughed out a sigh of relief and picked up speed. Barb and I rolled up to 65 miles per hour, or about half speed for the Suzuki.

Route 66 caught us by surprise. We had mistakenly counted on the state map, which was reasonably detailed, to show any remaining sections of the old highway. There were none on the map, and I-55 travels nearly straight and level across Illinois, so we assumed the new road had been laid down over the old. Not so.

Just north of McLean, Illinois, Barb gave me a jab in the ribs and pointed to our right. There, cutting a narrow concrete swathe across meadows, through clumps of trees and across creeks on small bridges, was an abandoned highway with tufts of grass growing between the slabs of patched pavement. It was clearly the one and only original Route 66 of song, novel, and television. One look and you knew it was the real thing.

We got off at the next exit and found a spot where the old highway crossed a country road. The intersection was unmarked—no stop signs, no manicured apron at the corner, no signs of any kind to say what the highway was. Sixty-Six was a Highway With No Name. You had to drop down over a low dirt shoulder from the country road even to get on it. The highway was just there; nameless and heading off inviting and empty through the rural countryside. We shut off the bike, removed our helmets, and sat for a few minutes looking down the road. There was no noise, just the wind through the trees, and it was somehow ghostly; the busiest road in America recently gone silent. You could almost hear the fading echo of a 327 Corvette rumbling off into the distance.

We put on our helmets and headed southwest.

The old road was in remarkably good shape despite weeds, grass, wild oats, and the occasional sapling growing up through the seams. The concrete slabs were solid, showed little weather damage, and were in relatively good alignment. The road was made from thousands of squares of white concrete laid end to end and joined with small strips of black tar. In a few places the broken white and solid yellow lines were still visible, but most of the paint was weathered away.

We started cruising tentatively, watching for chuckholes and broken glass, but soon found the road clean and smooth enough for normal speeds. After twenty minutes we were cruising at 70 or 75 miles per hour, or anything we felt like. The highway was like a science fiction dream, or a scene from one of those post-nuclear novels where a few people find themselves alone on an empty Earth; a road of your own, a fast motorcycle, and nothing to slow you down.

Almost nothing. True to the Last Inhabitant fantasy, the only risk came from animals. Conditioned to an unused road, they'd grown bold around the pavement; living, hunting, and nesting and generally carrying on as animals will in the long grass beside the highway. The dipping, erratic flight of roadside blackbirds had Barb gripping my sides as they narrowly missed our windscreen. Rabbits, chipmunks, strolling pheasants, and something that looked vaguely like a mud hen were all stirred up by the passing commotion of our big Suzuki. Uncomfortable with my sudden role as bull in Nature's own china shop and general despoiler of woodland tranquility, I backed off on the throttle.

None too soon either. We crested a rise and I clamped on the brakes. The highway had ended. The road was cut off by a black and white striped barrier and then disappeared under the soil of a cornfield. Ahead was a high embankment formed by an exit ramp from the nearby I-road. Short of jumping the barrier and plowing corn for 50 yards with the Suzuki, there was nothing to be done. We turned reluctantly around and backtracked for five miles to the last entrance ramp, climbed onto the Interstate, returned five miles, and took the very exit ramp that had blocked our path. On the other side of the cloverleaf we were able to dirt track our way onto old 66 again.

The scene was repeated over and over again. Route 66 ran roughly parallel to I-55, and each time I-55 threw off an exit ramp 66 ended. Sometimes you could play dirt bike, go around the barrier and cross the exit ramp to the other side, where 66 resumed; sometimes there was a dirt road detour off the old highway, especially near small towns, so you could circle around the exit; and sometimes, most of the time, you just had to go back five or ten miles and get on the Interstate. A dirt bike with knobbies and a pair of wire cutters might have helped, but not always. Particularly in one spot, where a washed out bridge had been left washed out.

At every chance, we left the freeway and traveled down the boxed-in sections of old 66, genuinely resenting having to mingle with the vacationing boat-towing masses on the four-lane. Sixty-Six was never very far from the Interstate, but close enough to farmhouses and trees that it could be said to go through the country rather than over it. Its curves and hills followed the topography of the land and the roadcuts were small. The bridges, smaller and more elegant, were built as overhead trestles or reinforced cement work, craftsmanship lost on public works since the days of the WPA. Depression bridges were best.

We had hoped 66 would take us through a lot of small towns, but found we couldn't count on it. Even back in the old days, 66 was a fast road. It went past a lot of towns rather than through them, affording only a passing, sidelong glance down the main streets of small farm communities on the roadside. You could go into the towns, but you had to want to. It was a road in a hurry that paralleled the railroad tracks and didn't dump you off in every burg and speed trap from Chicago to L.A. Which is why our highway ended so often at exit ramps instead of taking us into town.

An exception was McLean, Illinois, where 66 brought us right up to the front door of the Dixie Trucker's Home, a truck stop and restaurant recommended in *Road Food. Road Food* is a guide book that lists and describes eating spots deemed worthy of the cross-country traveler's patronage. It said the Dixie Trucker's Home had, among other things, good fried chicken. The truck stop was crowded and busy, one of those gleaming clean places where you could eat off the floor, as my grandmother used to say, but they had plenty of tables and plates so we didn't have to. The chicken was very good.

We followed 66 wherever possible through the afternoon and rode into a warm, soft summer evening in Lincoln. It was just sundown and baseball diamond lights came on brilliantly as we passed the city park. A drive-in theater along the highway began its show and we caught a glimpse of the wordless previews to *The Long Riders*; much noiseless shooting, smoke, and commotion going on. We decided to press on a few hours longer to Springfield. After a hot day, the merely warm evening felt so good we hated to give it up.

After a five-mile stretch of old 66 and another sudden dead end, we chose to ride on I-55. The strain of watching for barriers, broken glass, and red animal eyes on the deserted highway took too much concentration at the end of a 500-mile day. We stopped for the night in Springfield, Lincoln's hometown, at one of those budget (read: cheap) motels with a dollar figure in its name, of which inflation has now made a mockery. The sign out front advertised "Good Rest, Sweet Dreams," a seductive promise. The rooms, balconies, and restaurant upholstery were mostly turquoise and orange, colors that somehow came to denote modernness in the late Fifties. The painted cement block construction and the colored steel balcony panels with traces of rust gave the place the subtle flavor of a post-war barracks for officers in the New Army. We had good rest, but in the morning could recall no dreams.

We stayed on 66 all the way into St. Louis the next day, where the highway lost its identity somewhere in a maze of cloverleaf bridges, and we found ourselves in a minor manufacturing district near the old Cahokia Indian Mounds. We got back on I-55 and crossed the Mississippi, past the big arch that is the Gateway to the West. The arch glinted golden in the noon sun. "I'm suddenly hungry for a hamburger," Barb remarked.

We stopped at a truck stop in St. Louis—glaring, barren place with bright fluorescent lights. I had a perfectly square block of hash browns and a perfectly round hamburger dwarfed inside a perfectly round bun. A perfect meal.

In the beautiful rugged hill country west of St. Louis, Route 66 suddenly reappeared beside the main road, curving in and out of the woods and climbing hills beside the (now) I-44 roadcuts. It looked too inviting to wait for the next exit, so we just pulled off the Interstate, wallowed the big Suzuki down a rain gully, and launched ourselves up onto the time-scarred pavement of 66 again.

Near Stanton, Missouri, we swept down through a wooded glen, rounded a hairpin turn at the bottom, and crested the next hill to find an amazing collection of old motels, all abandoned except for the Ozark Courts, where the restaurant had been turned into a home. We stopped to take a look around and a nicely dressed woman and her daughter came out from behind the motel to talk to us. The woman said she and her husband ran the restaurant for 10 years before the highway came through in 1963. The motel closed, as did the others nearby, and the restaurant went broke. Her husband, she explained, now works at a McDonald's in Stanton.

"The place was really jumping back then, before they built I-44. We were open 24 hours a day and the counter was always full. There was a bad stretch of road near here, though." She pointed east down the road. "That curvy section you just came through, where it goes downhill through the trees, that place caused a lot of accidents. People would cross the yellow line and hit head-on. Seems like there was an accident nearly every other night, especially when it got foggy down there. Must have been 20, 30 people killed there over the years." She brushed a strand of hair out of her eyes and pointed to the traffic droning by in the distance on I-44. "That new road is a whole lot safer," she said quietly. "It was bound to come."

She wished us good luck and she and her daughter walked around to the back of the empty, windowless Ozark Courts. The restaurant in back had been converted into a very nice house, but from the front it was impossible to tell anyone lived there.

Central Missouri was Jesse James country. Competing signs wanted us to visit one of several true James Gang hideouts in the nearby river caves. By mid-afternoon, the heat in Missouri was astounding and the idea of hiding in a cave began to have a lot of appeal. We didn't know it at the time, but we were seeing the first weeks of one of the hottest, driest summers ever in the Southwest; a livestock killer. We stopped at the Windmill Restaurant near Stanton, a restaurant that really has a huge windmill (motor-driven, in an odd twist of technology) and drank a few gallons of iced tea in the cool darkness of the place. When we left, the heat and sunlight hit us like a pail of white steam.

Wine country signs for the Rosati Winery began to appear along the highway, so we stopped in the little town of St. James to buy some wine in celebration of our anniversary. A sporting goods store advertised "Minnows, Worms, Packaged Goods." Not being all that fond of bait, we settled on Packaged Goods and bought a bottle of Rosati Concord.

In western Missouri, old 66 had some trouble deciding which side of the Intersate it wanted, so we had to do some switching at overpasses and exits. Much of the road is still used as a sort of frontage road, or an alternative for local farmers who don't want to bother with the limited access of I-44, and the pavement is in good shape. The old concrete slabs have been paved over with a smooth, salmon-colored tarmac of some kind. The road was unpatrolled, but we slowed down a few times when we found ourselves under scrutiny by state troopers on the nearby Interstate. The rest of the time it was an exhilarating high-speed roller coaster through the hills.

The Suzuki was hard to hold at low speeds. It cruised so smoothly and effortlessly at 90 miles per hour and above that other speeds felt willfully slow. At around 75 miles per hour, the air behind the Silhouette fairing became almost still. We could hold high speeds without fluttering to death, and a pleasant sense of tranquility, almost a speed euphoria, set in. Above 80, we'd draw ourselves into a silent shell in all that motion; the engine and wind noise seeping past our earplugs with the sound of a bullet whine. High speed has a serenity of its own, a relaxed flow not found at lower velocities. And when the radar detector went off, as it did approaching one small town, it was like having a phonograph needle suddenly skate across the grooves of your favorite record. The spell was broken. You slow down to 55 and it feels like covered wagon speed; you are sure you could hop off the bike and run alongside picking flowers. Climbing back to 90, you are always amazed at the shortness of distance between two towns. You get into high gear and suddenly you are downshifting again. Barb and I talked about it at lunch; the smooth, abandoned highway was turning us into speed junkies.

By nightfall we were headed into Joplin, Missouri, and 10 miles from town we passed a small, badge-shaped sign that read 66 West. It was the first written admission on the entire trip that there was indeed a highway by that name. In every other town and intersection, it was either nameless or stuck with some dull municipal title like Frontage Road or Business 55. Somehow it was unfair to pin those unimaginative new names on the old road. A sense of tradition would have left it Route 66, just as Kennedy Airport should have remained Idlewild (Lord, what a beautiful word that was to have erased from our maps). But here, on the edge of Joplin, was a sign that said 66 West. We got off to take a picture.

We'd planned to celebrate our anniversary in Joplin by staying at a nice old downtown hotel, going out for dinner and maybe a movie later, and opening our bottle of Rosati Concord. On entering town, our hopes faded. We could find no movie theater anywhere near the center of town and the only downtown hotel looked like it had been closed since the Korean War. There were no people on the street and very little traffic. The only activity we found was a revivalist tent meeting in a windswept field at the edge of town. It was another city where the open-all-night life had been drawn away to the junctions of highway and interstate. To travelers, the town was not Joplin, Missouri, but Joplin Next Five Exits, and no one strayed very far from the exits.

We gave up the search and headed out of town to the Interstate, where we found a motel and a nearby restaurant staffed by some high school girls who seemed to be getting the most out of their grape gum. We had a dinner of enchiladas out of a can sprinkled with a kind of cheese product. The enchiladas were cold, but were served with hot lettuce; proof that lettuce heats faster in a microwave oven.

The number of people in the restaurant business who can't cook to save their lives is staggering. If they were plumbers, our houses would all be flooded. If they worked for the government, things would be just as they are now.

Back at the motel we celebrated our anniversary with the Rosati Concord from our tankbag. It was good; mellow without being too sweet, and had a nice full flavor of red grape. A little island of quality that almost made up for the lack of movie, grand hotel, and good dinner.

West of Joplin, 66 is a real highway with traffic and road signs. It enters Oklahoma past a sign that reads "Entering Indian Country." Where 66 and the Interstate cross you are offered a choice: "Will Rogers Turnpike. Toll Ahead," or "Free Road, 66 West." We figured Will Rogers himself probably would have chosen the Free Road, so we took that. Oklahoma is the Sooner State, named after those enterprising types who jumped the gun in the land rush, and we passed Sooner Cafes, Sooner Hotels, Sooner Used Cars, and Sooner Bars and Grills in the dozens of small towns along the highway. The land flattened out a bit and a new state technical college in one town advertised, among its other accreditations, a New Storm Cellar. The western sky was full of high cirrus clouds and we passed through a landscape of small, slag mountains from zinc mines. Another road sign read "Buffalo Ranch Ahead. Live Buffalo." That last apparently to discourage traveling flies.

True 66 continued all the way through Tulsa and Oklahoma City, I-44 taking most of the traffic load so 66 could carry the local traffic. Oklahoma City, true to song, looked oh so pretty but was very hot at noon.

We were both sleepy by mid-afternoon and pulled into a coffee shop in a small town west of El Reno. There was no one on the street and the sidewalk was raised high off main street, Dodge City style. A strong late afternoon wind was blowing and a faded Greyhound sign creaked in the wind above an abandoned waiting room. As we took off our helmets, a late-1940s DeSoto pulled up and a woman and little girl, both in cotton print dresses, got out of the car. The wind swirled up a cloud of dust in their faces and the little girl covered her nose and mouth with a white handkerchief as they went into the coffee shop. A chill passed over me. I hadn't imagined a scene like this since the last Woody Guthrie album I listened to. This was dry country and it was suffering through an unusually dry and hot summer. I had a feeling the dust bowl and the Great Depression might be over, but the weather here wasn't so sure. The wind in Oklahoma certainly did come sweeping down the plain.

We stopped for the night in Shamrock, Texas, "The Most Irish City in America," and checked into the Shamrock Inn and then rode into town, which actually had a working movie theater. *Foxes* was playing. A man and wife and their little boy climbed out of a pickup and bought tickets just ahead of us. The man collected his ticket and said, "I shore do hope your air conditioner's workin', or else we've just wasted five bucks." The girl in the booth smiled. "It shore is," she said, "and the movie's just fixin' to start."

The street was dead when we went into the movie, but we came out to find a virtual parade of pickup trucks going nowhere, cowboys and their dates honking at one another. The main street bars were busy and Waylon Jennings' heavy thumping bass runs could be heard from the sidewalks. We had a beer in a friendly, crowded bar, then went back to the motel for a late dinner. At midnight the air was still wiltingly hot. On the wall of our room was a shamrock-studded Irish blessing that began "May the road rise to meet you . . ." As a motorcyclist, I wasn't so sure I liked that image. But it ended with a promise of wind at our backs.

When you travel 66, you have different feelings about the changing landscape. In the Midwest, your thoughts and observations are largely botanical in nature, full of trees, valleys, and rivers; in west Oklahoma and Texas the theme is agricultural, all cattle ranches and big farms; but in the Southwest, very near the border of New Mexico, the landforms become mystical. The flat-topped buttes and the layered, painted sandstone, the purple tinge of distant ranges and the clean dryness of the place create a sense of peace and stillness that is more than a geography. Georgia O'Keefe had it in her desert paintings. You turn off the motorcycle and the loudest thing you can hear is your own breathing and heartbeat.

Where Route 66 is not the only highway across New Mexico, it splits off from I-40 and runs parallel to it in unused isolation. We stuck to the old highway, an endless succession of concrete slabs divided by tar seams. Broken up, they would make enough patios for all of Long Island, or enough foundations for all the tract homes in suburban Los Angeles, or the parking lot for one really large K-Mart. We are a rich country, I thought, that can abandon 2,000 miles of pavement (our own Appian Way), buy an entire new right-of-way nearby, and build another 2,000 miles of four-lane. A lot of measuring, grading, and contesting of property rights must have gone into both roads. ("Sorry folks, the new road has to go right through the front porch of your homestead.")

For the photographer of bygone Americana, Old 66 offers a lot of opportunities in the Southwest. The road is littered with the bones of truckstops, cafés, and motels left high and dry by I-40. It is a virtual gallery of Art Deco signs, architecture, and old American sedans left overturned in the dying cockroach position, usually riddled with bullet holes. We saw the remains of our first Burma Shave signs in New Mexico, everything weathered away but the word *Shave* on the last sign.

A brilliant red desert sunset had us about 30 miles east of Gallup on I-40. Barb nudged me and pointed to the railroad track that paralleled the highway about a quarter-mile away. We were being passed by *El Capitan*, the flagship passenger train of the Santa Fe Line, a train I rode to California as a kid.

"How fast do you think it's going?"

"About 80 or 85."

"Let's find out."

I rolled on the throttle and pegged our 85 miles per hour speedometer, but the train continued to pull away. The tracks were straighter and flatter than our road.

"We're going to beat that thing to Gallup," I shouted to Barb. "Hold on."

There are few opportunities in life, I reasoned, to race the *El Capitan* down Route 66 with a fast motorcycle into a blazing red desert sunset. At 6,500 rpm, which computed to about 105 miles per hour, we began to gain on the train.

We crested a rise in the road and suddenly noticed a mean-looking guy in mirrored sunglasses surrounded by a police car. He was parked in the median strip. I jumped on the brakes hard enough to leave permanent scars in all three brake rotors. The cop either didn't notice us, or thought we always traveled down the road with smoke pouring off our front tire, front suspension bottomed, rear tire chattering, Barb climbing up my back, and our facial features distorted from negative G-forces. He didn't follow, so we shrugged and rolled back up to speed. We beat the train into downtown Gallup by about 30 seconds after 30 miles of unmerciful flogging of the Suzuki, which handled the job easily.

We found our grand hotel in Gallup. It was a place called El Rancho, a big old lodge on Gallup's main street, full of dark timbers, balconies, log furniture, and Indian rugs; a sprawling, gracious place. The waitress at breakfast told us Hollywood movie crews used to stay there on location. They made *They Passed This Way, Red Mountain, Ambush,* and *Billy the Kid* just outside of town. Gregory Peck, Alan Ladd, Robert Taylor, and many others had stayed there, and as a teenager she had waited on their tables.

We left Gallup in the morning, planning to push all the way to L.A. We wound through the beautiful Painted Desert on I-40. Old 66 was nowhere in evidence, and apparently buried beneath the new pavement. We stopped to gaze down into the famous Winslow meteor crater and enjoyed the signs on the way in: "Free Petrified Wood With Fill-Up. See Painted Village Indian Teepees. See the Live Buffalo. See Winslow Crater, Established 20,000 B.C. Prototype of Lunar and Martian Craters." Established? Prototype? Oh well.

Leaving Winslow, we saw a sign that read, "Red Man Tobacco. America's Best Chew." That's quite a claim, I thought, and amused myself for the next 40 miles trying to picture the entire staff of *Consumer Reports* and the Consumer Protection Agency turning green around the gills and retching for a solid week as they sampled every known brand of chew to determine if Red Man was really America's Best. "Simpson, that's my spittoon you're using." "Sorry, Miss Jones." "Aaaaarrrrgghh . . ."

We climbed the mountains into Flagstaff, where we stopped for lunch. I ordered a milkshake and got one that contained no milk and hadn't been shaken. It was a plastic cup of whipped non-dairy product, and I felt ashamed for eating it instead of making a scene and berating the management. Barb and I vowed to visit a non-dairy at the first possible opportunity, to see where the cows were *not* kept and tour the missing barns and stanchions.

East of Kingman we hit the last really big chunk of Route 66, a loop that circles north of I-40; 80 miles of nearly empty highway that arced through the rugged desert country just south of the Grand Canyon. It passed through 10 small towns struggling to survive in the barren landscape, some doing better than others. There was no shortage of gas stations with plywood nailed over their windows.

We descended into the lower desert heat at Needles and crossed the California border at Lake Havasu, as the dammed-up remains of the Colorado River are known there. The higher mountain landscape gave way to Joshua trees, cacti, and the occasional palm.

We crossed the California desert in heat that strained credibility. The air rushed past us like something vented from a restaurant kitchen fan, the one over the oven and deep fryer. I wasn't sure that an air-cooled engine would keep running when the air got hotter than peak combustion temperature, but the Suzuki seemed less bothered than we did. Darkness on the desert brought almost no relief. At 11:30 that night, I almost crashed swerving to avoid a black pavement patch I mistook for an animal and decided Barstow would be a good place to find a motel.

In the clear morning desert sunlight, we came off the high desert at Cajon Pass and began our long descent into Los Angeles. The steep downhill highway was riddled with cops, apparently looking for fast coasters wasting gas. The landscape suddenly began to look like the Los Angeles of legend: the Biblical trees, tall Lombardy poplars, eucalyptus, palm trees bent like sails in a breeze, vines and red flowers overgrowing the bridges, and that particular brand of L.A. sunlight that turns everything into a muted, sun-softened pastel tone. Gone was the stark, glaring sharpness and spininess of the desert. Irrigation works wonders when combined with the sun.

Suddenly we were in San Bernardino, still on Old 66. The remnants of a main route into a big city are still there, such as really old gas stations and motels, mixed with valuable new services like poodle breeding, Tai Kwando instruction, and billiard table refinishing. We rambled past the beautiful old Spanish buildings of Rancho Cucamonga, the oldest winery in California, and endless developments of encroaching earthtone housing developments. Stuck here and there in all the newness and commercial glitter were a few early Spanish-style homes and ranch houses, small remnants of taste and elegance looking as out of place on the highway as Catherine of Aragon at a Donut Hut.

Then we rode through Claremont, where huge eucalyptus trees line 66, past the Equestrian Estates of Glendora where highly paid executives play evening cowboy on their five-acre spreads, around the manicured Santa Anita racetrack, past Azusa City Hall, the Conrock gravel pits, the nice old homes of South Pasadena near the Huntington Library, and into what Ross Macdonald called the sun-blinded streets of L.A. Sixty-Six got lost somewhere in those streets, so we took the San Diego Freeway south to the *CW* offices in Newport Beach and our nearby home. After 2,500 miles of heat and drought, it was cool by the coastline and an early afternoon fog was rolling in.

We parked the bike in the garage, then unloaded the pack and tank bag and we leaned them against the living room wall to be unpacked when we had more energy. We got the mail, mixed up a pitcher of margaritas, and sat out on the back porch to relax.

When you've just finished a big trip, it seems only right to have some conclusions. I thought about the trip, looking back at it through that long, slightly hazy tunnel that surrounds a highway journey, especially a disjointed Lost Highway journey. After some rumination and half a pitcher of drinks, I decided the trip had left me with two impressions.

First, as long as there *are* so many of us, we are lucky to have four-lane highways. It's easy to romanticize over the old two-lane, but today it would be like any other overcrowded highway, and the romance would soon cool. Those sections of 66 where the old two-lane was still the only highway were a dusty, hazardous alley full of truck blast, train crossings, potholes, detours infested with orange flags and loose gravel, slow campers, trundling mobile homes, and dangerous frustration. There was too much traffic for the old road. We had it best, being able to choose between the empty freedom of the abandoned highway or the smooth efficiency of the Interstate. People who didn't like the old road didn't have to use it, but at least it was there (or parts of it were). As Chuck Berry said, "Anything you want we got it right here in the USA."

Which led to another thought on the trip, and that was the tremendous variation in towns, restaurants, hotels, and people along the highway. There were prosperous farm towns, pretty little places out of an Andy Hardy movie lot, with white picket fences, tidy main streets, and bandstands in the town park. And then there were towns slightly gone to seed, where eroded expectations had allowed everything built in the last 20 years to be done the cheap, easy way; towns founded by pioneers with great expectations and inherited by people who didn't seem to care. There were good restaurants, terrible restaurants; nice hotels, poor hotels; good coffee, bad coffee; real milkshakes made with ice cream in stainless steel containers, and plastic cups of whipped non-dairy product.

The contrasts were most vivid at the end of a trip. If you got out of your house, out of your town, and traveled down the road, you would notice the sharp changes in quality. While you were out traveling, the good things raised your expectations a little, so when you got home you remembered them and wanted to concentrate some of those good ideas in the place you chose to settle down and live.

At the end of the trip I thought maybe that's what Todd and Buzz were searching for. Why they left their homes and towns and traveled Route 66 in a Corvette, other than for the sheer fun of traveling. Maybe they were just taking the long way home and bringing something back when they got there. They were finding out how a real milkshake should taste, so when they finally settled down they would never, ever accept a plastic cup full of semi-soft, non-dairy ice milk food product as a substitute, and if someone tried to give them one, they'd have enough sense to raise a little hell. They knew that travel is a gift you bring home.

June 1981

SPEED, FAME, SAND, AND SWEET MAGNOLIA

Daytona 1981

This was a short color piece I wrote about my first visit to Daytona Bike Week, and it still sums up how I feel about the place, 20 visits later.

Upon arriving in Daytona Beach from a cold climate, as much of the crowd does every year, several things are immediately apparent. First, the air is warm and there is no snow. In the daytime you can see palm trees everywhere and at night you can hear their dry rattle in the soft tropical breeze. The water along the shoreline is not frozen. In fact, there are people right in the water and some of them aren't very heavily dressed. The water is blue rather than slate gray because the sky is blue rather than slate gray.

Gulls and pelicans glide up and down the beach in formation, and above them an old Aeronca Chief labors slowly into a headwind, chugging up the coast trailing a sign that reads, "Solarcaine for Fast Sunburn Relief." Motorcycle riders, alone or in twos and threes, idle along the broad white beach while others stop and go wading, pantlegs rolled up and dark clumps of castoff boots and socks behind them in the sand.

On the streets, motorcycles are everywhere, cruising or parked in numbers at every restaurant, bar, and hotel. The sounds are a mixture of four-cylinder snarl, two-stroke crackle, and Harleys going cha-chuffa cha-chuffa. There are café racers with clip-ons, mom-and-pop touring rigs with twin American flags and matched helmets, and choppers done up in Basic Stark or Postwar Fringe for the aviator hat and tankshift crowd. There are British Singles restored to look better than they did new, silver metallic boxer Twins with riders in costly doeskin leathers, college guys in worn Adidas with $300 econobikes, legendary and salt-of-the-earth machines all mixed together in two-way traffic.

Everywhere people are clumped around parked bikes, discussing and looking, or riding by and being looked at. The drone of passing motorcycles is occasionally broken by a short tire chirp and the random irrepressible wheelie, but mostly the bikes are just cruising and no one is in a hurry. The weather is too nice for hurrying. No matter where you are, it's as pleasant as wherever you're going.

Just beneath the relaxed magic of the sun and palm trees is a special tension that keeps people alert, their eyes moving. Daytona is full of famous people, at least if you follow motorcycle racing. At the hotel coffee shop you rear the rapid ups and downs of a British accent and turn to see Mike Hailwood sitting at the next table with a friend. He is engrossed in conversation, fortunately, and doesn't notice the forkful of grits and melted butter you've just dumped on your lap.

At a crosswalk on Beach Boulevard, a van pulls up and its driver turns out to be, on second take, Gary Nixon. While dining on sweet and sour shrimp at the Hawaiian Inn that night, our perfect view of four hula dancers doing a floor show is interrupted by the entire Yoshimura family filing in, led by Pops himself. Wes Cooley joins them a few minutes later, and Rich Schlachter drops by to say hello, or whatever very fast and famous guys say to one another.

They are everywhere. No other art, sport, or craft brings its finest participants together in such concentration as Daytona. Oscar night in Hollywood doesn't attract showbusiness people as thoroughly and completely as Daytona does motorcycle people. Anybody who is, was, or would like to be something in the motorcycle firmament is there. Tuners, sponsors, ex-World Champions, and hot young riders; helmet, tire, and oil people; motocrossers, road racers, and dirt trackers are all there to compete.

The crowd in Daytona is truly international. The British arrive in droves, escaping the same lousy weather as the Americans from the north or the eastern seaboard. There are lots of French. In the hotel lobby, a French reporter with a fistful of notes is shouting a race report long distance to Paris or somewhere ("C'est Cooo-leee! Non, non Cooo-leee!") while a blonde woman who somehow escaped from a designer jeans commercial clings to his arm, pouts, and generally looks French. Canadians are everywhere, with plenty of red maple leaves on their luggage so no one mistakes them for Americans. At the

International House of Pancakes, a group of Italian men wearing Meccanica Ducati T-shirts argue among themselves over the meaning of Cheese Blintz or Buckwheat Strawberry Delight and a man behind us in line says, "By God, this really is an International House of Pancakes."

The city of Daytona Beach is Florida at its best, a crazy combination of beach resort, small town, and Old South. The architecture mingles beachfront posh, done up in Tiki Hut and Ponce de Leon chic, grand old Southern homes hidden in the willows and Spanish moss, needing paint in that slightly dissolute tropic colonial tradition, like sets from a Faulkner story or a Tennessee Williams play. There are country boy bars, Skunk Hollow homesteads back in the pines at the edge of town, new ranch house subdivisions, retirement communities, trailer parks, and even a proper Main Street with small, nicely kept shops. A few miles in from the coast, just off Volusia Street near the airport, is the speedway.

When you approach the speedway, Daytona is transformed from a beautiful but sleepy Florida beach town into an exciting Florida beach town. No matter how many races you've been to, the hardest part is waiting in line at the gate when you can hear bikes screaming around the track, but you can't see them. The sound of three or four superbikes wailing around the banking gets the heart going and drives patience away. A friend walks over to chat, but it's hard to concentrate on what he's saying. You just want to get into the track and *see* the machines that are making all that wonderful noise. After parking on the infield, it takes adult restraint and false dignity not to break into a run on the way to the nearest corner.

Cooley, Crosby, and Spencer are out on the track practicing with their superbikes. They come around the banking in a tight knot, brake for Turn One, and throw their bikes into the curve like one large inseparable raft of noise and machinery. When they are gone, another man leaning on the fence shakes his head and says "Damn!" in a low reverent tone.

Damn indeed. The sun is shining, fast bikes are on the track, the beach is three miles away, the air smells of Castrol R and Coppertone, the town is full of motorcycles, the soft tropical breeze is still rustling the palm trees, there's no snow, and the nearest trace of frozen water is in the margaritas back at the hotel bar where the four hula dancers do their nightly floor show in the Tiki Room. And if that isn't being in the right place during the Ides of March, I don't know what is.

April 1982

ADRIFT IN LOTUS LAND

If It's Sushi, This Must Be Japan

This was my first trip to Japan, and it left me with an abiding respect for the open-minded ability of the Japanese to recognize quality when they find it in any part of the world, to bring it home, and to mix it with their own culture. To me, that is the main benefit of travel. The trip also left me with a lasting appreciation for Japanese hospitality, sushi, good sake, and the wide-open spaces of the American West.

"How would you like to go to Japan for a week and ride the new Yamahas on their test track?" the Editor asked me.

In the big league of rhetorical questions, this one ranked right up there with, "How about a tremendous raise and a free company car?" and, "My parents are in Tahiti; would you like to come in for a drink?"

"Why yes," I said agreeably, "I think I'd like that."

Japan.

What I knew about Japan could fit in a sake cup, with quite a bit of room left over for sake. My knowledge of Japan and its people consisted mostly of confused images left over from *Teahouse of the August Moon, Shogun, Tora! Tora! Tora!* and dinner at Benihana's of Tokyo. Not to mention various Kurasawa movies populated by quick-tempered Samurai-heroes who go for their swords when agitated by mortal enemies, argumentative wives, or excessive bar tabs; the men who first elevated grumbling and muttering to the status of the seething threat.

And then there were the products of Japan. I knew about those. There was a time when objects manufactured on those islands had a reputation for all the enduring, peerless quality of party favors on New Year's Eve.

There were toy cars that said Blatz on the inside when you peeled away the painted tin, cap guns made of those uniquely Japanese materials, chromed plastic and slag by-product, and discount tool tables piled with Allen wrenches that twisted like candy canes, hacksaw blades with teeth of butter, and rubber mallets with heads that flew off. Mattel and Estwing did it better. The words *Made In Japan* branded on any consumer item suggested a sort of active, spontaneous disintegration going on within the molecular structure; if the product did not actually fail as you were leaving the store, it would almost certainly collapse in service. Japan was the fountainhead of the stripped head.

But sometime during the late 1950s or early 1960s, that image began to change. Names like Sony, Nikon, and Honda began to appear in the stores and showrooms, names that inspired cautious admiration rather than a quick dismissal. Many Japanese products progressed from being cheap copies, to good for the money, to just plain good. The Japanese became masters of industrial design. The handmade, carefully crafted items from America or Europe might have more romance, prestige, or lasting value, but in some cases the Japanese developed mass-produced goods of such quality they set new standards for others to follow. The *Made in Japan* stamp gradually shed its early, derisive overtones.

This slow blossoming of acceptance, or maybe its full bloom, led to a very strange moment I had in my own living room a year ago. I was listening to Mississippi John Hurt on my Japanese stereo system, thinking how nice it was to have a new Japanese turntable to replace the more expensive old English one that had never worked correctly from the moment I lifted its unfortunate hulk out of the Styrofoam packing. My attention wandered and I looked around the room. Next to the stereo on a guitar stand was an inexpensive (but nicely made) Japanese guitar, and on the bookshelf sat a Japanese 35mm camera. Our china cabinet was piled with Noritake cups and dishes, and stored in the basement below were some Japanese skis. Looking out the window I could see our Japanese car in the driveway, and in the garage was a Japanese motorcycle (next to a slightly less reliable one from another country). My wife, Barbara, wandered in from the back porch and said, "Would you light the hibachi?"

"Sure," I said, glancing at the pulsing LED numbers on my absurdly cheap Japanese watch. "What are we having?"

"Teriyaki beef."

It was alarming.

Through no conscious pattern of our own design, the house was virtually swamped with Japanese paraphernalia. Our very home was a heavy spot, a lead weight in the wheel balance of world trade, capable of throwing the globe into a crazy tank-slapper.

Who were these Japanese, anyway, and how had they done it? How had a country the size of California, halfway around the world, produced so many things we wanted or needed? (In all fairness to the productivity of California, we also owned a Beach Boys album and a half-empty jug of Gallo Hearty Burgundy.) How had these people managed to get a hand in every aspect of our lives?

These questions were obviously too complex for anyone to answer, least of all a motorcycle journalist on a one-week Yamaha junket, so I decided to forget all about them and concentrate on having a good time.

The 747 airline flight was pretty routine, if extra long; 11 hours of short naps punctuated by endless bottles of Almaden Pink Chablis, nice little meals in plastic sectioned trays served at odd times, and reading the airline magazine from the seatback pouch to learn "How the Dutch Raise Their Tulips" and that "The Spirit of Strauss Lingers on in Old Vienna." Sanitized headphones were handed out and we watched *Breaker Morant*, a wonderful and depressing Australian movie, while the airplane whirred and hummed and buffeted. The pilot announced that the Space Shuttle was, at that moment, somewhere off our port wing on its landing approach to Edwards Air Force Base, so we all looked out the window but couldn't see it.

A Japanese gentlemen across the aisle from me rose to go to the men's room, but first put a white surgeon's mask over his nose and mouth. I was told that the Japanese, leery of germs, often wear these masks in public places. He returned to his seat and put on the stethoscope-like headphones to resume watching the movie. He looked like a Japanese Marcus Welby, checking on the health of his own chair. I suppressed a temptation to have him look at my tonsils.

There is a lot of Pacific Ocean between the U.S. and Japan. That the Japanese and American fleets ever found each other in WW II is a testament to man's perseverance in seeking out and attacking his fellow man. The peaks of the Aleutian Islands rose out of the haze here and there, but the rest of the flight was hours of empty water. The pilot spoke on the intercom to explain that, while we'd left L.A. at 11:30 Saturday morning, our 11-hour flight would put us in Tokyo late Sunday afternoon. I am sure this is possible, but someday I'm going to get a dark room, a flashlight, a grapefruit, and a piece of string, with perhaps eight volunteers to represent the other planets in motion and we'll all give it the Mr. Wizard treatment to see if it makes sense. Drinks will be served.

We spotted the hazy coast of Japan at sunset. A childhood spent viewing the coast of Japan through periscopes in submarine adventure movies had led me to believe this event would be accompanied by the clanging of a huge gong, followed by the sinister chiming of Oriental stringed instruments. This does not happen. You look at the coast of Japan for the first time and it just sits there. It's nothing but a big piece of land with people living on it and a lot of buildings and roads. No music.

The plane landed at the New Tokyo International Airport at Narita, a place of great controversy in Japan because of all the farmland it absorbed. Tight security in and around the airport showed they were still worried over threats of violence against the new facilities. The nine of us, five American and two Canadian journalists, plus Ed Burke and Dan Dwyer from Yamaha, got through customs quickly and boarded a special tour bus for Tokyo (Narita is about two hours from the center of the city). A Japanese woman guide described the points of interest en route, though we couldn't see them because it was dark outside and the bus had bright neon lights inside. We could see our own reflections in the bus windows, however, and some of us looked quite good. The guide explained that we needn't be afraid of drinking the water anywhere in Japan because it was all clean and safe.

We were delivered to the imposing Hotel Pacific in downtown Tokyo and given time to find our rooms, change, shower, and gather our wits. before dinner. The room was nice, sort of American style, but simpler, with less gilding and Spanish woodwork. It had a color TV, a big modern bathroom complete with disposable razor, toothbrush, and toothpaste, and a handy wall telephone next to the toilet. This despite the good quality of the water. Every room was supplied with a robe-like kimono for each guest (or at least my room was; I was too tired to check the other 300 rooms to see if this was true). A card on my desk said "Massage in room: 3,300 Yen for 50 minutes." That was about $14. I could have used a massage, but had heard that another member of the motorcycle press had taken advantage of this service the previous year and they'd sent him home stretched across two airline seats. He was only now accepting visitors.

I turned on the TV and there was Lee Marvin, dressed as a small town cop, arguing in Japanese with a torch-bearing mob of American rednecks. I switched around and discovered that nearly all Japanese television ads contained some English, usually in their slogans. A Japanese housewife serves instant soup to her family, then holds the package up to the camera and says, "It's nice!" An ad for blue jeans announces, "They are cool!" The neon signs on Tokyo streets are also loaded with American phrases. I switched over to the news and managed to decipher an announcement that William Holden had just died. They showed lengthy clips of his films.

The porter brought my bags, bowed politely, and left without the normal throat-clearing hesitation and tip ritual. I learned that tipping is seldom practiced in Japan, and restaurants add a 10 to 20 percent service charge to the bill automatically. This certainly simplifies travel and mental calculation, and the service is generally so gracious everywhere that the American tradition of withholding a tip in revenge for rude treatment doesn't apply.

We had dinner that evening in the hotel's traditional dining area. "Traditional" meant private rooms with sliding rice paper walls, no shoes, waitresses in Madame Butterfly garb, and low tables (some with cheater footwells for Americans who can't kneel through a three-hour meal—or for those who *can* kneel through a three-hour meal but are never able to walk again if they do). We had sushi first, raw fish and vegetables cooked in a soy-flavored sauce at the table. The beef was excellent and we were told it came from Kobe, where the cattle are fattened on a beer diet and massaged by hand to help marble the meat. This is different from the American agricultural system where the farmers drink all the beer, the cattle go thirsty, and the average Hereford or Angus finds a good massage hard to come by. But then beef in the U.S. is cheaper, too. Kobe beef costs between $40 and $80 per pound, depending on whose exaggeration you believe.

Kirin, a good Japanese beer, was served from huge bottles, along with plenty of sake, hot rice wine poured from steaming stone vessels into tiny cups. Sake was served every night on this trip, and on cool autumn nights it quickly promotes a spreading warmth and a sense of well being not found in Diet Sprite, for instance. I began to like sake, then look forward to it, and by Friday I'd developed a regular craving for the stuff. If seven o'clock rolled around and I hadn't had any sake, I began to suffer a nervous tic in my left eye. The use of sake should be outlawed in the U.S., just to make sure everyone gets a chance to experience this enjoyable habit.

The traditional Japanese meal takes a long time to eat and drink; hours are spent stirring things, dipping sauces, sipping from cups, and all the while carrying on a lively conversation. I looked at our friendly Japanese hosts, laughing, talking, and eating; I wondered if they realized they were missing *Dallas*.

After dinner we retired early, as it was now mid-morning back in L.A. and we were all clobbered by jet lag. I went up to my room and turned on the T.V. *Dallas* was on. An overdubbed J.R. was busy losing the Ewing family fortune over the phone and everyone else was off cheating and sleeping around in Japanese. I switched channels and found sumo wrestling.

Sumo is an ancient sport where two very hefty men in loincloths try to shove each other out of a small circle, after a lot of pre-fight posturing and ritual. Our guide told me these men live a very rigid lifestyle and are trained (overfed) from youth. They do their workouts in the morning and in the afternoon drink beer and receive massages. I began to wonder if there was any living thing in Japan that didn't drink beer and get its back rubbed. I also wondered what a 350-pound sumo wrestler does for a living when his ring career is over and he has to hang up the loincloth. I asked one of our Yamaha friends.

"Anything he wants," was the reply.

I'd just finished dressing in the morning when there was a knock at the door. I peered out and a wizened little woman in a chambermaid's outfit waved a vacuum cleaner nozzle at me.

"Hoover?" she inquired.

"No thanks," I joked, "we're Democrats."

This cut no ice with the little lady, so I let her in and she Hoovered my room while I went downstairs to Hoover up a little breakfast.

We boarded an elevated train near the hotel and rode down to the Ginza district, an area of huge, classy department stores, theaters, camera shops, etc. It was Tokyo's own Fifth Avenue. The best entertainment of the morning was watching the renowned motojournalist, Dale Boller, blow thousands of dollars on oddball camera attachments, pearls, and multi-purpose wristwatches. Dale can now take underwater flash photos of marine life at depths that would crush a submarine and play ping-pong on his wrist.

Tokyo is a huge, clean, mostly modern city, a hodgepodge of new skyscrapers, small parks, ancient temples, modern apartment buildings, traditional old residential neighborhoods full of artfully curved red tile roofs, colorful sidestreets of tiny shops, manufacturing plants, railroad yards, and busy streets. The city is notably devoid of garbage, graffiti, litter, and unkempt buildings. Our guide, Mr. Ikeuchi, told us we could go anywhere at any time of the day or night in Tokyo, as street crime and violence are extremely rare. Walking around the city, we all noticed that no matter how plain or humble a shop, restaurant, house, or courtyard might appear from the outside, it was always much nicer inside. Japanese interiors have a simple serenity about them that is very restful.

Viewed from the elevated train or the freeways, Tokyo is unimaginably large. Its flat expanse stretches off to the horizon in all directions, a vast landscape of factories, towers, and houses. L.A. is a big city too, but it has a downtown of skyscrapers clustered together, surrounded by miles of one- and two-story structures. In Tokyo, the tall buildings go on forever. The city is terribly crowded, but the people seem to handle it better than citizens elsewhere in the world. Politeness is rampant.

We caught a taxi back to the hotel. Tokyo's streets are full of new-looking Japanese cars, many of them large luxury models only now beginning to appear in the U.S. You hardly see any rusty, dented, or half-primered old cars for some reason. The beater, the Japanese counterpart of every car I've ever owned, is absent from the streets. There are a lot of motorcycles, but not as many as you might expect in this bike-producing country. You have one big group of 50 to 250cc commuter and delivery bikes, ridden mostly by students, or construction workers who wear tall rubber boots, helmets that look like hardhats with liners, and big gloves, many smoking cigarettes as they ride. There is another class of sporty Twins and Fours in the 400cc range, owned largely by well-dressed young men in full-face helmets and nice leather jackets. Above that, you have the truly committed crowd, men 30 and over who have spent the money and taken the trouble to buy big foreign iron: Harleys, BMWs, and Ducatis. Or they have re-imported big Japanese bikes, brought back from abroad to get around the 750cc maximum rule for domestic motorcycles. A couple of Harley riders we saw were older men dressed in state trooper look-alike regalia. A lot of the smaller bikes do delivery duty, piled high with crates and boxes on pallet-sized luggage racks. Few women are seen riding motorcycles larger than those in the moped class.

In the afternoon we boarded the Super-Express, the famous "Bullet Train," and headed south to Iwata at what was supposed to be 135 miles per hour. The luxurious train was so smooth and quiet, it was hard to gauge the speed. The tracks use concrete ties and the rails are seamless. How they do this, I don't know. There are no visible welds. Journalist Ken Vreeke fantasized a sort of rolling steel mill, extruding tracks as it went along. Then he opened another bottle of Kirin.

South of Tokyo, fields and farms opened up, dotted with small villages stuck in the valleys and hills. Rounded hedges of tea plants were everywhere, in back yards and along the roadsides. You have only to look at the Japanese countryside to see where their landscape art comes from. The hills have a rugged, hazy look, dotted with rock outcroppings and small growths of trees above the tea and rice fields, all with a slightly mystical look.

Even in rural areas, the country is well populated. Villages are close together and the farms are small. There seem to be few open roads where you could ever get a CBX or an XS11 much past third gear without running into another pocket of civilization.

Traveling cross-country in Japan, you begin to understand the volume of competitively priced Japanese goods in American stores and homes. As England realized at one time, a small, crowded island country with few natural resources has to survive on its wits and innovative energy. Trade is essential. They have to figure out what the rest of the world will buy and then make it. That produce-or-perish mentality may not be as strong in other parts of the world because the lesson is harder to teach. The Japanese need only look out their windows to understand. It's crowded out there.

Cabs took us from the train station to our hotel in Iwata, the home of the Yamaha motorcycle plant. Riding in a Japanese taxi is one of the few things that will make a grown motorcycle road racer cry. On the way to the hotel our cab driver careened through the narrow streets of Hammamatsu honking at blind intersections, swerving around pedestrians and bicyclists, and scraping between delivery vans and the walls of buildings like a runaway fire truck in a silent movie. You have to ride in Japanese cabs with a relaxed fatalism or you'd go mad with fear. At one point our guide said, "We are almost there," and a voice in the back seat muttered, "Don't count your chickens."

We were asked to suit up in our leathers right away and a bus took us just out of town to the Yamaha test track. The track is a beautiful, smooth road circuit that winds around a wooded hilltop in a setting similar to Watkins Glen. We were given a briefing on track safety and layout and then turned loose on the track with five of Yamaha's new U.S. road models: the 650 Seca, XJ650 Turbo, 550 Vision, 920 Virago, and the 750 Maxim. We took the bikes out for 15- or 20-minute sessions, then came in, talked to the engineers for first riding impressions, traded bikes, and headed back out. The following day we were given a number of tech sessions and six or seven hours of track time. Long enough to find out Yamaha has produced some impressive street bikes this year, much to the satisfaction of the journalists on the tour. A day with the engineers is always much more pleasant when you genuinely like what they've done.

Before Bullet Training back to Tokyo, we were given tours of the Iwata motorcycle factory and the Nippon Gakki plant where Yamaha pianos are made.

At the bike factory the stamping and machining of gears, shafts, etc. is mostly automated, but the final assembly line is handwork and the most interesting to see. There's something strange about watching bare frames come down from the ceiling on hooks at one end of the assembly line while at the other end, just a few hundred feet away, completed machines are started up and ridden away. Last time I restored a bike and assembled it from parts it took me about six months, and starting the rebuilt engine for the first time was a dramatic event to rival the first manned flight. Yamaha was turning out a new living, breathing 550 Vision about every 30 seconds, fully expecting each one to start and work just fine.

Not all of them did, of course. While we were there one bike came off the line with a loud exhaust leak and another one developed a steamy coolant leak while it was being run up on the dyno. Several others were sidelined for coolant leaks. "Bad batch of hose clamps," the guide explained. "We're replacing them all." The combined Yamaha assembly lines turned out 8,000 bikes a day, or one every 3.4 seconds.

The green-clad employees in the assembly line were models of careful work and concentration. No one gave the tour group and its flashing cameras more than a passing glance. The women in the line all wore multi-colored aprons with cartoon characters on them. In English lettering the aprons were emblazoned with such titles as, "Tweety Pie," "Tom & Jerry Tennis," and "Happy Cats." Happy Cats was a big favorite.

The most exciting bit of assembly line technology for the visiting journalists, because so many of us have spent time chasing ball bearings under workbenches, was the installation of steering head bearings. The workman was dipping a ring-shaped vacuum attachment into a huge keg of ball bearings, shoving them into the grease of the steering head cups, and then releasing the vacuum. We watched in amazement. "So that's how they do it," said Editor Larry Works, "they have a bearing Hoover."

We visited a soundproof room for sound testing, a frosty refrigerated room for temperature testing, and walked past a 250 Exciter being torture tested by a mechanical rider whose electronic brain was strapped to the back seat. We watched a technician throw a frame design up on a green computer screen and then feed cornering stresses into it, causing the frame to flex and twist with mathematically exaggerated severity. In each department people appeared to be absorbed in their work, moving steadily and efficiently but never rushing. "We make our assembly line so workers don't have to hurry too much," our guide said. "Not good for quality to hurry. Also, we have 10 model changes a day on different assembly lines. That way workers don't always do the same thing."

After the tour we were bussed to Lake Hamana, where Yamaha Corporation owns a resort called Marina Hamanako, a vacation spot for company employees who join a recreation club. A cocktail party was thrown so we could meet all the Yamaha executives. If this has all the makings of a stuffy affair, it wasn't. The Japanese take their work seriously during the day, but at night they relax and become good-humored, affable company. Throughout the trip I can't recall meeting a single sour or ill-tempered personality. Such people are either rare in Japanese society, or they were being hidden for our visit. Even Yamaha's upper-level executives, no doubt burdened with considerable responsibility, were largely an easy-going, likable group whose good nature and wry humor made it through the language barrier with no problem. Meeting these gentlemen, it is easier to understand why Japan has fewer conflicts between labor and management than many other countries. As executives, they seemed remarkably free from pretensions of authority, bluster, and other overbearing behavior, acting instead with a sort of alert humility that suggests they got to the top on merit and hard work; they live in a society where actions speak louder than loud words.

I may be wrong about all this, of course. But after a few drinks they all seemed like a splendid bunch of fellows.

We took the Bullet Train back to Tokyo, eating salty dried squid (Japanese counterpart to pretzels) and drinking Sapporo beer from a vending cart that rolled through the train. The Tokyo skyline loomed into sight, a grim and sobering reminder of how many Japanese monsters, from Godzilla to Rodan, have devastated that landscape in their clumsy battles; squashing cars, running afoul of high-tension lines, swatting down jet aircraft, shrugging off white phosphorus rockets, and shaking the terrified passengers out of elevated railway cars after first peering into the windows. Sure, the crime rate was low in Tokyo, but those monsters! Talk about vandalism.

On our final evening in the country our hosts took us out to a little sidewalk café on a sidestreet in Tokyo, practically under the girders of the elevated railway. We drank beer and sake, and had dozens of courses of skewered meat and vegetables cooked over an outdoor charcoal brazier.

And of course, plenty of raw fish, which, like the evening sake, had grown on most of us during the tour. Mr. Ikeuchi suggested we sing some songs, and it turned out that he and another Japanese gentleman who was with us not only had excellent voices, but knew dozens of American folk songs by heart. We sang *Swanee River, She'll be Comin' Around the Mountain, Davy Crockett,* and other standards. They knew most of the words better than we did. A group of college students at the café moved their table next to ours so they could join in the singing. One of them said, in halting English, that his sister was going to college in Santa Barbara, California, then stood up and did a perfect imitation of Frank Sinatra singing *Strangers in the Night.* Then we all toasted him and his sister and Frank Sinatra and Santa Barbara. People passing by on the sidewalk stopped and joined us in some of our songs. They knew the words too. Other people stopped and bought us rounds of drinks.

This sort of thing doesn't happen to Americans in Europe, or anywhere else I know of, including America. The Japanese may not always understand the crazy Americans, but they know a lot of our culture and freely adopt many of its better aspects. There is a friendly, open curiosity at work here, and that may be the great strength of the Japanese. They would rather learn about something new than complain about it. (I personally prefer to learn just one or two simple things and then leave well enough alone.)

At Narita airport we sat in the restaurant and waited for our flight home. A tour group of middle-aged American women sat down at the next table and it took them about five minutes to reduce our young waitress to tears because (a) she didn't speak English clearly and this was, after all, an International Airport and (b) because she brought the wrong order to a 300-pound matron who had a fox fur around her neck and didn't have to put up with this kind of treatment. I wondered if they thought the American waitresses at the airport coffee shop in L.A. all spoke fluent Japanese. Or any Japanese. Or even good English.

We couldn't watch any more, so we got up and left. After we'd been around the graciously polite Japanese for a week, these women seemed about as civilized as a gang of buffalo hunters. How, with all the wonderful Americans we had back home, did we always manage to produce a dismal brand of tourist?

These women aside, we were all anxious to get home after a week in Japan, for various reasons involving families, clean socks, and chocolate milkshakes. One of my own reasons was the old elbow-room problem. In the U.S. many of us might be crowded into cities, but in the back of our national mind we knew the open spaces were out there, just over the next hill; mountain ranges, prairies, and half-empty states with wide-open roads. Our sense of geographical scale was all different. The parts of Japan we toured, beautiful though they might be, were like one continuous neighborhood, broken here and there by hills and fields. Such places give me a sort of geographical claustrophobia. I could enjoy living there for a time, but not forever. No one has to be knocking around in the wilderness or riding down lonely roads all the time, but it's nice to know such places exist when you get in the mood.

Clicking a fast machine—say a Turbo 650—into fifth gear on an unpopulated, unpatrolled country road is important to some of us; it's a state of mind and a kind of evening sake to the human spirit. Not a strictly legal thing to do, but as Americans we have a tradition to uphold. Leaving any foreign country, I've always come away with the conviction that irreverence is still our finest export.

October 1982

OLD STONE, GREEN TREES, & SPEED

Cycle Week on the Isle of Man

In my world view, I suppose the Isle of Man comes as close as anywhere on earth to being Holy Ground. It's a beautiful, civilized place of almost Druidic charm and antiquity that encourages motorcycle road racing over its streets and country lanes, a route lined with friendly pubs that serve some of the world's best stouts and ales. I wasn't kidding about wanting to retire there.

"Why would you want to go to the Isle of Man?" the voice on the other end of the phone asked me. "It's a cruel, dangerous place to race and most of the top international riders avoid it. Why don't you go to Assen instead and see some real racing?"

"I want to go because it's the last real roadrace," I explained. "There are other races on public roads, but they're really just street races where the track is easy to learn. The Isle of Man Tourist Trophy runs on 37 miles of real road. I've seen the pictures. It goes through villages, over bridges, past farms, up and down a mountainside, and so on. It seems to me there's nothing else like it."

"All the same, I'd go to Assen if I were you. Forget the Island. No one should race there."

The man on the phone was entitled to his opinion. As a team manager who had been to the Island many times, he'd lost a few acquaintances there and his best friend had been seriously injured in an accident, never to race again. He'd earned his right to dislike the place, while I (the world's oldest novice at nearly everything) had never been there.

He was not alone in his feelings. Many top roadracing stars have badmouthed or boycotted the race for years, so much so that the TT was finally relegated to minor league status. People like Sheene, Roberts, Mamola, and

Luccinelli didn't race there now. The best riders at the Isle of Man these days raced there because they loved it or because they considered the starting money worth the effort, or both. True road racing has always demanded peculiar skills and a different type of concentration than short-circuit racing, so many riders have probably continued to come to the Island simply because they are very good at it.

Added to that is the sheer romance of the place. For most of the twentieth century, the TT has been the world's supreme motorcycle race. To win at the Isle of Man was to become legend, and every great rider of the past has been required to master the fast, difficult circuit to cement his reputation as a roadracer. Names like Duke, Read, Agostini, Hailwood, and dozens of others are inextricably tied to the TT, and the very bumps, corners, bridges, and hills of the circuit itself are as famous as the riders. Ballaugh Bridge, Windy Corner, Creg-ny-Baa, and Sarah's Cottage are as well known to TT fans as the name Mike Hailwood. A mental map of the track, with all its strange-sounding Manx place names, is a permanent fixture in the minds of most racing enthusiasts in the British Isles and elsewhere.

The race has been held since 1907, when England refused to allow such craziness on its own public roads and the largely autonomous Manx (they have their own parliament called the Tynwald) offered their lovely island to the Auto Cycle Union for the Big Race. So the TT has been around a few years longer than the Indy 500. Not a bad tradition.

"Thanks anyway," I told my friend on the phone, "but I think I'll go to the TT rather than Assen. I've been reading about Ballacraine and Cronk-y-Voddy since I was twelve years old. There's a picture on my wall of Agostini and his MV airborne at Sulby Bridge. At home I have a TT record album with the sound of Mike Hailwood screaming down Bray Hill on the Honda Six. It's a place I've wanted to go ever since I gave up shooting frogs with a BB gun, and now, after all these years and at the advanced age of thirty-four I am finally going, by God, to the Isle of Man."

There are a lot of ways to get to the Isle of Man, but I naturally took the Easy Motojournalist Route, which involved flying to London, borrowing a GS650G from the nice folks at Heron Suzuki GB Limited, riding halfway across England to Liverpool, and taking the Packet Steamship Company ferry to the Isle of Man. My wife, Barbara, came with me.

We left notoriously sunny L.A. in a gloomy rain and arrived in famously gloomy London on a hot, cloudless day. A friendly gentleman named Ray Battersby signed over the Suzuki and drew us a detailed labyrinthine map to guide us out of Greater London. And make no mistake, London is Great. We threw our only luggage, a tankbag and some soft saddlebags, on the Suzuki and headed northwest.

Ray's last words as we pulled out of the parking lot were, "Drive on the left!" As it turned out, I had no trouble remembering to drive on the left, but all week I kept looking the wrong way as I stepped off curbs. There are many different types of horns on English cars, and most of the cars have superb brakes.

After looking at Ray's map, I suggested to Barb we pay a cab to drive to Liverpool and then follow him with the bike. The map worked fine, however, and after an hour we were free of London and its endless high-speed roundabouts. We avoided the big Motorways and headed toward Liverpool on the more interesting two-lane winding secondary roads.

England isn't a very dull country to cross on a motorcycle. The land is so condensed in the overlapping layers of its own history that the name on every road sign seems to be famous for something—be it a battle, king, school, bombing raid, sporting event, novel, factory, or rock group. Our route took us past Hampton Court, Windsor, Blenheim Castle, Henly, Rugby, Oxford, Stratford-on-Avon, Birmingham, and into Liverpool. England is an old country with an animated past and men with something on their minds have been tramping around on its soil for a long time.

We rode into a cool, grey Liverpool late in the afternoon, following signs to the Liverpool Car Ferry with a motorcycle throng that grew larger as we got closer to the docks. We were either on the right road or every motorcyclist in England had been seized with some kind of lemming madness. Policemen on the wharves directed us into an immense holding shed with a glass-paneled roof, where guards at the entrance checked the fuel level in our tank and gave us a *Tank Inspected* decal. You no longer have to empty your tank for the Isle of Man ferry, but the fuel has to be low enough that nothing sloshes out in a rough sea. The boat company doesn't want a cargo bay full of gas fumes and expensive motorcycles, especially in a country where virtually everyone smokes.

We handed over the tickets we'd ordered in advance (about $38 round trip for two people and a bike) and rode down a steep ramp into the cargo hold. Loading men lined the bikes up on their center-stands, slid them into tight rows, and then strapped each row down with rope about the thickness of a fire hose. They pack about 500 bikes into each shipload, which is a lot of chrome, mirrors, fairings, and handlebars crammed into a small place.

Up on the passenger deck, the ferry boat had the look of a troopship for some kind of motorcycle army. The deck was packed with a crazy mixture of Barbour suits, boots, helmets, racing leathers, touring leathers, and fringed leathers, the predominant color being black with a sprinkling of Kenny Roberts Yellow and Barry Sheene Red. There were hard- and soft-looking women, bespectacled school teachers carrying pudding bowl helmets, wild rocker types in fringed leather who looked like Ted Nugent with more tattoos, mature Germans with BMW patches on full road leathers, and vintage men with chests full of meet pins glittering on their thornproofs. If there was a uniform on the boat, it was black roadracing boots worn over Levis and topped off by a Belstaff or leather roadracing jacket and a full-face helmet with a racing-theme paint job.

While some elements in American motorcycling take a lot of trouble to select riding gear that makes them look like skiers or snowmobilers, European and English bikers are less apologetic in their choices. They wear first-rate, expensive paraphernalia that leaves no doubt they are Serious Motorcyclists; they like going fast or appearing to go fast, and dress the part when they are riding.

Their bikes reflect the same attitude. It costs money to go to the island and stay there for a week, and most people are using a week or more of precious vacation time to be there, so once again you get a committed rather than casual brand of motorcyclist. Big sport bikes and classic restorations predominate, while the full-dress touring bike is all but absent.

The harbor lights of Douglas, the largest city on the Isle of Man, appeared out of the mist just after dark. As we eased into the dock a voice on the PA instructed riders, in three or four languages, to report to their bikes. We went down into the cargo area and picked our way through the mass of bikes to the Suzuki. The same burly guys who tied the bikes down were removing the ropes.

If Federico Fellini ever gets a little farther out and wants to film a truly bizarre spectacle taken from real life, he should bring his camera crew and sound men into the cargo bay of the Isle of Man ferry on a night when approximately 500 motorcycles are being cranked over or kick started all at once, packed together in a steel room about the size of a small gymnasium and lighted by a dim row of 40 watt light bulbs.

The microphones would pick up an ear-splitting confusion of shrieking RDs, high-revving unmuffled Fours, and the general chest-pounding thunder of Ducati 900s, Norton 850s and 750s, Harleys, Triumphs, BSAs, BMWs, and piston-slapping British 500 Singles, all of it bouncing off the walls in an incredible rising and falling wail. The camera crews would get footage of several hundred leather-clad people flipping down face shields and punching starter buttons, with others in the mob of bikes heaving up and down on kickstarters like erratic pistons in some kind of insane smoke machine, headlights flaring on to make a blanket of brilliance and flashing chrome at the bottom layer of the smoke cloud. They could catch the bikes launching themselves row by row up the ramp into the dark night, people spinning their tires on the oil-slick steel ramp or catching traction and disappearing in half-controlled wheelies.

What no film could capture is the mixed smell of Castrol R, several dozen brands of two-stroke oil, and all the other choking thick exhaust fumes, or the instant, furnace-like heat given off by hundreds of motorcycles lighting their engines in a confined space. Also, they'd have to film it through the distorted starburst pattern of a really scratched yellow face shield, just to get the last effect of profound unreality. You wouldn't want to witness this scene if you'd been smoking anything funny or you might just go mad and never recover.

Always quick to notice the obvious, I turned back to Barb and shouted, "This is really something!"

I don't think she could hear me, but I think she knew it was really something.

Our turn came and we slithered up the ramp with a wave of other bikes. We landed on the docks and the white gloves of a row of nearly invisible policemen directed us onto Manx main street, the Douglas Promenade. We were on the Isle of Man.

Douglas is an old seaside resort town with tall, narrow Victorian hotels lining the curve of the bay. The hotels are built wall-to-wall, but you can tell one establishment from the other because they are painted different colors. Sidestreets with more hotels and rooming houses climb the steep hillside of the bay to the park and cemetery that border the start/finish line of the TT course. The city is one of those places where you could hide the modern cars, take down the TV antennae, and imagine that World War I is still about five years away. There are only two or three modern structures in town and naturally these are made of concrete and are ugly as hell. The rest of the city is charming.

We checked into a hotel we had picked at random from a travel brochure. It turned out to be a great choice because the staff was a wonderful bunch of people and the pub and restaurant downstairs were both good. The only problems were an occasionally moody water heater and an elevator with a bad memory, so we spent a few evenings scaling a great numbers of stairs to reach a cold bath. (Not everyone can claim to have taken a bath "because it's there.") We discovered throughout our trip that the reliable heating of water is something of a mystery on the other side of the Atlantic, though the English and Manx are way ahead of the French, who handle hot water the way we handle expensive cologne.

Stepping out onto the street, we discovered the great TT Week pastime—strolling up and down the Promenade at night looking at the thousands of motorcycles parked on the street. In one pass, you can see an example or two of nearly any motorcycle ever made in every stage of restoration from ratty to concours. For instance, the people staying at our hotel owned—among others—an Ariel Leader, two Hesketh, a Hailwood Replica Ducati, a John Player Norton (not a replica; the ex–Peter Williams bike), a Honda CB900, a 350 Superhawk, and a BSA Gold Star, those being a small contribution to a row that went on for two miles.

The other great discovery was the people on the street and in the pubs. They formed an impression the first night that lasted all week. The crowd is generally polite, knowledgeable, and enthusiastic. Even with all the drinking and pub-crawling at night, there never seems to be any ugliness; none of the usual fistfights, throwing up curbside, or shouting clever things at passing women. Even the roughest-looking characters never seem to get publicly drunk or nasty. People stand around in groups of friends, pints of Guinness in hand, looking at bikes and talking about racing. I've never seen so many people drink so much and have such a good time without anyone getting out of control. They could obviously use some Mean and Stupid lessons from race fans in other parts of the world.

It probably goes back to the cost and commitment of getting to the island. In order to get there you have to (a) love motorcycles and (b) be smart enough to read a steamship schedule, both severe obstacles to a large part of the human race. The Isle of Man crowd is a fun collection of people.

In the morning we walked downstairs to the hotel dining room, which proved much easier than walking upstairs from the pub at night, and had a full Manx breakfast, i.e. two eggs, two strips of bacon, two sausages of strange consistency, toast with orange marmalade, juice, half a fried tomato (yes), and a pot of coffee or tea. In England this is known as a full English breakfast, and in Ireland it's a full Irish breakfast.

The Formula One race (for bikes like U.S. Superbikes and/or AMA Formula 1) wasn't scheduled until 3:00 P.M., meaning the circuit was open to traffic all morning. We climbed on the Suzuki and rode up to the start/finish line to take our first lap in the brilliant morning sunshine.

Briefly, the circuit is a 37.7-mile rectangle that looks as though it's been shipped parcel post through the U.S. Mail (crushed and dented in spots), running up one side of the island and back down the other. Most of the narrow pavement runs through villages, farms, and wooded glens in gently rolling countryside, but at the north end of the island it climbs the side of Mt. Snaefel and then descends in great sweeping stretches all the way to the start/finish line in Douglas.

There are only about a dozen slow corners on the course, so the rest of the circuit can be taken about as fast as memory and icy nerve allow. If you can remember what's around the next blind corner or over the brow of the next blind hill (and most people can't), you can ride large sections of the course flat out. If your memory isn't so good there are a lot of walls, churches, houses, and other fine examples of picturesque stonemasonry waiting to turn you into an ex-motorcyclist.

A first lap around the island is a revelation. Anywhere else it would be a scenic drive through the countryside of a lovely island. But knowing it's a racetrack changes your perspective on the road and its corners. The narrowness of the road and the close proximity of walls and other roadside obstacles would make 50 or 60 miles per hour seem plenty fast under normal touring circumstances. Corners, cars, and pedestrians are upon you almost before you see them.

At about 70 miles per hour the hedges and walls and overhanging trees begin to blur around the edges of your vision and the road becomes a sort of green, stone, and sky-blue tunnel. On a street bike, anything over 80 miles per hour begins to feel insanely fast, like a wild roller coaster ride, and the forks and shocks begin to hammer and kick the bike around. It bottoms in dips and loses contact with the road over rises, making it hard to pitch the bike into blind corners that unfold in front of you, revealing their peculiarities only after you've hit them.

On our first lap, my faithful passenger agreed that 80 miles per hour felt quite fast and hinted something a little slower might be more fun (I still have the bruises on my ribs). Racers, of course, go about twice as fast as we did. Really fast guys average about 115 miles per hour around the island, just under 20 minutes per lap. Our best lap was about two hours, with a stop for lunch in Ramsey.

Vance Breese and Mike Ross are two American riders who came to the island for the first time this year, bringing a pair of 1,300cc Harley-Davidson roadracers with them. Their race bikes were late in arriving during practice week, so they borrowed a couple of big street bikes from some sympathetic Manx enthusiasts. After the first practice lap they pulled into the pit lane in Douglas, took off their helmets, and both said, "I hope our bikes don't arrive in time for the race." After a few more laps, however, they began to develop some cautious enthusiasm and decided it might not be so bad after all.

"I was unprepared for the speed of the place," Breese said. "On the map the course looks like it's all corners, but most of those corners can be taken flat out—if you know where you're going."

"You can take one corner on the right line," Ross added, "but it'll ruin the line for the next two, so you'll have to back off to make it, and that can cost valuable seconds. You have to know where you're going all the time and be thinking ahead."

The TT course has to be ridden, at any speed, to be appreciated. Coming back into Douglas after that first trip around the circuit, it didn't feel as though we'd merely done a lap of a race course; it seemed we'd been gone on a week's vacation and were home at last. One lap is good for more changes of scenery and geography than most people see on a long summer holiday. Thirty-seven miles on the TT circuit is a long trip, and each time you come back into Douglas you feel a little older for the experience. The competitors no doubt feel a lot older.

That first lap also instills a combination of awe and respect for any rider who can set a competitive lap time on the circuit, because a fast lap time is irrefutable proof that the rider has both superb concentration and great courage. A short circuit just doesn't tell you as much about the people who lap it quickly.

We watched the Formula 1 race from the grandstand on the start/finish line. Compared with the mass-start mayhem of a GP event, the start of the TT is a relatively relaxed affair. The bikes are numbered according to starting order and are released in pairs every 10 seconds. They then race for six laps against the clock, rather than directly against one another. After the bikes are gone, an attentive quiet spreads over the crowd and everyone listens to the progress reports over the PA system, settling back for the 20-minute wait for the leaders to come blazing through town again.

It didn't take long for Mick Grant to establish himself as the leader in the F-1 race. Three quarters of the way through the first lap, he was reported 12 seconds ahead on the clock, and as his Yoshimura Suzuki came howling through Douglas it was announced he'd set a new lap record of 114.93 miles per hour at 19 minutes, 48 secconds—from a standing start. Joey Dunlop and Ron Haslam were second and third, both on Hondas. Before all the riders streaked into pit row for fuel, Grant had built up a huge 30-second lead. But on the last lap he parked his bike at the Hairpin with ignition trouble and Haslam took over the race as Dunlop slowed with handling problems. Haslam took the race, with Dunlop second, and New Zealander Dave Hiscock third.

Circle track fans might have a hard time adjusting to a race where the leaders come by every 20 minutes or so, then disappear over the hill for another 20. Hearing race reports from distant parts of the track, you sometimes feel a little like a civilian listening to war news from the Falklands. Yet every 20 minutes the war comes through town for a few brief seconds, and when you see the speed of the bikes on the narrow road it gives you pause to realize all those riders have been *out* there riding like *that* the entire time you've been sipping your warm pint of Okells Bitters and relaxing in the shade. The speed of the bikes (relative to the stationary nature of trees, pubs, and your own perch on the wall) is enough to raise the hair on the back of your neck.

In the pub that night everyone was talking about the race, and Mandy the barmaid was explaining to me that a 50/50 mix of Guinness and bitter ale is called a brown split by some and a dark-over-bitter by others. I tried several versions of both and couldn't make up my mind which was better. Everybody was buying endless rounds for everyone else. I discovered you can never sit in a Manx pub without at least two pints awaiting your attention.

Amid all the racing talk in the pub, two names surface over and over again, floating through the acrid smoke and endless variety of upper- and working-class British accents. The names were Mike Hailwood and Pat Hennen; Hailwood because he was the absolute smooth master of the circuit, and Hennen, the American, because he rode his heart out with an abandon that is still fixed in the memory of everyone who witnessed it.

"I saw Hennen pass a guy in midair at Ballaugh Bridge and then take the next corner with everything dragging and twitching . . . I mean he was *scratching*, mate. I never saw anything like it. He just bloody well *attacked* the course . . ." and so on. Hennen was seriously injured on the TT circuit and retired from racing several years ago, but no one who was there seems to have forgotten the smallest detail of his aggressive riding style.

Some pub conversations are easier than others. While it has been said that the Americans and British are two people separated by a common language, it is actually the British themselves who are separated by a common language. There is more stark contrast between the accents of two Englishmen from neighboring shires than there is between a Cajun alligator hunter from Louisiana and a New York stockbroker. Class and education throw up further barriers in language. While some British speak with the clarity of Prince Charles or John Cleese, others can approach you with such a broad regional dialect that conversation is all but impossible. Just before closing time I had the following chat with a man who seemed to be from England:

"Ha pen the nay thrraa queekum?" he asked me.

"Pardon?"

"Ha pen the nay thrraa queekum?"

"Uh . . . oh yeah. Sure."

"Aye?"

"Aye."

"Yer a foofa deekin, then?"

"Yeah. You're probably right. I'm a foofa deekin."

"Ah. 'Tis a shame . . ."

I bought the guy a beer before I sank any lower in his estimation. Then I crawled off to bed. I had no idea whether we were discussing piston rings or his wife, so I decided to clear out before I admitted something terrible.

I walked into the hotel elevator and punched the 5th floor button, but the elevator didn't want to go anywhere, so I decided to walk up to my room. I stopped for a smoke break on the 3rd floor landing and the elevator went by with no one in it. By the time I got to my room, the cold bath felt good.

The next day was Mad Sunday, when the track is open to the public and the police with their radar guns look the other way. Barb and I joined the stream of speeding bikes for a quick lap. Most of the riders were relatively sane, under the circumstances. The only hairy part was the downhill off the mountain. Every time we came up behind some slow vintage bike, like a smoking Scott Flying Squirrel, I'd check the mirrors and find we were being passed by a Honda 900F going 90 being passed by a Guzzi Le Mans going 100 being overtaken by a Bimota Kawasaki going flat out. This telescoping speed range can make things exciting on Mad Sunday. We passed some kind of accident and later learned a German rider had hit a car and lost his leg.

Much is made of these accidents when the TT is under fire, but when you see the number of people on the island and the amount of driving and riding they do, mishaps are amazingly rare. Americans and their cars seem to do themselves in at a much higher rate on any given holiday weekend in summer, and it would make about as much sense to cancel the Fourth of July as the Tourist Trophy because of the accident rate. This year there were, happily, no racing fatalities. And hundreds of competitors raced thousands of miles.

Races were scheduled every other day for the rest of the week. On the off days everyone rides around to the numerous vintage and owners club rallies held in various villages around the island, or people simply go sightseeing. The Isle of Man is such a pleasant vacation spot it's worth a week of anyone's time, even without the races.

The whole island is like a landscape created for a Tolkien novel or a Cat Stevens song. To say the island is quaint does it an injustice; that's like saying

Nastasia Kinski is good-looking. There's more to it than that. The combination of seacoast, fishing villages, farms, forested glens, cottages, and villages all fit together to provide a kind of bone-deep charm. There is nothing contrived or artificial about the Isle of Man. Brooks tumble, cattle and sheep graze, roses, wisteria, and lilacs grow around cottage gates and churchyards, and every time the sun comes out the island glows about fifty colors of green. Throw in a motorcycle race and you've got an island that's first on my list of Places I'm Going to Move When I Get Filthy Rich or Retire.

Norman Brown won the 500cc Senior race (for pure GP bikes) on Monday, riding a Suzuki that was quite a bit faster than ours. A dark-horse entrant and pub owner from Ireland, Brown rode a brilliant race, beating South African Jon Ekerold by only 8.6 seconds. New Zealander (people come from all over) Dennis Ireland finished third. Mick Grant had led the race for three laps before colliding with a slower rider and crashing without injury. A happy sidelight to the race was that veteran Charlie Williams, after being sidelined with a kinked fuel line during the race, went back out and set a new lap record of 19 minutes 40.2 seconds at 115.8 miles per hour. Another fast veteran, Tony Rutter, won the 350 Senior convincingly. Rutter turned in another fine ride on Wednesday, winning the Formula II race on a Ducati 600 Pantah. Dave Roper, one of a small contingent of Yanks racing the island, took 12th in the Formula III race on his borrowed 350 Aermacchi, making some of the nicest thumping noises of the week and looking very smooth and fast.

The last race of the week was the Classic—virtually unrestricted bikes—on Friday. After a gloriously sunny week (unheard of), the island woke up to rain on Friday morning. But it cleared off by noon and by race time the track was dry except for a few treacherous wet patches under the trees. Charlie Williams led most of the race, but retired on the fourth lap. Dennis Ireland took the win, with Jon Ekerold second, and Tony Rutter third. The fast guys did well no matter what they rode.

Two of the most interesting entries, at least from an American point of view, were those 1,300 Harleys of Breese and Ross. They'd had a tough week with very little practice and the bikes arriving late. A blown motor on Breese's bike and various mechanical problems had precluded even a full lap of practice on the bikes they were to race. Breese started the race with a hot street motor to replace his blown race engine. Ross retired on the first lap with engine problems and Breese soldiered through with a missing ignition to finish 38th.

"This is really an endurance race," Breese said later. "Two hundred and twenty-six miles is a long way to go on this road. Next time we'll be ready for it."

Breese and Ross had each completed only six laps of practice when the green flag dropped on their race, yet we watched both bikes come thundering through the glen at Barregarrow quicker than they had any right to, bottoming out on the sharp dip and flying off through the corridor of walls and trees. With all they'd been through, just being out there was an accomplishment and finishing was a minor triumph. And they sounded good.

We took the boat back to England on Saturday morning and stayed on deck long enough to see the green island disappear in the ocean haze.

I think my friend on the telephone was wrong. It isn't that no one should race on the Isle of Man. It's just that no one should *have* to race. There is no doubt the circuit is difficult and demanding, so perhaps a rider should race the TT only because he enjoys it and loves the challenge of a true road course, but not because his contract demands it. The Isle of Man is far too nice a place for people to race against their will.

I was partly wrong too, of course. The Isle of Man isn't important just because it's the last real road race on earth. It's important simply because there's nothing else like it anywhere, and if it disappears there will never be anything like it again.

Try to find another green island in a misty ocean with 37.7 miles of breathtakingly beautiful road and good draught ale, where the friendly inhabitants welcome a contest of speed with open arms and the word lawsuit is still regarded with proper disdain. And nowhere else on earth will we find another motorcycle race where the charming ladies of the Women's Church Guild serve tea and scones on blue and white fine-bone china to the race fans sitting on the churchyard wall.

September 1983

WOLVERHAMPTON DETOUR

A Look at the Old Norton Home

More Holy Ground. Nortons have played a big part in my life; it was a story about a Norton breakdown in Montana that got my writing career started, and the beauty of these bikes still stops me in my tracks whenever I see one. Also, nothing sounds and feels as good as a Norton during those charmed moments when everything is working right.

There's nothing quite like chasing a violent thunderstorm halfway across England in June to make you feel like a charmed motorcyclist. Fifteen or twenty miles ahead, angry black clouds tower over the landscape, shooting pitchfork lightning and shaking the ground with thunder. Meanwhile, just behind the passing storm front, you ride in a serene, sunlit world of blue skies, glorious rainbows, wet streets, and villagers emerging from their homes to inspect the fallen branches and missing shingles.

My wife Barbara and I were riding a borrowed Suzuki GS650 from North Wales toward London and we'd been sweeping the storm southeast all afternoon. We'd been to the Isle of Man and were on our way home. The storm had passed over us at sea, rocking the ferry boat and sending more than a few people to the rail, and now it was leading us like an unwieldy, grumbling Star of the East (talk about your delusions of grandeur) in the general direction of Gatwick Airport.

Late in the afternoon it appeared we were catching the storm. Despite stops for scenery and tea, the Suzuki was simply making better time than the foul weather. Rather than creep timidly behind the front or ride straight into the wind and rain, we decided to stop for the night. It so happened this roadside decision was made directly in front of a large road sign that read WOLVERHAMPTON 5. An arrow pointed left off the main highway. The cathedral steeples and industrial chimneys of the city were just visible above the trees of the hilly countryside, so we set off in that direction. After riding around the factories, shops, and charming old residential districts of Wolverhampton for half an hour, we finally found a nice hotel called the Goldthorne not far from the center of town. The well-dressed patrons in the lobby gazed at our mud-spattered Belstaff gear and appeared to be wondering whether it was we or they who had chosen the wrong hotel.

An hour later we were cleaned up, relatively presentable, and seated in the hotel dining room. After we ordered, I said to Barb, "Do you know where we are?"

She sensed a riddle but decided to play along. "Wolverhampton, England?"

"Exactly. Does it ring a bell?"

"No bell in particular. I read it on the highway signs."

"Where else?"

"I give up."

"On the owner's manual of our Norton Commando!" I effused.

"The one that blew up in Montana or the other one?"

"Both. Wolverhampton is the last home of the late Norton factory of Norton-Villiers-Triumph. This is the city where Commandos were made. We are on Holy Ground."

"I wondered why you wanted to stop here for the night. We could have gone another 20 miles."

"It was the storm," I said. "We were chasing it."

I sipped on a pint of nearly chilled ale and considered our past Nortons. We'd had two of them, a yellow 1971 750 Commando and a black and gold 1975 850 Interstate, which for all their small problems and peculiarities, remain in my mind as two of my favorite motorcycles. They were beautiful to look at and listen to, and they provided a sensation of thrilling power delivery and instantaneous torque that faster but smoother multis could not quite duplicate. They were British Twins of great charisma. Eventually, I sold them both to pay for the Japanese Fours I used in Box Stock roadracing. Purity sacrificed for expedience.

Both Nortons came with owner's manuals, and the home address of the company was stamped on the cover: *Marston Road, Wolverhampton, England.* I saw these words every time I consulted the owner's manual, which was often, and always spoke the name of the city silently to myself. Wolverhampton. It was a perfect name. It sounded like the kind of place Nortons should come from; a word of antiquity and industrial quaintness with an undertone of ferocity.

When the young waitress brought our dinner I asked if she knew the whereabouts of the Norton factory.

"Sir?"

"The old Norton motorcycle factory. Norton-Villiers? I believe it was located in Wolverhampton."

She bit her lip, thinking a moment, then shook her head. "I don't know of such a factory, sir. All of the motorbike garages in town sell Japanese machines—like Hondas or Kawasakis. My boyfriend," she added brightly, "has a Kawasaki."

I successfully resisted a strange temptation to leap from my chair and grab the poor woman by the throat. She meant well, but how could anyone live in Wolverhampton unaware of the fate or existence of the Norton company? She was like a Dubliner who didn't know if James Joyce was dead or alive. Disgraceful.

In my mind's eye, these many years, I had imagined Wolverhampton as a city whose very existence hinged on the success or failure of Norton motorcycles; a place where framed paintings of James Lansdowne Norton and speeding Commandos hung above the glittering rows of bottles in every pub, and workingmen toasted their memory; a town where mothers and children included Geoff Duke, Peter Williams, and Bob Trigg in their bedtime prayers. Never mind that the factory had moved from Birmingham to Woolwich before landing here in 1969, amid the ceaseless turmoil of British corporate division and amalgamation, or that much of the final assembly was done at Woolwich. I had nevertheless expected to find Wolverhampton a solid Norton town, still mourning its loss. Instead I'd discovered a large, busy industrial city that could swallow a motorcycle factory whole without blinking, and a waitress who didn't know Nortons from Maytags.

I cleared my throat, "So you don't know of the Norton factory?"

"No sir."

A middle-aged waitress who was clearing the next table overheard our conversation and stopped in her tracks. She stared at the younger woman quizzically for a moment, then turned to us. "The Norton factory," she said quietly, "is across the street." She pointed out the restaurant window. "That wall is the back of the Norton works. The main gate is just around the corner, on Marston Road. The factory occupies most of that block. It's been closed now for over five years."

The woman left us staring out the window at a high red brick wall with wrought iron trim. "Amazing," I said. "Across the street. Looks like we picked the right hotel." It was nearly dark, so we put off exploration until the next day.

It was a sunny morning with Sunday church bells ringing when we stepped out of the hotel after breakfast. The streets were quiet and nearly empty, except for random couples and families out for morning walks in their church-going finery. We crossed the street and strolled up Marston Road, following the brick wall until we came to a pair of elaborate iron gates with the name Villiers fashioned in wrought iron. The gates were locked, but we could see an office building flanked by long brick assembly-line structures with skylights and multi-pane windows. A large green lawn with a circular drive extended from the office building to the gates. The factory had a civilized, friendly look about it, as though it might have been the entrance to an old prep school or university.

We walked farther up the street, almost to the corner of the factory where Marston Road intersected with Villiers Street, and found an open gate. Beside the gate was a small time clock shed with many broken windows and the door swinging idly on its hinges. Inside, the floor was scattered with old Norton record books, technical bulletins, old teacups, magazines, and industrial safety posters (Protect Your Eyes!, Safety is Everybody's Business, etc.). A huge key closet was open, with keys marked Storeroom #4, Milling Tool Room, Paintshop Main Door, and so on, hanging on cup hooks. Rain had blown in the broken windows and dampened the record books scattered on the floor.

I picked up a large volume entitled Detail Occurrence Book and began reading. Some typical entries, from October of 1974, written with a black ink pen in a florid hand: "Number two engines running experimental tonight" and "Radiator in piston shop requires attention; leaking badly" and "All toilets in D Shop under canteen blocked except one" followed by "two engines still running experimental after weekend." They had more nerve than I'd ever had, leaving their Norton engines running all weekend.

We walked outside and wandered around the factory buildings, most of which were gutted and empty. One, however, had all its windows intact and was filled with machine tools and parts bins. We walked around the corner and found a construction crew sitting against the building, taking a tea and cigarette break. They explained that several of the factory buildings had been leased to small industrial companies. Lawnmower engines were being produced in this particular building, they said. Several more buildings would soon be fixed up, and these men were part of the renovation crew hired to put them in order. The wiring, they said, was a mess.

As we walked back toward the gate, a dump truck rumbled in and backed up to another of the buildings. Several workmen jumped out and began shoveling a pile of debris from a loading dock into the open truck. The old factory was getting to be a lively place on a Sunday morning.

We passed the time clock shed and started out the gate, but I turned around and went back into the shed. I came out carrying a water-soaked Detail Occurrence Book. Usually I'm not much on looting and souvenir hunting, but I thought at least one memento should be saved from the scoop shovel and the dump truck. We went back to the hotel and I stuffed the book into the Suzuki's tank bag. I later dried its pages back into wrinkled parchment on a hotel radiator in London, lightening our luggage by about five pounds.

We checked out of the hotel, climbed on the Suzuki, and slowly circled the block. Adjacent to the Norton-Villiers plant were other buildings representing the great industrial names of England: Fafner, Spicer, and Lucas, as well as several metal plating and aluminum casting companies. The Norton people didn't have to walk far for their bearings, electrics, and other specialized components. We completed our circle of the block and found that a large plywood realty sign had been nailed over the Norton-Villiers name at every corner of the factory.

I tried to ride away from the Norton plant with a minimum of self-inflicted wistfulness and irony, but there was no denying that those peaceful brick buildings on that warm Sunday morning were inhabited by their share of ghosts. Just beyond vision and barely above the aural range of the human ear, the place was probably alive with the clamor of industrial production; it was possible to imagine cartloads of 750 Combat engines being hauled in gleaming rows from the assembly plant, or triangular timing gear covers with the lovely Norton emblem being buffed to a high luster in the metal finishing shop, or Peter Williams walking through the gates to look at his new Isle of Man ride.

Battlefields, historic racing circuits, famous movie locations, and the homes of poets and artists surround themselves with a similar aura. They continue to ring with the presence of great endeavor long after the principal characters have left the scene. They become, if not sanctified, at least Certified Important Places on Earth. Nortons had been great motorcycles, in their own English way, and greatness does not desert a place just because bank managers and financiers decide the game is over. Nailing a realty sign over the Norton-Villiers could now have little effect on the place. The Norton name, peeking out from behind, was simply more powerful than the realtor's. (In fact, I worried for the health of the man who nailed it up there; risky business, like messing around with a pharaoh's tomb.)

I liked to imagine that it was just a matter of time until all this was put right. Sometime after the turn of the next century people would realize that the Norton factory was a part of the national heritage. They'd return with painters, carpenters, and bricklayers and a large bundle of historical photographs to reconstruct everything just as it was in 1975. The Norton works would take its place beside Ann Hathaway's cottage and the Bronte homestead on the roster of historical landmarks. Tour guides in 1975 period costumes (bellbottoms, etc.) would say things like, "It was at this drawing board that Bob Trigg designed the Isolastic engine mounts," or "This is where they put the gold pinstriping on the gas tanks."

It would take a while for us to realize that our loveliest industrial designs were as great a contribution to Art as the poetry, painting, and sculpture of the twentieth century. In the meantime, the romance of an old British bike factory, like the call of motorcycling itself, was as selective in its appeal as a silent dog whistle. You had to have owned a Norton—or have wanted to own one very badly—in order to hear it.

June 1985

THE EMERALD TOUR

Ireland on Five Gallons a Day

On this tour of Ireland, I must admit that the beauty of the country and the graciousness of the people was offset somewhat with the rain and cold and our semi-permeable waxed cotton Belstaff suits. Between the wet clothing and unheated rooms, restaurants, and bathwater, we never got warm for a moment during our week of touring. I would like to go back and do it again with a better rain suit.

Ireland. The name provoked all kinds of response in England. You'd sit in a bar in Birmingham and the man who'd just bought you a pint would say, "Well, where are you two adventurers riding next?" You'd answer "Ireland," and a strange hush would fall over the pub. A few people would shake their heads, the bartender would raise one eyebrow, and your drinking friend would equivocate, "Well . . . that might be a nice trip. I guess. But I don't mind telling you I wouldn't go there myself."

"Ever been there?"

"Nope." The answer always came with stunning quickness, like the standard medical questionnaire response: "Any mental illness in the family?" "Nope." "Ever been to Ireland?" "Nope."

A friend in Liverpool reacted the same way. So we asked, "Aren't you curious about a big island right next to your own?"

"Nope. Never been there. You see . . . (a how-shall-I-phrase-this pause) it might be very well for you Americans, but if I walked into an Irish pub or hotel with my English accent, I can't say how I'd be treated. I'd be on edge all the while."

Others told us, Americans or not, to stay away. A crazy, dangerous place of no consequence. Trouble. Don't go to Ireland. Tour England.

"We've already toured England. Twice."

"Tour it again, mate."

I learned a long time ago to take this kind of advice with a large grain of salt. I'd been warned by Frenchmen to avoid Italy like the plague, by northerners not to ride through the Deep South, by mature adults to stay off motorcycles, by country folk not to walk around New York City, by all kinds of people not to fly airplanes, and by clergymen to stay away from girls in high school. I eventually learned that these advisors had two things in common: First, they had almost no experience with the thing they mistrusted; and second, they were always dead wrong.

There was, no doubt, trouble to be found if you went looking for it in certain select industrial neighborhoods of Belfast in Northern Ireland, but our plan was to tour the south of Ireland, reputedly peaceful since it became a republic in 1922. We had a motorcycle, a few hundred dollars, and exactly one week of remaining summer vacation.

We left from Liverpool on a Saturday evening, following a line of cars up a steel ramp into the gaping maw of the Connought, our ship to Dublin. Cars were packed bumper-to-bumper in orderly lines, but a loading foreman directed our bike to one side and pointed to a thick coil of rope on the deck. "Take that," he said, "and lash your motorbike to the rail against the hull, in case the sea gets rough." Our motorbike on this trip was a shaft-drive Suzuki GS650G, kindly lent to us by our English friend Ray Battersby, who works for Suzuki U.K. and lives near London. We tied the bike down, padding the tank with gloves and scarves so it wouldn't scrape on the hull, and climbed onto the main deck.

There was no danger of rough seas. The ocean was mirror-like as we sailed out of Liverpool and into the Irish Sea, with moonlight shining through the scattered clouds. Traveling on the cheap, as usual, we hadn't paid the extra money for a stateroom, so we spent the night alternately sipping coffee at the snack bar, trying to nap in the reclining chairs on the enclosed foredeck, and looking at maps of Ireland. We pronounced the names of counties aloud, just because they sounded good: Wicklow, Wexford, Waterford, and Cork; Kerry, Limerick, Tipperary, Clare, and Galway. And then there were the Boggeragh

Mountains, the Slieve Bloom Mountains, Blarney, Dingle Bay, and the River Shannon. The whole island looked like a Tolkien invention, full of impossible, imaginary names and places.

Barb spotted Ireland first, just before dawn. She pointed out what I believed to be just another low bank of clouds, but it emerged as a lower, greener cloud lying in the early morning mist. Our ship steamed into Dublin Harbor and, after much roaring and reversing of the props, bumped solidly against the dock, as if to prove the island was solid and not just a hazy green vision in the Irish Sea. The ramp dropped and after a quick customs check we accelerated out into Dublin's streets, which were just waking up for Sunday church.

Greater Dublin, we discovered, sprawls over a large area, but its downtown is condensed into a pleasantly small area around the River Liffey. The city has an old, stately feel about it, with very few tall buildings and a lot of Georgian architecture. The houses of Dublin are famous for their neatly painted doors and window casings, contrasting with the gray stone and brass trim.

We rode around the largely empty streets for about half an hour, exploring and waiting for the restaurants to open. "I wonder," I said to Barb at a stoplight on O'Connell Street, "if there's anywhere around here you can get two semi-fried eggs, two undercooked sausages, two slices of boiled tomato, and a cup of truly terrible coffee."

"This is Ireland," Barb reminded me, "not England."

"I forgot. I wonder if they have the same breakfasts in Ireland?"

We camped at the door of a café whose sign promised the place would open soon, and met a young American couple named Steve and Kathy, who were also waiting at the door. We all went in and had the Breakfast Special: two semi-fried eggs, two undercooked sausages, two slices of boiled tomato, and a cup of truly terrible coffee.

Steve and Kathy gave us the phone number of a good bed & breakfast place where they'd stayed and suggested we call after breakfast. "Ask for Mrs. O'Donovan," Steve said.

Mr. O'Donovan answered the phone. "Ah, then," he said, "so it's a room you need. You'll be wanting to talk to my dear wife, then. She's just now returned from mass with our two young boys."

I held the phone and smiled to myself. In America, the man would have said, "Just a minute," and left it at that. In Ireland, people painted you small pictures with words, always in a soft, quicksilver cadence that was easy on the ears.

We found the address on a quiet residential street a few miles away, and Mrs. O'Donovan turned out to be a tall, sparkling woman with a beautifully kept house. She was not at all put off by our Belstaff suits, boots, and motorcycle gear, but seemed genuinely intrigued that a married couple would be traveling in this fashion. "Cold and damp, I should think," she said, bringing us hot tea.

I'd heard motorcycle touring in the British Isles described before, but never quite so succinctly.

After cleaning up and unpacking our luggage, Barb and I rode the much-lightened Suzuki back into the city center, where we ran smack into the annual Children's Day Parade pouring through the middle of Dublin. There were marching bands, soccer clubs, dance troupes, drill teams, etc., all children, marching to the scattered applause and flash photography of their parents. The older kids were confident and showy; the younger ones still wide-eyed and wary, wondering what kind of civilization they'd been born into that marched them down the street dressed like little pumpkins and leprechauns and drum majorettes.

We stopped in a pub for a glass of Guinness, and a man at the bar looked out the window and said it wasn't a very good parade. "They do it much better in Texas," he declared, "for the football games. Irish never learn to handle the baton properly as Texas children do. Look at them, dropping the things all over the street." I thought they looked just like the kids from my own grade school, but I'm not from Texas, either.

Barb and I later wandered over to McDaid's pub. McDaid's is reputed to be the erstwhile hangout of writer and poet Brendan Behan, who supposedly drank there as a young dog. There was a picture of him on the wall, and a collection of students, professors, scarved hangers-on, and other rowdy drinking-and-smoking classes at the bar. We discovered that first night that you have to be careful in Irish pubs because genuine draft Guinness is so easy to drink. Guinness Stout, if you're not already a convert, is a very heavy beer—like brew that has the taste of dark roasted malt with overtones of molasses and licorice and has a color that is closer to black than brown. A friend of mine who hates the stuff says it tastes like burnt wool athletic socks from someone's gym locker, but I've grown quite fond of it. Guinness is the official pub drink of Ireland and is also widely drunk in England, commonly mixed half-and-half with lighter beers and ales. Great stuff, as they say, but it certainly doesn't help you climb stairs.

In the morning, Barb and I packed our luggage, which consisted of a tank bag and two soft saddlebags, and said goodbye to the O'Donovans. On our way out of Dublin we stopped to see the famous Book of Kells, housed in the Long Room of the Trinity Library. The book is a richly illustrated manuscript of the four Gospels, believed to have been written around the year 800 A.D. in a monastery scriptorium. A woman ahead of me in line peered through the glass at the elaborate Insular Celtic script, intertwined with snakes, tendrils, and flowers, and said in a New York accent, "I wundah what it says?"

Her husband snapped back, "How should I know?"

I suppressed an urge to read it for them and make it up as I went along: "Gloria entered the room, flushed from her tennis lesson . . ."

We went south first, along the east coast of Ireland, through Bray, Gaystones, Newcastle, and Wicklow. It took some time to get out of greater Dublin, but once we were free, the two-lane road down the coast was wild and beautiful, sweeping down into one harbor after another and back over the cliffs. The weather was cool and overcast with the sun breaking through thin spots in the clouds occasionally, instantly changing the color of the ocean and the green fields. We stopped for lunch at a little town called Gorey. Lunch, the big meal of the day, consisted of roast pork, potatoes, peas, cabbage, tea, and strawberries with cream. There's nothing terribly subtle about the restaurant food in Ireland, but it's good and you get a lot of it.

We filled up our gas tank for the first time. Gasoline in Ireland costs about 1.55 Irish pounds (or Punts, as they are properly called) per Imperial gallon. Only a few years ago, when the Irish pound was worth around

$2.20, this was expensive fuel, but now that the pound is approaching parity with the dollar, Irish gasoline is becoming something of a bargain for Americans, if not for the Irish themselves.

There are no motorways or expressways to speak of in Ireland, so there is a fair amount of commercial traffic on the main roads along the coast and between larger cities. Leave the main roads, however, and the traffic drops off to a desultory mixture of sheep, tractors, the occasional car, cattle, donkey carts, and pedestrians, all traveling at roughly the same speed and spaced well apart. Irish drivers tend to be relaxed and easy-going, with none of the murderous seriousness you find on the Continent. There is a sense of good-natured flexibility and complete patience. Making time on Irish roads is not in the cards, however, and dragging your knee in corners isn't recommended unless you wish to become One with the back of a haywagon, or are especially fond of sheep.

We stopped for the night at Waterford and found a bed & breakfast place overlooking a small square, had dinner nearby, went to a well-acted production of *Stagestruck* at the Royal Theater, and then wandered around town, exploring at random.

We came across an Egan's Pub and, naturally, dropped in for a pint. The Egans of my own family were supposed to have migrated to the U.S. from Waterford during the great potato famine. I have to admit that I've always been a little bit skeptical of the Roots Movement, since most of the people I know who are overly concerned with the accomplishments of their forebears seem not to be up to much of anything themselves. Still, it's fascinating to wander the streets of a foreign town and imagine your great-grandparents walking down to the docks and sailing off to a new life in America. My own relatives ended up in Minnesota, apparently because Ireland wasn't cold enough for them, or had too few mosquitoes.

Waterford, like many of the cities we rode through, is laced with ancient walls, fragments of towers, bits of old monasteries, and other ruins. Old stone structures that would be national landmarks in the U.S. are so common in Ireland that no one pays them much mind, and they are often integrated into lesser but more modern buildings. The ruins of a thirteenth century guard tower become the north wall of a tin-roofed auto repair shop; part of a medieval city wall is used as one side of a pink stucco beauty parlor, and so on. It's an odd mixture of the old and the new, the elegant and the garish.

On the way back to our room in the evening we stopped to talk to an old woman who was leaning out the front window of her small house. "It's good to see a young man and wife walking together," she said. "Now that the pubs serve food and allow women inside, there's no reason a'tall for a man to come home to his family anymore . . ."

If she thinks it's bad now, I thought, wait'll they discover *Space Invaders.*

In the morning we rode out to the Waterford Crystal factory at the edge of the city and watched the glassblowers and cutters at work. I'd never seen such a cheerful, good-natured bunch of workers in any factory, but then, the last factory I worked at was a gunpowder plant, where anxiety was our most important product. Barb and I bought a crystal salt-and-pepper-shaker set, after voting them most likely to succeed in a tank bag. Wine glasses and chandeliers were out of the question.

We rode south through Dungarvan and Cork along the coast and then inland to Killarney. Killarney had a large tourist trade because it's the jumping-off point for a beautiful loop of roads around the mountainous Kerry Peninsula. The route is called the Ring of Kerry. We found a nice old hotel in Killarney, and after dinner went looking for some authentic Irish folk music. "This is a big tourist town," I told Barb. "They've got to have a good club somewhere."

We found a pub with a big sign that read Live Music Tonight and sat down inside with a drink. A band showed up—four guys in cowboy shirts and bandanas—and proceeded to set up their equipment, then launched into a half-hour of Waylon Jennings and Willie Nelson tunes. "Not exactly the Boys of the Lough or the Sands Family, are they?" I said to Barb over the thumping Fender bass and the whining steel guitar. When we left, they were singing "Don't Let Your Babies Grow Up to be Cowboys" in perfect Texas twang.

In the morning we rode south along the forested shore of Lake Leane, in the first real sunlight of the trip. When we came to open meadow and mountain country near the coast, we stopped on a hilltop to look over the landscape. If Paris, as Henry Miller said, is composed of a hundred different shades of gray, then Ireland has at least as many shades of green; grass green, moss green, tree green, meadow green, etc. When the sun comes out from behind a cloud, the effect is stunning, like the switch from black-and-white film to color in the *Wizard of Oz.* There's a shifting, moody quality to the light, and the sky seems to move over the island at a faster-than-normal pace.

Partway down the Kerry Peninsula we decided to get away from the tour buses and turned inland on a narrow road that wound through a mountain range with the strange name of the Maggillycuddy's Reeks. This almost empty road took us through a rugged landscape of rocky valleys, sheep farms, peat bogs, abandoned houses, cemeteries filled with Celtic crosses, old stone churches, walls, and the ruins of walls. We came to several Ys in the road and made our choices at random. The scenery and the road were so perfect for motorcycling, we really didn't care where we were going.

Until late in the afternoon. We suddenly decided it was time to start wending our way back to civilization or we'd be sleeping on the moors; just us, the Suzuki with its empty gas tank, and whatever it is that howls on the moors at night.

Luckily, you're never far from friendly advice, even in the remotest parts of Ireland. In the countryside everywhere there is a class of individual we came to call The Solitary Walking Man. You see them miles from anywhere, walking along the roads in neat caps, ties, and jackets, walking with canes, walking with hands behind their backs, or strolling along smoking pipes. A sociologist would probably tell us this phenomenon is economic—the cost of fuel, the cost of cars, etc. Personally, I'd like to think that most of the people walk from one place to another because the country is so lovely that a ride is simply a missed opportunity.

We were pointed toward the coast by an old gentleman in tweeds who was walking with his sheepdog. By nightfall we'd found a nice bed & breakfast place in the little town of Tarbert, at the mouth of the River Shannon. When we signed the guest register, the landlady looked at what I had written and said, "Ah, you're American. I thought you were English. You have English registration on your motorbike." I looked back at the bike and wondered how many other people had made that same mistake. Probably quite a few, but no one on the highways or elsewhere had shown us anything but courtesy and hospitality. In some places I could think of, just being a motorcyclist would have lowered the level of warmth and charm. This lady had cheerfully showed us a room thinking we were English motorcyclists.

There is a saying in Ireland that if you don't like the weather, just wait a minute. Generally that's true, but sometimes the weather takes more than a minute to change. Sometimes it can take several hours. And if it's gusting a cold, driving rain off the North Sea and you're on a motorcycle, it can take days. We rode toward Galway on a couple of those days.

Barb and I were both wearing Belstaff jackets of the black, waxed-cotton variety, with matching Belstaff pants. They worked great in those famous one-minute Irish showers, but in a steady, lashing rainstorm they began to wick moisture through the inner lining, and by the time we reached Limerick we were so wet we didn't care anymore. In an effort to close the barn door after the horse got drenched, we stopped at a Limerick sporting goods store and bought the closest thing we could find to Dry Rider suits—a couple of rubberized canvas duck-hunting outfits, olive drab in color.

Slightly warmer, we rode through some of the prettiest scenery on the trip—thatched cottages, the towering cliffs of Moher, endless castle ruins, etc.—all glimpsed through face shields streaming with water and fogged from within. It just wasn't a motorcycle day. We sloshed our way into Galway late in the afternoon and took a room at the first structure with a Hotel sign on the wall.

Our hotel turned out to be, essentially, an old men's rooming house with a few extra rooms. It was the kind where the wallpaper, carpets, and paint were all finalists in some long-forgotten eyesore contest. We draped our wet jackets and riding gear around the room to dry and went down the hall for a hot bath. The hot water was cold, so the hotel clerk said to wait an hour and it would be warmer, which we did, but it wasn't.

The heating of water seems to be something of a black art in most parts of the world I've visited, except for Switzerland, Germany, Japan, and the U.S. The English and the Irish manage to get it sort of hot at certain hours of the day if you give them plenty of notice, while the French succeed in heating water only in coffee makers. Spaniards (as nearly as we could tell during the month we spent touring the Iberian hinterlands) are not aware of any process by which potential bath water can be heated. I've often thought that some benevolent American plumbing magnate should send a missionary to Europe with a cutaway water heater and a pointer, just to pass the technology along and get the ball rolling.

Ireland is a country of not much heat, but plenty of warm blankets, so our pneumonia was relatively mild the next morning and had not spread to both lungs. We poked around Galway, then had lunch at a pub, sharing a table with two old retired farmers. One had no teeth or hair, and the other had one eye, a badly scarred lip, and a bandaged hand with yellow iodine stains around his fingers and wrist. We bought each other a couple of drinks and then settled down to a potato, cabbage, and bacon meal.

"So you're American," the one-eyed man said, dropping some food on his lap and deftly returning it to his plate with the side of a butter knife. "Did you know that John Wayne once came to Galway and had his famous fistfight with Victor McLaglen right here, and that John Ford came in this very pub when he was filming a famous American movie called *The Quiet Man*?" I confessed we hadn't known. "Aye," he said, "I saw them all, and I've been to America myself to visit my brother in Baltimore." He dropped some food and searched for it with his good eye, but the food had fallen out of range. "The Americans ask for a lot," he continued, "but they give you a lot when you go there."

"Ah well," said the bald one agreeably, "They work hard and save their money and deserve a good time."

When we'd left the pub, I said to Barb, "There are times when this country makes me feel like Jim Hawkins in *Treasure Island*. At least one of those guys should have had a parrot on his shoulder."

It was almost time for us to go back to working hard and saving for a good time, so we had to turn away from the coast and the stark beauty of Galway to head back toward Dublin. Central Ireland, south of Lough Ree and through Westmeath, is gently rolling country with relatively straight roads, so we made good time.

Regardless of the roads, however, speeding across the countryside is difficult, and I told Barb that the Tourist Bureau should issue horse blinders to travelers who have to follow a schedule, especially if they own cameras. That's the tragedy of traveling in Ireland with a camera: You could stop anywhere in the country and shoot up a roll of film while turning on your heel in a 360-degree arc. You are surrounded everywhere with achingly beautiful scenery, ancient buildings, interesting people, and whatnot. You just have to shrug it off and breeze by castles, ruins, churches, and charming villages without a second look. There just isn't time to investigate everything.

One thing we did stop to investigate, however, was a pub in the little town of Moate, which had a sign that said "P. Egan" over the door. We went in and the owner, a quiet, friendly man in his forties, introduced himself as Peter Egan. "That's my name, too," I said. We bought each other drinks, and he gave me a handful of Guinness labels with our mutual name printed at the bottom. "These are left over from the days when we used to bottle our own stout for customers," he said. I gave him a couple of *Cycle World* business cards with the same name on them, and then we said goodbye.

We rode hard for the rest of the afternoon, looking neither to the left nor to the right, averting our eyes from the scenery. We had a boat to catch in the morning and could not be distracted. The Suzuki had run so flawlessly and needed so little maintenance (i.e., none) in our one week of touring that I'd stopped expecting anything else. It occurred to me on that last stretch of road that a 650 was almost exactly the right size for two-up tour in a country the size of Ireland, and possibly at the upper limit of necessity. The narrow, winding roads, the mixture of rural traffic and animal life, not to mention the frequent need to stop, park, and explore, made maneuverability far more useful than huge reserves of acceleration and horsepower. Speeding through Ireland made about as much sense as rushing through a good dinner or a close friendship.

We made it to Dublin late in the afternoon and checked into a bed & breakfast place on the north side of the city. We cleaned up, put on our last change of clean clothes, and rode out to a peninsula named Howthh Haad. We found a famous old place called the Abbey Tavern, had a wonderful salmon dinner, and stayed to hear the Abbey singers do Irish ballads and folk songs. After a couple of Irish coffees, we rode back to the bed & breakfast late in the evening. In the morning we had a breakfast of two semicooked eggs, two undercooked sausages, two slices of boiled tomato, and a cup of truly terrible coffee.

"From dust we came . . ." I said to Barb.

"I'm beginning to like these breakfasts," she said.

"So am I. Time to go home."

Our departure from the island was like a movie played backward. We tied our bike down in the ship's hold again and went up on the deck to watch Ireland move east on the horizon. Perhaps ten miles out, the land became that same low, green shape on the water, and in another five miles the clouds and mist had swallowed it up. I stood on the deck for a long time, watching seagulls and the wake of the boat, and thinking what a pitifully short time one week was to spend in a place like Ireland.

A motorcycle is almost always one of the best ways to see a country as it should be seen and to get under the surface. And yet, in leaving Ireland, I almost felt as though we'd seen it from the train. It was too complex, an island of too much depth and too many layers. It was a place that demanded a summer of our time, at least, and maybe a slower motorcycle. Or one that broke down a lot.

As our boat approached the coast of England late in the afternoon, I thought about all the well-meaning people who had advised us not to go to Ireland, and I wondered if they were related, in some spiritual sense, to the same people who warned us never to ride a motorcycle.

February 1984

THE TWO-WHEELED UNDERGROUND CANADIAN RAILROAD

Sometimes the Longest Trip Begins With a Really Long Trip . . .

This is a Vietnam-era story about a trip I took just before joining the Army, and about the absence of one's country and friends making the heart grow fonder. Two of the people in this story, Pat Donnelly and Jim Wargula, still live nearby and—35 years later—we are still good friends and riding buddies. Strangely, we all own red mid-1990s Ducati 900SS-SPs and play Gibson electric guitars in the same blues band. Proof that similarly addled minds work alike, almost indefinitely.

The summer jobs were over and Donnelly and I were rich. Three months on a railroad section crew, shoveling gravel halfway from Milwaukee to the Twin Cities, had earned us each a tidy $1,400. In 1967, that was a lot of money. It would pay for our room, board, and tuition at college, with change left over for a few student luxuries like cigarettes, pizza, and gas for our motorcycles. I had a slightly beat Honda CB160 and Donnelly had a Honda 305 Dream, a little less beat. We both wanted Triumphs but had settled for these used Hondas because they were amazingly cheap, having been bought late in the second semester from other desperate students.

It appeared we were all set for a junior year at the University of Wisconsin. I was an English major and Pat Donnelly was in Political Science. What we hoped to do with these majors, I have no idea. We weren't thinking very far ahead. The war in Vietnam was going on, so between that and various other social perils, it wasn't fashionable or especially worthwhile to make plans much beyond the age of 21. There was plenty of precedent for disappearing just a bit earlier than that.

The idea at the time was to join the army if you flunked out of college or happened to think the war was a good idea, or to stay in college if you weren't entirely convinced it was a wonderful thing. Donnelly and I were not entirely convinced. A few years earlier we'd gotten out of high school with a fairly solid collection of patriotic notions. My freshman year in college I'd gone so far as to sign up for the ROTC because I wanted to become a Navy fighter pilot. But two years spent reading newspapers and watching the war on TV at the student union had eroded my enthusiasm for the conflict. By 1967, my conventional military fervor had turned to a sort of heartsick malaise. Donnelly, my roommate and best friend from youth, felt the same way.

So when I say it appeared we were all set to go back to school in the fall, I mean we were tossing around some other ideas. One of those was moving to Canada. That was a big step, of course, a trip of no return that slammed the door on families, friends, girlfriends, home towns, and calling ourselves Americans. Neither of us had ever been to Canada, nor anywhere else outside the U.S. for that matter. We wanted to see this Canada before we attempted to move there; to see what life looked like from across the border, to smell the Canadian air, drink Canadian coffee, and meet some Canadians. Did Mounties still wear red outfits? We were told they looked like FBI agents now. We needed a scouting trip to check it out.

That trip was planned for early September, between the end of railroad labor and the start of the fall semester. In retrospect, our preparations for the trip seem almost quaint. We changed our oil, adjusted valves, lubed our chains, and each took $60 out of the bank. To the rear seat of my CB160 I strapped an army surplus duffel bag containing a flashlight, a sleeping bag, and Big Pink, a faded red pup tent from my childhood, a tent originally designed to make a pair of dwarfish 9-year-olds mildly claustrophobic. Its lack of water repellency was legend among all who'd been doused within its tiny pink walls.

Rain gear?

Forget it. Motorcyclists didn't wear rain gear in those days (unless they had an ounce of common sense or were older than 18). We saw motorcycle rain suits as an extravagance for people who worried about all the wrong things. No, Donnelly and I had our blue jeans, work boots, Bell helmets, leather jackets and gloves, and that was enough.

The first part of the trip went pretty well. We left early on a gray morning and had breakfast in a truckstop on Highway 51, heading southeast from Rockford. Our first stop for the night was to be Arlington Heights, a suburb of Chicago. Another roommate of ours, Hugh Wessler, lived there. It took us half the day to blunder into greater Chicago and the other half to find Arlington Heights amid the suburban sprawl. We finally found Hugh's house and, with typical courteous forethought, called from a gas station about two blocks away to let the Wesslers know we were in town. Yes, I admitted, we sure could use a place to stay for the night, now that you ask. Hugh's mother wanted to know if we were hungry. I told her not to go to any trouble in a tone of voice that implied if she had a side of beef or maybe half a dozen pizzas around, we'd probably eat them.

When we got to Hugh's house he was in the basement, listening to his Heathkit stereo and making an electric guitar in his woodworking shop. Hugh was an engineering major who could make anything, including, it turned out, a living when he got out of college. We had a marvelous dinner concocted by Hugh's mom on short (no) notice, and let ourselves out the back door the next morning, leaving a thank-you note propped between the salt and pepper shakers on the kitchen table. We wanted to be in Canada by nightfall.

If you've never been there, Calumet City and Hammond are lovely at six in the morning viewed from the elevated Chicago Skyway, especially with a light rain falling. The air is scented with aroma of Bessemer furnaces, industrial arc welding, and coke production, and rain glistens on the axles and driveshafts of overturned cars with their wheels gone. Open gas flames billow from tall chimneys and everything, including your motorcycle, face shield, and very teeth, acquires a fine patina of cinders and ash. We skirted the south end of the lake through Gary and headed northeast into Michigan on Highway 60.

Traffic was heavy on 60, but at last the factories and scrap yards gave way to green pastures and wooded farmland. Our bikes were running well. Oddly enough, my CB160 was quicker through the gears than Donnelly's single-carb 305 Dream. True to its touring image and ethereal name, however, the Dream cruised at a more relaxed pace on the highway and had a few more miles per hour right at the top end. Both bikes topped out in the neighborhood of 90 miles per hour and cruised at 70 or more without apparent strain.

The only real problem with my 160 was a dead battery, meaning I had to bump start the bike every morning in a sort of Hailwood-at-the-TT imitation. Once the engine was warm, the kick starter worked all right. With no battery to regulate things, however, the brightness of my headlight varied on revs, so I tended to flicker and dim at stop signs.

Michigan was my initiation to a basic maxim of cross-country travel. Stated simply: Maps are small, while the earth, on the other hand, is quite large. It looked like a short jaunt to Detroit in Rand McNally, but it took us all day to get there. Our original plan on this trip was to ride across eastern Canada all the way to the fishing villages of the Gaspé Peninsula on the Atlantic coast. Halfway through Michigan, we began to see Montreal as a more realistic goal.

After a late hot dog dinner at some godforsaken shopping center in Jackson, we rolled into Detroit at exactly midnight. I don't remember much of Detroit from this trip. We were pretty tired. The enduring image is miles of broad avenues with streetlights throwing a cadence of glare and shadow across my scratched yellow face shield; parked cars, honking and weaving cars, sirens, and the slickness of rain on manhole covers. We looked neither to the right nor to the left, but straight ahead, and passed through Detroit at midnight.

I remember the Canadian border very well, however. I wasn't too tired to remember that.

We pulled up to the U.S. Customs station on the Detroit River and a uniformed official signaled us to stop. He looked us over for a minute and then leaned into the office and said something. Two more uniformed men came out. They asked us to get off our motorcycles and push them over to the side of the office, under the lights. We were instructed to remove all our luggage from the bikes and bring it in the office. There everything was gone through. I should say we were instructed to go through everything by the officers, who did not deign to touch our motorcyclish belongings.

It was, "Take off those leather jackets. Okay, now open the duffel bag. Unroll that pink thing. What is that, a tent? A pink tent? Unroll it. What are those?"

"Tent stakes."

"What's that other thing in there?"

"A flashlight."

"Let's see it. Take the batteries out. That's it. Put them on the table."

And so on.

Then we were searched and told to empty our pockets on the desk. Driver's licenses were checked, social security cards, draft cards of course, and we were told to count our money. We were questioned as to travel plans, home towns, and possible criminal records. One officer took our ID material into his office and began dialing phone numbers. He talked, nodded, dialed, lit and snubbed out numerous cigarettes, all the while watching us through the glass partition with unblinking reptilian eyes that said he'd seen guys like us before. It was 1967, a war was on, we were of college age, this was the Canadian border, it was midnight, and of course we were on motorcycles. All wrong.

When we had been found unarrestable, they quickly lost interest and told us to pack our scattered belongings and go. After only an hour's delay, we were on the road again. For about 20 seconds.

The Canadian customs officials were more efficient. They took about 20 minutes to go through our luggage, grill us as to our plans, and have us count our money. Only one phone call was made, and then we were free to pack and go.

We crossed into Canada at 1:30 in the morning. The drizzle had stopped and a warm autumn wind was clearing the sky, revealing a nearly full moon. We were so tired Donnelly claimed to be hallucinating various restaurant foods as we stopped for a light in downtown Windsor. I suggested we take Highway 401 out of the city, hit the first likely exit ramp, and find a place to eat and camp.

About 20 miles from Windsor, we peeled off into a little town called Tilbury. For two in the morning, the main street of Tilbury was jumping. Crowded cars cruised the strip, groups of people mingled and walked on the sidewalks, and there was actually an open café. We parked in front of the café, found ourselves a booth inside, and ordered breakfast. "Lot of people out tonight," I said to the waitress.

"Hops picking season," she said. "Teenagers and migrant workers from all over, and they all come into town on Friday night."

Our bacon and eggs had just arrived when I looked out the café window and realized that three guys in leather jackets of the multiple-zipper persuasion were messing around with our bikes. They looked drunk. One was trying to unhook the bungee cords from my pack and another was kicking the spokes on Donnelly's 305. The third was watching. We put down our forks and laid our napkins on the table with weary resignation. "Well, let's get this over with," I said.

As we left the restaurant, the waitress and a cigar-smoking cook and several patrons came to the front window to watch. "Be careful," the cook said. "When those boys get drunk, they're really crazy."

The three guys wore motorcycle jackets and heavy-duty engineer boots, but they didn't seem to have any motorcycles nearby. I walked up to the one who was meddling with my luggage and shoved him away from the bike. "What are you doing?" I said. He threw something back at me in garbled French and shoved me back, and then I shoved him, and so on . . . the usual boring pre-fight choreography.

Meanwhile, Donnelly was dealing with the other two. The one who'd been kicking his spokes was a short, stocky guy with a blue stocking cap and curly red hair that stuck straight out from the sides of his head. The other one, who stood back a bit, was slightly larger with a sort of weasel-like demeanor. Donnelly had pushed them away from his bike and was trying to talk to them in our excellent University of Wisconsin Conversational French, sophomore level. He wasn't getting very far. Another shoving match was developing. So much for the U.N. approach, I thought.

Then I saw the knife.

Right. A knife. The short guy with the shocking red hair had produced a very long, very open switchblade and was playing it unsteadily around Donnelly's throat, moving him back against the restaurant window. The waitress, cook, and five customers stood watching on the other side of the window glass. The cook was sipping coffee and munching on a donut. Just behind him was a phone on the wall, but no one was using it.

The knife changed everything. My absurd shoving match slowed to a halt, and even the guy I was shoving stopped to watch and his breathing tightened up. This wasn't fun anymore.

Donnelly looked down at the knife and then back into the face of the red-haired man. Donnelly was a naturally obliging, easygoing person but he had a rather explosive flash point and I had personally seen him lay waste to much larger individuals who gave him unsolicited trouble. And at that moment I could see the anger rising in his face.

I think the man with the knife sensed this, even through his glazed, drunken eyes. The way things were shaping up, he'd either have to do something terrible with that knife or get himself all ripped apart by Donnelly. He backed up a few steps and blinked. Glancing uneasily at his pals, he suddenly made a motion with his head and said, "*Allons.*" They all backed away from us, then turned and staggered off down the street.

When they were a half a block away we heard the switchblade snap shut. They crossed the street, piled into a yellow and white 1959 Chevy, and drove away.

We both let out a long, low whistle and went back into the café. Back to our ice-cold bacon and eggs with the grease congealed on them. The customers returned to their seats and the cook said, "You don't want to mess around with those boys. They get crazy when they're drunk."

I said, "Yeah, well, thanks for all your help."

He apparently sensed my insincerity because we didn't get any more coffee.

Returning to our bikes, we saw a cop car cruise by, so we flagged him down. We explained the entire incident, complete with the knife descriptions and the color of the 1959 Chevy. Everything but 8x10 glossies, as Arlo would say. He listened to our story without emotion and without writing anything down, all the while looking at our boots, jackets, and motorcycles. Then he asked to see our driver's licenses. He wanted to know what, exactly, we were doing in Canada and where we were going. He took out a pad and wrote down our license plate numbers, then went to the patrol car and made a radio transmission. A few minutes later came a radio squawk reply we couldn't understand. The cop gave us back our licenses, said we were free to go, and drove away.

I looked at Donnelly and shrugged. "Looks like we're innocent . . ."

"Yeah. Third time tonight."

As we rode out of town, a 1959 Chevy peeled out of a side street and dropped in behind us. It took us about three blocks to lose them forever. We turned down an alley, across a parking lot, and through a schoolyard as fast as we could ride. Our friends in the Chevy were last heard running into some garbage cans with their car. They were in no condition to drive.

We took the first backroad we found out of town and rode about five miles before pulling off on a tractor path into an open pasture. We parked the bikes under a lone oak tree and by the light of the moon and the Dream began to unroll our tent. I was getting the tent stakes out when Donnelly grabbed my arm and said, "Do you hear voices?"

I did.

And laughter and the breaking of glass.

We turned out the bike headlight and climbed a nearby rise in the field. As our eyes adjusted to the moonlight, about 25 to 30 cars materialized, parked in the open field. Someone was pumping a beer keg and we could see cigarettes glowing or being lit. "Great," Donnelly said. "A goddam beer party. Let's get out of here."

We rolled up our tent, rode another five miles, found another pasture and pulled off. This time there were no voices. We put up the tent and climbed into our sleeping bags. As we drifted off to sleep it became apparent that some sort of drag race was being run on the nearby road. Eventually we heard what sounded like a serious car crash off in the distance. Lots of traffic sped by and later there were sirens. We didn't care about any of this. We were too tired.

"Welcome to Canada," Donnelly said, and we more or less laughed ourselves to sleep.

Bathed in pink tentlight, we awoke at about 11:30 the next morning, gasping for air. We ripped our way out of the hothouse tent to discover a beautiful autumn morning. We rode under clear, sunny skies toward Highway 3 and the shores of Lake Erie. The warm, fall air smelled like the fields of stubble and cornstalks along the road, taking on a cool freshness when we got to the lake. The north shorelines of Erie and Ontario were lovely, and whenever possible we stayed on the two-lane shore road.

Riding again until long after dark, we had dinner in a place called Gananoque at the north end of Lake Ontario, then found a campground in a piney wood south of town. We stumbled out of our tent in the morning to discover ourselves camped about 50 feet from a tall shoreline cliff that overlooked the famous Thousand Islands, where Ontario narrows into the St. Lawrence River. Donnelly had thought to bring a small pan and a jar of instant coffee, so we made a campfire on the rocky cliffs and sat under the pine trees for a long time, drinking coffee and watching the sun rise over the U.S. side of the channel, burning the mist off the green islands. I smoked my last Marlboro, crushed the pack, and made a mental note to buy a pack of Players at the next gas station.

Following the St. Lawrence River, we crossed into Quebec Province and made it to Montreal late in the afternoon. After being turned down at three hotels with VACANCY signs burning, we learned to leave our helmets and jackets on the bikes while inquiring. In the end, the effort was wasted. We found a room in a downtown hotel so cheap that mere possession of helmets and jackets made us something of a success story within its dark hallways. Most of the patrons were elderly men who talked to themselves and seemed to own nothing but a jealously guarded brown paper bag. The rest were slightly younger women who kept funny hours.

For the next two days we walked all over the hills of Montreal, sitting in parks, poking abound in bookstores, and looking over the campus of McGill University. We climbed Mount Royal and looked out over the grounds of Expo 1967. The second evening we stopped in a topless bar, which at that time was a brand-new concept of great novelty. As we sipped on beers, a rather bored-looking woman climbed up on the bar and did some perfunctory topless dancing to Spencer Davis' *Gimme Some Lovin'*. Then she sat down at the bar and said "Give me a beer, Ernie." Donnelly and I looked down the bar for a moment and smiled politely. She studied us for a moment and didn't smile back. I don't think she liked my work boots. It was suddenly too quiet in the bar. What do you say to a topless dancer? That was nice dancing? We paid our tab and left. I felt Spencer Davis had somehow been compromised.

It was a long walk back to the hotel. The weather was changing and a cold, raw wind was blowing down the streets of Montreal. It was a

Monday night and the streets were almost empty, people all gone to their homes or offices, doing routine things. The city around me suddenly felt remarkably cold and indifferent to our presence, and it was my first inkling that foreign cities are not by nature hospitable to people without connections or money. I felt like Bob Dylan on the cover of *Freewheelin'*, except I didn't have my girlfriend clinging to my arm. She was back in Wisconsin.

As we entered the hotel, the manager stopped us and wanted to be paid *now* because he knew we were leaving in the morning. We paid him and tried to get some sleep in our taco-shaped beds.

In the morning we loaded up our bikes in the alley behind the hotel and I pushed mine across the street to a gas station, not wanting to do my mandatory bump-start until necessary. The gas station had signs in English and French, but the English words had been painted over with red paint. The attendant ignored us when we asked about filling up our bikes and buying a quart of oil. Our poor French didn't win him over. Another customer who'd been refused service, said "Don't bother. Go to an English station." The Quebec Separatist movement was at something of a fever pitch right then, and we'd also been refused service in a French Canadian bar the previous night. To Donnelly and me, who thought of ourselves as civil rights advocates, this behavior seemed unbearably provincial and small-time. It was another version of something we despised in the States.

We finally found some gas, got my reluctant bike started, and left Montreal on Highway 17, which follows the Ottawa River across the northeastern border of Ontario. Financially, Montreal had taken us beyond our point of no return. We each had about $25 and had to make tracks on the way home.

Somewhere near Ottawa, a hard rain began to fall; a chill autumn Canadian rain that angled down in drops like cold steel pellets. The rugged, wooden countryside along the river was beautiful, but much of its charm was lost on us, what with our relentless shivering and borderline hypothermia. We set up our wet tent in a dripping pine forest on the wet banks of the Ottawa River early in the afternoon because we were too cold to ride any further. We climbed into our wet sleeping bags with our wet clothes on and I think I spent the night wondering if it was physically possible to chatter your teeth into pure calcium dust. I slept briefly, dreaming of jackhammers and sidewalks.

Through some miracle of meteorology it managed to rain harder the next day while getting still colder, yet not quite snowing. We rode, with an uncharacteristic lack of cheer, for many long hours down the long, straight pine forest roads of Ontario. I got a flat tire around mid-afternoon, so we hid my bike and our luggage in the woods and rode Donnelly's bike 20 miles into the next town for the patch kit and tire pump I wasn't carrying. I replaced the tire, managing to put several permanent sprocket stains on my blue jeans, and we were off again. At 4:30 in the afternoon we were too cold to ride anymore, so we pulled off at a sign that said WRIGHT'S CABINS, near Pembroke. Sitting just back in the trees, this place had one large logcabin/office surrounded by a horseshoe of similar but smaller log cabins. We didn't have much money, but after two days of rain we had to get indoors for one night and warm up. We were both beginning to shiver and sweat at all the wrong times, when not busy coughing.

Always wary of being refused service because of our motorcycles, I was overjoyed to walk into the office and find that the place doubled as a Yamaha dealership, of all things. An elderly woman sat knitting by a kerosene stove. She explained that her son ran the Yamaha end of the business and she managed the cabins. Would we like a cabin for the night or motorcycle parts? A cabin? She'd get the stove and hot water turned on for us, then, and a clothesline to hang up our wet clothes. She explained almost apologetically that the cabin would cost six dollars for both of us. Was that OK?

It was OK.

We stayed in a tidy little log cabin with two feather beds and a bathtub on feet. In the morning the rain was hammering down on the green shingled roof and neither of us wanted to get out of bed. We discussed staying in the cabin until the rain stopped or until we died, whichever came first. Lack of money and a driving need for breakfast finally got the better of us, however, and we pushed onward into the morning rain.

At a coffee shop near Sturgeon Falls we ran into another traveling motorcyclist. His name was Ron. He was a free man, having just gotten out of the U.S. Air Force, and he was circumnavigating all of North America with his brand-new Harley XLH. His Harley had the biggest pile of luggage I'd ever seen lashed onto the back of any motorcycle. It looked like an overloaded pack burro. Prominent in this mobile heap of goods was a full-sized Coleman two-burner stove, an ice chest, and the biggest tent I'd ever seen outside a circus.

Ron sipped his coffee and looked in amazement at our damp jackets. "Don't you guys have any rain gear?" he asked.

"No." He shook his head.

"Strange . . ."

He invited us to travel with him and said he had a tent big enough for all of us. The weather at last began to clear, and the three of us cruised along the north shore of Lake Nipissing, across the barren yellow moonscape of Sudbury's sulfur mining district and down to the North Channel of Lake Huron. It took us a while to get used to traveling with Ron. He cruised down the road with his feet up on highway pegs, looking around at the scenery, never exceeding 60 miles per hour. It had never occurred to Donnelly and me that anyone would ever voluntarily go slower than 85 miles per hour, as long as there were no cops around. We rode everywhere flat out. And here was this guy, motoring along 5 miles per hour under the speed limit, appearing to enjoy himself. It took some getting used to.

It was strange too, listening to the ka-tuff ka-tuff of the low-revving Harley next to our wound-out smallbore Hondas. With his tall windshield, huge padded seat, highway pegs, and thumping engine, this guy was traveling in a different world from us. There was no sense of urgency in his riding. We were always in a hurry, even when I couldn't think of why. He was traveling, of course, and we were on our way home.

We found a perfect campground (Ron had a campground guide) on the shore of Lake Huron, and we put up Ron's tent. I had seen tents like this only in Sears catalogs—the photo where the whole family is playing cards around a table inside the tent. We laid out our sleeping bags, Ron erected his folding army cot (I'm not kidding about this), and then he insisted that we all park our bikes in the tent "in case it rained again." He had cardboard to catch oil drips. He got out the Coleman stove and ice chest and cooked us up a great dinner of Spam and fried potatoes, with bottles of Moosehead Ale. Later we had coffee and made a big campfire. For the first time in days Donnelly and I felt roughly like human beings instead of muddaubed barbarians of the northern rain forest. "This guy," Donnelly mumbled to me, "really knows how to travel."

"Next time," I said.

We sat across the campfire from Ron and I watched him, wondering what it would be like to be out of the military and free to travel; free to cross borders, work or not work, marry or stay single, go to school or quit school, bum around or save money for a brand-new motorcycle. Ron's face flickered in and out of the shadows and I watched his expression for some sign of the calm and serenity that must certainly come with that kind of freedom. In that light it was hard to tell. I grinned to myself and thought, *Ron is on the other side of the fire and we can't see him clearly.*

We parted company with Ron at Saulte Ste. Marie the next day. He was heading around the north shore of Lake Superior and we were crossing into upper peninsula Michigan.

We had no trouble getting back into the U.S. and were virtually waived through customs. *Right*, I thought to myself, *volunteers.*

The rain had gone away, but a cold piercing wind was blowing off Lake Superior and the later afternoon clouds had the pink-and-gunmetal look of winter. I was suddenly very tired of being cold. Once we crossed the border, our homing instincts set in and we rode absolutely flat-out across northern Michigan without regard for police and traffic tickets. Nightfall found us still a long way from home, so we took Highway 41 down to Oshkosh, Wisconsin. Another college friend, Jim Wargula, lived there and his parents were particularly understanding and good-hearted people. We rang their doorbell at 8:00 in the evening.

They had just finished dinner, so Mr. Wargula ran out and got us a huge bucket of Kentucky Fried Chicken. While he was doing that, Mrs. Wargula made fresh hot coffee, ran bathwater, got out towels, and put sheets on the guest room beds, all the while chatting cheerfully and asking us about our trip. Jim put the bikes away in the garage for us.

Mr. Wargula returned with the chicken and we all sat around the kitchen table. While we ate, he noticed that our leather jackets were all cracked and stiff from repeated rainstorms, so he went to the basement and returned with a can of neat's-foot oil.

While we drank coffee, he insisted on cleaning up our jackets and making them supple again. Jim helped him and Mrs. Wargula brought out a homemade cheesecake. She told us to take off our old, damp boots and brought us some clean, dry wool socks. Mr. Wargula put our boots next to the radiator—but not too close—to dry. He said he'd put some neat's-foot oil on those when they dried a little better. Mr. Wargula knew all about proper care of boots because he'd been a soldier in Europe during WWII, and he was presently a colonel in the U.S. Army Reserves. Mrs. Wargula poured more coffee all around and offered to run our road clothes through the washer and dryer later.

We sat at the table gradually warming up, and Donnelly and I exchanged a glance. Through bloodshot eyes from fourteen hours of riding that day and four days in the rain, it was the flat, neutral glance of two people who were thinking exactly the same thing, no expression required. Looking at these friends, I wondered how I had ever thought it possible to cut myself off from them. They were good friends, but would they be able to come to Canada to see us? Wave, perhaps from across Niagara Falls? It was hard to imagine.

When we got home the next day, the welcome mat rolled out all over again. Our parents were tremendously relieved to see us back, and I was quite content to be there. I called my girlfriend and we talked for a long time. She said she was glad I was home.

After the trip, Donnelly and I never mentioned moving to Canada again. The subject never came up. It took a special courage and conviction to leave everything behind, and I don't think either of us ever really had it. My parents eventually sold the Honda 160 for me when I was in Vietnam. I look at the Canadian trip now and no conventional description of the journey fits exactly; I can't see it as merely an adventure, a fall vacation, or a first motorcycle trip. In retrospect, I think it was just practice for subsequent journeys and other homecomings. A dry run.

September 1990

RESTORATION OF A TRIUMPH

Dialing Back the Clock to 1967

Most loving restorations are done by those of us who couldn't afford the bikes of our dreams when we were young. This is one of those.

A few months ago, my friend Brian Slark called to ask how the restoration was coming. "Great," I said. "I just got the seat back from the upholstery shop. I can bolt it on tonight and go riding tomorrow."

Slark chuckled. "Now the hard part begins."

"The hard part?"

"Right. Getting the rebuilt carb dialed in, finding the leaks, getting the chainguard not to rub on the chain, making the cables work—all the fun stuff. You've got it reassembled, but not restored. Right now, it's just a collection of parts, all bolted together."

"I suppose you're right," I said agreeably, but I didn't think he was.

Slark couldn't know how carefully I'd assembled this bike, how thorough and methodical I'd been in the restoration. How much expert help I'd had. I didn't tell him so, but I expected this particular Triumph to start and run just fine, right out of the gate.

Lord knows I'd spent enough time on it. Restoring my 1967 TR6C was the culmination of a personal dream. The dream is a fairly common one these days. It's called Owning the Bike You Wanted Way Back When, But Couldn't Afford.

When I was in high school and college, I owned a succession of small-bore Hondas, but what I really wanted was a Triumph. I spent half my time hanging around the dealership in Madison, Wisconsin, cooking up schemes to purchase either a 500 or a 650 Triumph. Those were the street scrambler years, the high-pipe era, when all my heroes were tough guys who raced Triumphs far away in the California deserts, or in the Jack Pine Enduro, or on TT courses all over America. If your streetbike couldn't jump and slide, it wasn't squat.

So naturally, I wanted one of the high-pipe Trophy models, either the nimble 500cc T100C or the big desert sled, the 650cc TR6C. The 650 was more expensive, of course, costing around $1,300 at most shops. The 500 was slightly more attainable at around $1,100, so I set my sights on the 500. As it turned out, I got through that entire phase of my life without being able to afford either one.

In the late 1970s, I finally bought a Triumph, a 1967 Bonneville, did a nice partial restoration, and even wrote a story about it for *Cycle World.* I like the Bonneville a lot, but it wasn't exactly the Triumph I wanted. The one I truly desired, based on my many hours of deep soul searching at the Triumph shop, was a 1967 TR6C.

Why that particular year? First I liked the color, the two-tone Mist Green and Alaskan White separated by a thin gold stripe. I also like the seat design—ribbed pattern, all black—which first arrived that year, the simplicity of the single carb, the look of the dual exhaust pipes, but without the mesh burn-guard of the later models. With its small taillight and no mandated side reflectors, the 1967 was a clean machine, pre-safety, pre-government mandates. I liked all the Competition models up through 1970, but 1967 was my absolute favorite. The Holy Grail.

So when *Cycle World* hired me in 1980 and I moved West, I sold the Bonneville. I'd surely find a Trophy TR6C in California, and when I did, I'd do it up right.

I discovered when I got here that most of the sixties Trophies had, indeed, gone to the desert. Their owners had sawed off the fenders, thrown the original pipes and mufflers away, tossed the headlights, padded the seats, installed dual-carb Bonneville heads, raked the steering heads, dented the tanks, and generally thrashed the poor bikes to death. (Which I suppose is what they were built for, after all.) Street-legal, original Trophies were in short supply here. I looked for a long time and didn't find one. Until two years ago.

I saw an ad for a 1967 TR6C in the paper, "All stock, beautiful shape, 1,300 original miles, second owner, $1,350." I left work, drove straight to the man's house, and bought the bike. It was all there, but a little loose mechanically. The tank had been repainted solid green, the knee pads were gone, the seat had a small tear, the fork leaked, and the sprockets were worn. It started and ran fine, but there was a strange, intermittent upper-end clatter that I thought might be a broken valve spring. I rode the bike for a year before I got the courage to deny myself its daily use and take it apart.

As mentioned in a previous *CW* column, I tried first to restore the bike in small increments, just to keep it on the road. Wheels came off first, one at a time. I had the hubs powder-coated and the wheels respoked in stainless steel, and then installed new tubes and new Dunlop K70 tires, made-in-Japan modern replicas of the originals. I installed new wheel bearings and a new rear sprocket and chain, had the brake drums turned, new shoes skimmed for a concentric fit, the hub cover rechromed, and the brake backing plate polished. Total cost, of just this wheel-related restoration, came to about $675.

A new primary drive came next—clutch basket, plates, primary chain, adjuster, tensioner, and sprocket. This set me back two weekends and $200 for parts.

Suspension was next, and this is the step that finally took the bike off the road. The triple clamps and rust-pitted fork came off, and new chrome fork tubes were ordered from Franks, at $100 each. Then I went to work removing the engine and disassembling the bike down to the last nut and bolt. I sent out all bolts and screws for plating in white cadmium and then began what I will always remember as the Summer of Endless Beadblasting.

Two friends, Chuck Johnston and Richard Straman, both had industrial-size beadblasting cabinets and allowed me to spend many hours using up their compressed air while blasting swingarm, shock covers, fender braces, footrests, and the nine or ten thousand small bits of hardware and mounting plates that all hold a Triumph, sandwich-like, together. The main frame section was too big for a beadblaster, so I sandblasted it outdoors.

With all the frame parts clean as bleached bones, I had to decide what finish to use for the black frame parts. Powdercoat? Not pure and original, some said. Looks too plastic. Use paint. Others said they wouldn't use anything but powdercoat. This being my first true ground-up restoration, I decided to go with a combination and judge for myself. The main frame section and swingarm were powdercoated ($250) and all other parts I primed with zinc chromate and painted in black Imron, with the help of Chuck Johnston and his paint booth. Cost of paints, abrasives, and solvents came to around $100.

Results? Both the Imron and powdercoat look fine. If it isn't put on too thick, powdercoat doesn't have that sealed-in-plastic look that has given it a bad reputation, and it's tough and doesn't scratch easily, which is good when you are installing an engine. If I were to do it again, I'd powdercoat the whole frame and use Imron (as I did here) on parts like fork legs and shock covers, where a perfect, high-gloss finish is needed.

For the engine rebuild, I deferred to my friend Denny Berg, who runs a motorcycle shop called the Time Machine. Denny has years of experience building Triumph dirt-trackers and making them last, and he agreed to do the engine and gearbox for $1,400, including new bearings, pistons, valves, guides, springs, etc., plus machine work, polishing, and installation in the frame. During teardown, he discovered the source of the phantom head noise: a loose valve guide moving randomly with the valve. With 1,300 miles on the engine, everything else was worn, but serviceable.

While Denny worked his magic on the engine, I started putting the frame back together and getting it up on its wheels. Here is where I discovered that the restoration books aren't kidding when they say to photograph and sketch everything before you take it apart. On the Triumph, some bolts have two washers, some have none; some go in from the left, some right; some use lock washers, some not; etc. With a photo or a drawing, you can assemble a section in about five minutes; relying on memory, you can spend two experimental hours on the same job. Then you later discover the four bolts you used on the axle caps belong on the handlebar clamps, and so on.

Fortunately, two books saved my hide. One was the indispensable *Triumph Twin Restoration* by Roy Bacon, which has hundreds of clear, close-up photos and a lot of good advice. The other was a Xerox reproduction of the 1967 Triumph parts book, supplied to me by Bill Getty at JRC Engineering. I also bought most of my Triumph parts from Bill, and he was kind enough to give me needed technical advice each of the hundred or so times I called to place an order. Still, my own photos and drawings would have been a big help. Another whole Triumph standing by for reference would have been even better.

With the chassis rolling, I dropped it off at Time Machine, and Denny bolted the rebuilt engine into its new cradle, hooked up the electrics, and started the engine. The crowning touches were the gas tank, sidecover, and oil tank. I decided not to try painting these myself (being a somewhat unsteady pinstriper) and had them painted by a local shop called Color Cycle. They charged $350 and did a beautiful job, with a clear coat over decals and tank paint.

The seat was something of a problem. The old one was torn and crumbling, so I took it apart, beadblasted the pan, painted it with Krylon enamel, and ordered a new cover and foam. The seatcover was backordered for several months from the supplier, and when it came it was a one-style-fits-all version, shaped more like the plump mid-seventies Bonneville seat than the flat, rakish sixties version. So I had a local upholstery shop make a replica from the original, using the original top panel, which was not torn. Cost: $150, plus $50 for foam.

My last item to rebuild was the old Amal Monobloc carburetor (I'd been using a new Amal Concentric before the restoration). I beadblasted the Monobloc body and installed new jets, needles, and slide, then cad-plated the fittings. Another $100, roughly. I bolted the carb on, fired up the engine, and went for a ride.

Here's where Brian Slark's admonition that a restoration is only a starting point began to come true.

During the first two months of riding, I fouled innumerable plugs (and walked many miles carrying a helmet and jacket) while trying to dial-in the jetting and needle height, and finding the ideal sparkplug heat range. Chronic weak spark from the old off-road, non-battery ET ignition system was part of the problem, and (being no electrical genius myself) I finally asked Denny Berg to install a 12-volt stator, new advance mechanism, and a Mity Max ignition box, which gives better spark and starting.

The bike is finally alive and well, and I've now done several hundred miles in weekend rides and commutes to work.

So, how does it feel?

It feels like . . . a Triumph. Light, narrow, agile, almost bicycle-like in its effortless sweep through corners; a balloon-tired Schwinn with a 650 engine slung low in the frame. The sound is a pleasant combination of vertical-Twin muttering snarl and light valve-train clatter. Brakes? Yes, but plan ahead. Power is moderate by current standards (original brochures say 45 bhp at 6,500 rpm) but the bike is quick enough to be fun. I went up two teeth from stock on the countershaft sprocket, so highway cruising at 65 miles per hour is done at a fairly relaxed 3,500 rpm.

Overall, the Triumph feels compact, solid, and slightly antique, even compared with my Norton 850 Commando. It is a bike that reflects nicely the technology and expectations of its time, which included an admiration for light weight, graceful simplicity, and a high state of finish in all the individual components, be they tank badges, choke levers, or timing cases. Very sixties, with strong hints of much earlier roots. Which is exactly what I wanted. The original idea, after all, was to build a brand-new 1967 Triumph—the one I never got to buy.

A fine goal, but is this one really brand-new?

Yes and no. There are still things left to do. Like silk-screen the Triumph logo on the back of the seat. Also, the instruments are original and faded (and will be until I can find somebody who knows how to rebuild them), and I've left the original chrome on the pipes and mufflers, which have the slightly burnished, hazy quality of age. I guess, after all, I wanted the Triumph to be new in function without losing every link to its own past. A few reminders of the bike's gathering antiquity seem worth leaving untouched, as long as it runs well.

Aside from those few shortcomings, nearly all the painted and plated surfaces are now appropriately shiny, and virtually every surface that rubs on any other surface is now new—bearings, chains, sprockets, swingarm bushings, forks, shocks, tires, cables, brakes, ignition points, etc. This is the core of a restoration. When you are out on the road, there is a place in the mind that wants to know that a machine is *whole*, that the pieces are working as they should and the noises you hear are all good ones. That the bike has life ahead of it as well as behind it.

There is a price to pay for this compulsiveness, of course. Spread over two years of work, the cost of restoring my Triumph came to just over $5,000, including the original cost of the bike.

When I first added it up, that sounded like a staggering amount of money to me, what with my notions of value lagging well behind inflation. The total made me shudder just to think about it. Then I began to rationalize. I made a trip to the library and found that, according to the Consumer Price Index, a $1,300 TR6C, if sold new today, would cost $4,890 in 1990 dollars. Turning that around, it seems I have paid the 1967 equivalent of $1,329 to have myself, essentially, a brand-new Triumph.

Not such a bad deal, really. I think I'll just consider the extra $29 over list as a fair price for storage. Twenty-three years' worth. My labor, of course, is always free.

June 1994

THE THREE-HUNDRED-DOLLAR JEWEL

Often Overlooked in Favor of its Bigger Brother, the Honda CB550 Four was (and is) a Minor Classic in its Own Right

This is a tribute to a favorite bike I somehow skipped over in my slow but relentless climb up the displacement ladder.

All right, I've wanted one of these bikes for a long time. The Honda 550 Four was a motorcycle I missed during my meteoric rise through the displacement ranks in the early seventies, having gone straight from a Honda CB350 Twin to a Norton 850 Commando. Nevertheless, I almost bought a 550 instead of the Norton, and spent many hours at Honda shops regarding the middleweight Honda from as many angles as possible and snagging brochures that could be pored over at home.

Why this enthusiasm for the 550 when the larger, faster, and more famous CB750 sat nearby on the showroom floor and could be had for just a few hundred dollars more?

The magic word was *Balance.*

You heard it repeated over and again, in the road tests of the time, in editorials, from the mouths of owners and in the small but expanding band of American riders tuned into the cult of the café-racer. The 550 was not too big, not too small, lower and narrower than the 750, nicely proportioned, and it handled effortlessly. Both *Cycle World* and *Cycle* remarked that it was probably the best-handling Japanese bike you could buy.

It's hard to fathom now, but there was a time when many of us thought the Honda 750 Four was just too big. I remember riding one in 1973 and being somewhat alarmed at its bulk and width. Compared with the light and narrow Twins to which I was accustomed, the 750 felt like an absolute refrigerator.

Climb on one now and you're amazed at how compact and diminutive it seems, like a pinto pony among the current generation of tall, fast warhorses. But in the early seventies, I had grave philosophical and aesthetic objections. It was the smaller Fours I admired.

Unveiled in 1971, two years after the 750, the mid-liter Four was originally introduced as a 500. *Cycle* magazine ran a wonderful cover shot of the bike, golden-green against a dark green background, a red-clad model with flowing blond hair sitting side-saddle against the bike. The photo seemed to glow from within. The cover blurb cried, "500 FOUR! THE HONDA MAGIC LANTERN LIGHTS AGAIN."

Years later, I was told by a former staffer that the cover model was a very sweet and polite young woman named Mary Kathleen Collins, who now goes by the name of Bo Derek. It doesn't quite look like her in the picture, but I'm certainly willing to buy into the legend.

In 1973, Honda made some improvements to the bike, widened the bore by a mere 2.5 millimeters for 544cc of displacement and called it a 550. Upgraded were the somewhat balky shift mechanism and the clutch, which could slip under hard use. The price was upgraded, too, from $1,345 to $1,600.

Except for the 550 Four logo on the sidecovers and subtle changes in paint colors and tank decals, there wasn't much, visually, to distinguish between the two. Performance didn't change a great deal, either. *CW*'s quarter-mile run on the original 500 was 14.74 seconds at 88.23 miles per hour, with an actual top speed of 98.46 miles per hour. The newer, bigger 550 turned a 14.27 at 91.55 miles per hour, and top speed (estimated, this time) was 105. Midrange torque was said to be slightly better.

Even at the time, this was not considered blindingly fast or quick, but the small Honda had a few other things going for it.

First, there was its bloodline. If you were a racing fan—and particularly a fan of Mike Hailwood and his screaming red-and-silver Honda GP bikes—there was a certain amount of magic in that half-liter displacement. Real GP bikes were 500s, and the displacement had a lean competition ring to it.

Okay, even if these bikes were barely related to anything Hailwood was riding, they had successfully appropriated some of the look, sound, and aura. You had four (count 'em) separate pipes upswept from the side in a fanned emblematic tribute to the Honda wing, and the mufflers had a lovely shape to them, necked down and then flared open into small megaphones.

Those mufflers were relatively quiet, but what sound did come out of them was intriguing. The Honda 750 growled, but the smaller, short-stroke 500s and 550s positively whooped. And quickly, all the way to their 9,200-rpm redlines. There was a muted electric fury to the sound that could hardly be lost on anyone who liked mechanical things.

There was also a glassy smoothness that implied—to us Britbike fans—a long engine life and a riding experience devoid of lost bolts, loose head-pipes, fractured gas tanks, and headlight filaments shaken to tungsten dust.

Also of interest and pleasure to those of us who used British motorcycles as a standard of aesthetics (if not smoothness) was the general shape and look of the 500 and 550. Hondas of this era looked less . . . well, Japanese, than they had earlier. They embraced a kind of architectural classicism that paid tribute to both British and Italian design, with just enough Honda thrown in to reassure those who hated walking.

From the side, the Honda, with its half-teardrop tank, flat saddle, rounded sidecovers, and upright cylinders, almost looked like a Triumph 500, albeit with a few too many pipes. It also had a few un-Triumphantly raw welds and seams, but the overall effect was good. Journalist Rich Taylor described it as having "an ethereal appearance," and added, "It just might be the best looking Japanese bike in production."

Good looks and good handling made the 500s and 550s the darling of the café-racer crowd. *Cycle World* described the 550's handling as "positively inspired for a 458-pound pleasure cushion aimed at a conservative clientele." Many of the owners, however, turned out not to be so conservative. The college town where I lived had half a dozen of them running around with clip-on handlebars, rearsets, 4-into-1 exhaust systems, good shocks, and the obligatory Dunlop TT100 K-81 tires.

The magazines also featured lovely café customs built around the CB500 and 550 with fanciful names such as "The Gentleman's Express," and "The Mantlepiece." If you were a true believer in the cult of knee-out cornering (a style of riding then just in its infancy), a middleweight Honda was the bike to have.

So, in one of the most extreme cases of delayed gratification in the history of the Western world, I finally decided to buy one, about two months ago.

My friend Bob Barr, the local Kawasaki/Ducati dealer, was having an autumn open house and Ducati Appreciation Day at his shop, so I rode my 900SS over for a visit.

In his lineup of used bikes was a 1975 CB550K, Candy Jade Green in color. It had a mere 10,000 miles on the clock, but looked a little rough around the edges: wrong-color sidecovers borrowed off an old CB500, cruddy 2-into-2 aftermarket exhaust system with bologna-shaped mufflers, old luggage rack, dirty engine, and a little light rust around some of the bolts. Naturally, I was drawn right to it.

"You've been looking at that old thing all summer," Bob said. "Why don't you just buy it, so I don't have to store it all winter."

I looked at the price tag on the handlebars. It said $795.

"Too expensive," I explained.

"I'm just waiting for an offer I can't refuse," he said.

"What offers have you refused so far?"

"None."

"How about $300?"

"Sold."

Five minutes later, I was riding the bike, which started, idled, ran, and stopped absolutely fine. It didn't even have the typical old Honda camchain noise from worn adjuster surfaces, which always sounds like an anchor chain being winched through a hawsepipe. Perfectly nice bike, just dirty and not quite correct. I wrote out a check, came back later, and rode it home that afternoon. On a lonely stretch of country road, I managed to hit an indicated 98 miles per hour.

Back in my own garage, I changed the oil and filter, and adjusted the chain, but there was very little mechanical fiddling needed. Bob had given me a shop manual and a batch of receipts that came with the bike, and I discovered the previous owner had spent about $500 at a local shop, one year earlier, on sticky brake hydraulics, tune-up, new chain, and a few minor electrical repairs. So I turned my attention to the cosmetics.

Off came the rusty luggage rack and the gnarly exhaust system. My friend David had an original set of pipes and mufflers left over from his own CB550, so I bought those for $150. (A new replacement set from Honda costs about $450.) One of the four pipes was rusty, so I ordered a new one from the dealer, for $112. The 550s were famous for rusting out low spots in the system because the four individual pipes seldom got hot enough to burn off condensation on short rides.

The old system fit perfectly, but the one new pipe from Honda was misformed, terminating a good half-inch from the cylinder head. I spent one long evening heating the pipe with a large rose tip on my welding torch, slowly bending it to fit and using up enough acetylene and oxygen to scrap out the carrier *Lexington*.

I also ordered new 550 Four badges and Candy Jade Green sidecovers from Honda for just over $100. The new sidecovers showed up painted an electric pea soup green that has never been seen on any known Honda, or in Nature, one hopes. I returned them for a refund and decided I will try to find the correct paint code and paint the old ones myself.

Until recently, one of the appealing aspects of restoring an old Honda was the factory's willingness to stock very old OEM parts and keep them on the books. My friendly parts man informs me, however, that Honda is now farming many of these parts out to small independent suppliers, so quality has slipped. Too bad. Still, not many companies stock any parts at all for bikes that are 20 or 30 years old, as Honda does.

So, my $300 jewel is now a $600 bike—though I could easily have left it alone and ridden it just the way it was. But it looks correct now (except for the sidecovers) and is ready to ride.

And how is the CB550 to ride, here in modern times?

Surprisingly nice.

In handling and steering characteristics, it reminds me most of the two Triumph 500s I've had. Which is to say you can swoop down a twisty country road with very little conscious effort or even awareness of cornering technique. The wide handlebars and rational, relatively upright seating position provide a perfect, balanced platform for almost effortless steering. In many ways, the 550 handles almost like a modern dual-purpose bike, but with a slightly heavier lump of engine down there, and a much lower seat height. It feels compact, solid, and secure.

Push a little harder, though, and you begin to scrape sidestand and pipes, and you can feel a little motion in the swingarm, probably from worn bushings. The old stock shocks are so ineffective as to seem absent. There were good reasons the café-racers—and roadracers—replaced the stock pipes and shocks and removed their stands. Still, if you don't get gymnastic, the bike can be ridden reasonably fast just as it is, with no great drama.

My 550 will just touch 100 miles per hour on the speedometer, but its happiest cruising speed is about 70, at 5,600 rpm. Try holding 80, and five minutes later you'll look at the speedo and find yourself at a serene 70 again, as though the twistgrip were spring-loaded to return to that setting. Maybe it is.

The CB550 is neither terribly quick nor very torquey in the depths of its rev band, but in full acceleration it woofs through the gears in a series of smooth, euphonious lunges with enough spirit to be fun. Fuel mileage—never a strong point in the 500s and 550s—averages about 35 miles per gallon. It was always worse than the 750 in this respect. Reserve is needed at around 100 miles, at which time you have about another 30 miles of fuel; only slightly better than a Sportster.

The wide, broad, flat seat is quite comfortable. The foam could be a little denser, but at least you can move around and change position. I'd have no hesitation at all in striking off on a long cross-country trip with this bike, as so many have. It's a pretty good all-day traveler.

Two of my friends took the 550 out for ride, and both of them came back to deliver almost exactly the same quote: "You know, most people really would never need any more bike than this. It does everything just fine."

Factor in that it's actually fun to ride, and it adds up to an awfully nice motorcycle, especially for a total investment of $600. I realize I got this bike at a friendly bargain price, but even pristine, low-mileage 500s and 550s seldom seem to climb much past the $800-to-$1,000 zone. Real rats can be had for almost nothing, and the world's most beautiful museum-worthy example might fetch $1,200 or so.

Why so cheap?

Well, Honda made a lot of them. But then, too, you have to look at the chrome on the mufflers and fenders. We aren't talking Brough Superior here. These bikes were mass produced and made to a price, and that price did not include chrome plating for the ages, polished castings for the passenger footrests, headlight shells hand-hammered by Druidic artisans, or hand-striping of the tank by someone who squints with one eye through cigarette smoke and wears his cap at a jaunty angle.

What the price did include was some very fine engineering, a jewel-like engine, long service life, beautiful shapes, and a plethora of convenient features all wrapped up into a machine whose appearance and performance transcends its individual parts.

And you can still buy one, if not exactly for free, almost for a song.

May 1995

IN THE LAND OF THE LONG WHITE CLOUD

Touring New Zealand by Triumph 1200 and F650 Beemer

Did I actually bungee-jump off the old Kawarau Suspension Bridge? Yes. Had to. It's the New Zealand way.

"Here's the key to your room, sir," the cheerful woman at the reception desk said. "Would you like some nice fresh milk?"

She held out a cold, dripping carton of milk.

Okay. Non-sequitur time. My mind was addled for a moment. Maybe because I'd been on an airplane for 17 hours.

"Uh, thank you," I said, taking the carton. Perhaps it was the custom here to slam down a carton of milk every time you checked into a hotel room. Good health practice. Yet no one else in the lobby seemed to be drinking the stuff.

"It's for your afternoon tea," she said, smiling. "There's a tea kettle in your room."

"Ah."

Needless to say, we weren't in Kansas anymore. We weren't even in Wisconsin or California. We were, in fact, about 1,400 miles southwest of Oz, on the Colorado-sized twin-island nation of New Zealand, which I am here to tell you is a long way from anywhere, but none the worse for it.

More specifically, we were on a Beach's Motorcycle Adventure tour called the "Maori Meander," Editor Edwards and I. We'd boarded an airliner in L.A. just before midnight of an October's eve and awakened to a clear golden dawn over the endless blue South Pacific. An hour later, the airplane banked and we could see New Zealand, or at least the long streaks of gray and white cloud that obscured New Zealand, off to starboard.

"Land of the Long White Cloud," was what the first Polynesian settlers, the Maoris (pronounced MAU-reez), had called these two big islands when they arrived in their open boats 1,000 years ago. The mountaintops rising out of the sea make their own weather, forcing the moist Pacific air to rise and deliver.

Through holes in the broken cloud ceiling we could see emerald-green sheep pasture and thick forest, then the mostly single-story houses and businesses of Auckland as the plane descended over Manukau Harbour (says the map) and landed. Lovely modern airport, but built on a human scale, just the right size. It's like landing on the set of *Casablanca.*

At the airport we hook up with Rob Beach himself, whose parents started this touring company (2763 West River Parkway, Grand Island, NY 14072-2087; 716/773-4960) in Europe, years ago. Rob, a former WERA roadracer, now lives in Niagara, New York, but leads New Zealand tours every chance he gets. He loves the country and has made a lot of Kiwi friends. We also meet the other seven members of our tour group—two married couples (the Werners from New Jersey and the Kulls from Florida) and several random single guys—and our other guide, a New Zealander from Christchurch named Bob Wilkins.

On the van ride from the airport it starts to rain. Hard. Someone asks Rob Beach what the weather forecast is like for the rest of the week.

"Hot and dusty," Rob says quickly, establishing a phrase that will be our standing joke for the rest of the tour.

It doesn't rain all the time in New Zealand, but it is seldom dusty. The climate, like the landscape, seems to combine elements of Washington state, Scotland, southern England, and the Canadian Rockies. Also, October is early spring in New Zealand, about like March or April in the Midwest. We will end up using our raingear about every other day.

To say I've been looking forward to this trip would be an egregious understatement. First, there's the appeal of seeing a new country, which I know only from stunning travel posters and by reputation for its legion of great racers, mountain climbers, bungee jumpers, yachtsmen, fighter pilots, ANZAC military heroes, and other rugged outdoor risk-takers.

It's a country where laughing at danger seems to be a national pastime.

And there is the added inducement that David Edwards and I are to ride a pair of new and (for us) untried bikes: a British Racing Green Triumph Trophy 1200 and a BMW F650 "Funduro." A big roadburner and a lightweight, agile single. Perfect ying-yang combo.

The afternoon rain clears and we drive over to a large Harley/Honda/Triumph dealership called, ambiguously, Shaft Motors to pick up the Trophy 1200. There we meet New Zealand's Triumph importer, a bearded, affable fellow named Geoff Robinson and I get to see my first new-generation Triumph in the flesh. It's stunning. Luminous dark green with Union Jack emblems. Handsome also are the Laverda-orange Speed Triple and the black Daytona. Hot damn—the Brits are back in business!

Geoff Robinson tells us the bikes have been virtually troublefree, and have been selling well to Harley owners who want more performance. The bikes, he says, have great appeal to traditionalists, as well as sport-bike buffs. It turns out we will be borrowing two Triumphs, at least for the time being. One of Rob's BMW K75s has failed to make it to the hotel (trucking problems), so Shaft Motors is lending us the orange Speed Triple for a day or two. David and I do not protest.

As we leave the hotel the next morning, Beach reminds us about riding on the left side of the road. "All day long, I want you to say to yourself, 'Ride left, look right; ride left, look right,' so we don't have any accidents."

I smile to myself a private know-it-all smile, having had lots of experience riding in England. Then I almost pull out in front of a truck. "Ride left, look right; ride left, look right," I tell myself for the rest of the day. The mantra of the still-living.

On the first day of the trip I'm on the Trophy 1200 as we head southeast out of Auckland, along the coast and then back inland to Rotorua, which sounds to me like a kitchen appliance but is actually a very nice resort area. The Trophy is a big, fast comfortable sport-tourer, with hard Givi bags attached for plenty of luggage room.

The motor makes no particularly interesting sounds, but it has the kind of torque you could use to move your house to a new location. It feels and sounds somewhat like my old ZX-11, but pulls a little harder and more usefully at the bottom end and is not quite so silky and explosively fast near redline. No handling vices, a big-hearted motor, and ergonomics that are just right for all day sport-touring.

Where the 1200 Trophy exudes a kind of solid, head-of-the-family virtue, the Speed Triple is the wild, good-looking son who smokes cigarettes, runs around with girls, and stays out too late. It is a lithe, low, and fast café-racer that feels dense and compact, as if cast from a single billet. It also has one of the most charismatic engines to enrich our sport since Ducati got back on its feet. Responsive and punchy, it has a growly, torn-canvas exhaust note that cures depression, boredom, and ailments of the nervous system.

The riding position looks extreme before you get on the bike, but it isn't. It's at least as roomy and moderate a layout as my 900SS, and the seat is better. I manage to hog this bike for the entire afternoon and would gladly ride it on the whole trip if it didn't have to go back to the dealer. This is a motorcycle with enough personality to warrant its own Richard Thompson song.

That first night on the road we stop on a lake near Rotorua—an area of geysers, bubbling mud ponds, and steam fissures spewing forth sulfurous gasses—and go to a Maori territorial meeting house called a Marae. At the edge of the property we are greeted by a fierce-looking Maori warrior who does a traditional threatening speardance of warning and/or greeting, depending upon our intentions, which are good. So he lets us into the Marae for a visit and a dinner cooked on hot rocks in a large underground pit.

The Maori are a lively, self-assured people who did not exactly roll over and play dead when Captain Cook first landed Englishmen on these islands 200 years ago. In fact, a few early landing parties were greeted, measured up, cooked, and eaten.

These days, the Maori are famous for their musical talent (Kiri te Kanawa, the great opera soprano, is Maori) and they sing for us some of the most beautiful, rhythmic, multipart harmonies I've ever heard. Our group is handed a guitar and expected to sing a song. After a brief huddle, we burst forth with "Michael Rowed the Boat Ashore." It turns out Ralph Werner of our group is an excellent guitar player and Mary Ann Kull has a professional-class voice. The rest of us muddle through and everyone is happy. Thank God for scout camp musical training.

In the morning we rise early and don wetsuits for a whitewater raft trip down a nearby river gorge. Our raft guide is a lovely woman of outdoor radiant health (does no one look sickly in this country?) who says her name is "Ista."

"Beautiful name," I remark. "Unusual."

"Not unusual here," she says. "Ista is a name from the Old Testament."

Edwards and I look at each other for a minute, blankly. "Ah," David says, "Esther."

"Right," she says, "Ista."

After years of canoeing in Canada, I have learned to be wary of water that moves fast enough to rip your arms off. Nevertheless, we go through some heavy rapids, then over a 20-foot fall with me in the front of the raft and nose straight into the roiling water below like a Stuka with a broken elevator cable. I am flung out of the raft (holding onto a rope) and then flung back in, with a little help from Ista. Thrilling stuff, even if I have sprained my thumb and will spend the rest of the trip putting on my right glove with my teeth. Such is the price of glory.

Riding south toward Taupo, the road takes us through high timber country with areas of towering green volcanic cones and wonderful winding roads. The roads in New Zealand are nearly all paved with a coarse-grained blacktop that seems to provide excellent grip, wet or dry, and they are smooth and unblemished by frost heaves, expansion strips, or potholes. A dream surface through a fantastic landscape that lends itself to endless curves. This is a great country for sportbikes—or any bike that is quick and light. As I discover.

Midway through the morning, I trade my 1200 Trophy for David's BMW F650. It takes me about 10 minutes to decide that this, like the Speed Triple, is a fine motorbike. Having written a whole column on this bike (see *Leanings,* April), I won't belabor the subject, but on tight, winding roads I can actually keep up with the flying Mr. Edwards, and I find myself laughing at muddy-road construction sites and awkward parking spots. The F650 looks ugly as a warthog to me, but it is pure pleasure to ride, and it has a great engine. As the week goes on, its handling and maneuverability cause me to reconsider my whole concept of motorcycle design, back toward the lean and spare.

Just north of Lake Taupo, we come across Huka Falls, where there is a geothermal power station, a prawn farm, a waterfall, and some jetboat rides. So David and I naturally take a wild jetboat ride to see the waterfall and the power station, then eat prawns in garlic butter at a riverside restaurant. We are in the country of doing stuff, so we must do it. God forbid we should go half an hour in New Zealand without a new thrill. I manage not to sprain my thumb, but now have garlic breath.

After Lake Taupo, it's back to the east coast, along Hawke Bay to Napier. Vineyard country. New Zealand now produces a tremendous number of topflight wines, both red and white. Like the U.S., New Zealand has had a sort of revolution in food and wine over the past two decades, going from a meat-and-potatoes fifties culture to a land of fine restaurants and great wines.

The Kiwis may be a long way from anywhere, but they travel a lot (every young person is expected to have an OE, or Overseas Experience), and they bring good ideas home with them. The result is a remarkably cosmopolitan, open-minded, and with-it population. Everything is up to date in Wanganui.

There is an oft-repeated (by Americans) myth that New Zealand is just like the U.S., only 25 years behind the times. But it seems to me we are ahead of them only in population growth, nihilistic violence, mean-spirited talk radio, and the production of really stupid television shows. With any luck, they'll never catch up.

A sunny, late, cool afternoon finds us in the old mining town of Waipawa. David and I tour an old museum of local history and then meet our group in a nearby parking lot, where we are to meet our hosts for one of New Zealand's traditional "farm stays." It's a program that allows tourists to meet real people and stay on farms or sheep ranches. Our group is split in two, and David and I ride to the sheep ranch of Barbara and John Bibby, a 4,000-acre slice of heaven on steep green hills overlooking the ocean, in terrain that reminds me of the California coast around Big Sur, but greener.

The Bibbys are charming, lively, well-traveled people whose children are grown and out of the house. John takes us on a late-afternoon Land Rover climb through the spectacular steep hills and then we have a roast lamb dinner that can't be beat and after-dinner drinks by the fireplace.

The Bibbys, for some reason, find themselves answering questions about local property values and the economics of sheep ranching. It has not escaped anyone's attention that this is a wonderful place to live. Imaginations soar into the night.

More supremely beautiful roads take us south toward Wellington, where we will board a ferry to go to the South Island. On the way south, we stop for lunch at a biker bar with a row of Harleys out front. Here we encounter the only New Zealanders of the trip who do not respond when we say hello. They've seen one too many American movies with bad actors playing dim bikers, and know exactly how they are supposed to behave. Life imitates artlessness.

Elsewhere on the road, we pass roving bands of vintage British bikes, Japanese sportbikes, and a fair number of dual-purpose bikes rigged out for hard travel. New Zealand is a highly motorsports-conscious country, and seems to have far more than its fair per-capita share of motorcycles, sports cars, racetracks, and transportation museums. English heritage and good roads make it almost inevitable.

Wellington, at the south tip of the North Island, turns out to be a lively port town with a Seattle flavor—and wind. The day we arrive, you can lean on the wind, unsupported; Marcel Marceau imitators are everywhere. This city is supposed to have 40 days a year when the wind blows at more than 60 miles per hour. All of New Zealand, in fact, has been quite windy on this tour. The sky moves overhead quickly and, like England, it often feels more like a ship at sea than a large island.

We lash our bikes down in the hold of the car ferry, Isle-of-Man-style, and watch the North Island disappear as the South Island hoves greenly and mountainously into view. Everyone has told us if we like the North Island, we will love the South Island. It's less populous, studded with the snow-capped Southern Alps, and generally wilder; kind of a large national park with the occasional city.

First impressions bear this out. Leaving Wellington and arriving at Picton is sort of like leaving Upper Michigan for Alaska. As we wend southward, deeper into the island, the ever-changing landscape becomes an unreal mixture of seashore, subtropical rain forest, cloud formations, volcanic peaks, pines, palm trees, and giant fern-like fans of vegetation that seem left over from the Age of Dinosaurs, all held together with those same smooth, twisty, grippy roads. You don't know whether to ride or gape, so we do some of both.

We stay at Nelson and Westport, then head on to Fox Glacier, which is a product of the towering Mt. Cook. I dirt-track the Trophy down five miles of wallowing wet muddy road in a rainstorm to see the glacier, while Edwards rides the F650. Someday I will get even. The glacier is big. It is raining and cold.

We ride into clearing windy weather down to Queenstown, a pretty mountainside resort town on Lake Wakatipu, packed with expensive shops and hordes of Japanese tourists buying woolens and sheepskin coats. Unable to resist, I have my first hamburger of the trip at a café called Wisconsin Burger. I ask the waiter why it's called "Wisconsin Burger." He says, "I guess it just has a nice ring to it."

One of our group, Steve Reustle, returns to the hotel at night having just made a bungee jump from a high bridge on the nearby Shotover River. David and I look at each other. Our eyes narrow with resolve.

On the ride out of Queenstown, we stop at the famous old Kawarau Suspension Bridge (built 1881) on the Shotover Gorge, where the world's first bungee jump was made. The bridge is 143 feet above the river. We join a big busload of Japanese tourists who are watching some of their own tour-mates bungee jump off the bridge. It is freezing cold, dark, and windy, and David and I are wearing motorcycle boots, leather pants, and nine layers of underwear and sweaters. Not dressed for it, we tell ourselves.

"Besides," David says, "it has never been my lifelong desire to commit suicide in front of a busload of Japanese tourists." We decide not to jump and ride on.

Twenty-five miles later I pull over, flip up my shield, and say to David, "I've been thinking about that jump."

"Me too."

"Let's go back and do it. We'll never be here again."

"Right."

So, we ride back, pay our money, get weighed (for bungee length), walk out on the bridge, and get in line, David first. They wrap a towel and a nylon strap around the ankles of his motorcycle boots and latch the bungee to the strap. David tells them, "I'm kind of worried, because my boots are about two sizes too big for me. They're pretty loose."

The kid who hooks up the rope says, "If it feels like you're going to slip out and fall into the river, just curl up your toes."

David does not laugh as hard at this joke as you'd think.

The man just ahead of David jumps off the bridge and disappears from our sight. The kid looks over the edge and cries, "Oh, NO!"

"What happened'?"

"Ripped both his legs off!"

David smiles wanly. Then it's his turn.

He bravely jumps without hesitation and disappears into oblivion. Then I see he's been lowered into the tethered raft on the river below and returned to the riverbank. He is actually waving and smiling.

My turn. I hop to the edge of the bridge platform, my feet tied together, and look down.

If there was ever anything that goes against 5 million years of human evolution, it is the concept of diving head first off a 143-foot bridge over cold rushing water with your feet tied together. There is a special place in your brain set aside for the express purpose of telling you not to do this thing.

Nevertheless, I jump. The moment of jump is an odd existential experience, but the stretch and triple recoil of the bungee is pure and simple whoopdee-doo fun, like being tossed in a blanket, and is surprisingly unstressful on the joints, muscles, and spine. When you are lowered into the raft (like a side of beef) you feel relaxed, refreshed, and loose. Another triumph of endorphins over reality.

David and I have a celebratory Been-There-Done-That Coke from a vending machine, put on our riding jackets, and hit the road, feeling years younger.

Farther down the road we stop for coffee and hook up with our sometime riding partner Wayne Henneck, and then we come across Steve Reustle and Guy Crossley, two riding buddies who signed up for this trip together. It's one of the nice aspects of this tour that you can ride in a big group, a small group, with a partner, or even alone (though this isn't recommended). You have a map and a bike, and the only requirement is to show up that evening at the next hotel.

On a couple of days we ride with Rob Beach, who is one of those fast, smooth, skilled riders who can go at any pace you care to set. But most days we just meander, going fast or slow as roads, mood, and scenery dictate.

As on the Alpine trips I've taken, every night is essentially party night at the hotels, which are well-chosen for their local charm and color as well as mattress and shower-stall quality. We eat well, drink lots of good New Zealand beer, wander through towns, and sit around fireplaces telling true stories. And making friends. It is an unavoidable part of group motorcycle tours (this is my fourth) that you make friends for life. This is a natural byproduct of hanging around with examples of the world's only known species of consistently superior human, the avid motorcyclist.

Cost of a two-week trip like ours, for solo riders, is $2,700, and an extra $1,975 for a passenger, including motorcycle with unlimited mileage, dinner, breakfast, and hotel. Airfare, lunches, and gas are on you, as are drinks and roadside snacks. Single riders can also add $200 to that if they are not willing to share a room. For those who have time, Rob Beach prefers to lead a three-week tour ($3,775 solo and $2,850 for a passenger; $275 extra for private single room) because you can see so much more of the country, and there's a lot to see. Maybe when I retire.

On our last day we ride from Lake Tekapo to Christchurch, a lovely city on a bay, backed up by steep mountain ridges and looking northwest onto a coastal plain of Kentish-looking farms and fields. We have some time to kill before flying out, so David, Bob Wilkins, and I make a visit to the superb New Zealand Air Force Museum.

Naturally there is a guy there giving aerobatic rides in a nice old yellow Tiger Moth biplane (one of my all-time favorite airplanes), so I am forced by fate to sign up, put on a sheepskin jacket, and go for a ride. Besides, it's almost lunchtime, and I haven't risked my life since breakfast.

Christchurch looks lovely upside down from 3,000 feet on a crisp, sunny October day. It's an odd view, what with the green, rugged horizon hanging above the blueness of deep space, but a fitting last vision of the Land Down Under.

May 1997

CHARGE TO CHIHUAHUA!

Touring Northern Mexico in the Footsteps—and Tire Tracks—of the Revolution

After years of exploring the Baja Peninsula, I finally made it to mainland Mexico, a place to which I will soon return. And probably again after that.

Friedrich Nietzche once said, "Without Italy, Germans would go crazy." There is some evidence that Germans occasionally go crazy anyway, with or without Italy, but one can understand his meaning.

Those of us who live in uptight, highly organized northern climes seem to require a place in the mind that is more relaxed and Latin in temperament, where the trains do not always run on time. A warmer, more spiritual place where good food and drink temporarily induce a kind of memory loss and make time stand still. Not to mention the elevator in the hotel. Mexico, for a lot of *norteamericanos*, is that place.

It has been for me, for a couple of decades now. When we lived in Southern California, I fell in love with Baja and the modest, courtly good manners of its people. I became a student of the place, reading books and maps and exploring the whole peninsula by motorcycle and jeep. But in all those years, I never made it to mainland Mexico.

So I was naturally gratified and beside myself (see Dualism) when my old riding buddy Gil Nickel called from California to say that this year's ride of the Napa Valley Touring Society (NVTS) would take us on a late-October "Charge to Chihuahua," led by Skip Mascorro of Pancho Villa Moto-Tours.

The NVTS—which, curiously, looks like "NUTS," spelled in Roman letters—is an interesting mix of people. Several members are in the wine business in Napa Valley, but the rest are from all over the U.S. and Canada. Essentially, it's just a bunch of Gil's riding pals, the only consistent theme being an irreverent sense of humor and a fierce, abiding veneration for the cocktail hour. And the several golden hours that follow, to include dinner.

Previous NVTS trips, organized by different members, had taken us through the Ozarks and the Canadian Rockies. This year's Mexico trek was orchestrated by Stan Rosow, a semi-retired lawyer from Chicago who is using his spare time to explore the four corners of the Earth on a motorcycle.

After Gil invited me on this latest adventure, I walked over to my Rand McNally wall map of North America to ponder my options. The trip was to start in El Paso. All very well, but that's four days' ride from my home in Wisconsin, and four back. Added to eight days in Mexico, that was a long time away from work, deadlines, and family. Too long, maybe.

Gil to the rescue. He offered me his prized yellow BMW K1 (just repainted) and said he and his wife, Beth, could ride their other bike, a red BMW R1100RS. Stan was hauling a truckload of bikes from Napa to El Paso, and there was room for one more. Perfect. I could fly to El Paso and ride from there.

So on a Friday in late October, I said goodbye to my long-suffering wife, Barbara, whose job prevented her from going along this time, and left Madison in a blinding snowstorm. The plane landed in a warm, dusty, sunbaked El Paso, where our Ryder truck full of sardine-packed motorcycles had just arrived at the Airport Hilton.

After the usual warm greetings and fraudulent compliments about not looking any older, fatter, or more senile, our reunited band of 16 riders and passengers began the nerve-wracking task of backing 10 bikes—eight BMWs, one Harley, one Yamaha FZR1000—down a tall ramp. Much advice, many outstretched hands (picture, if you will, the Biblical distribution of the loaves and fishes), but no fatalities, hernias, or ruined backs. Good start.

At the hotel I met Skip Mascorro, the friendly, affable fellow who owns Pancho Villa Moto-Tours (685 Persimmon Hill, Bulverde, TX 78163;

800/233-0564), and his co-guide, Kenneth Upchurch. Interesting guys, both, with a solid background in Mexican culture.

Seems Ken Upchurch's great-grandfather, an American sugar magnate, not only founded and laid out the Mexican city of Los Mochis on the Gulf of California, but also helped pioneer the trans-Sierra railroad line that joined the Pacific Coast to Chihuahua. As a result of these long family ties to Mexico, he speaks Spanish so fluently I can barely understand it.

Skip is also a Mexican history buff. He's from San Antonio, but his great-grandfather was Mexican, so Skip gradually developed an interest in his Hispanic roots, traveling in Mexico and teaching himself the ways and language. It's no accident that he's named his company after Pancho Villa.

Villa, of course, was the famous Mexican revolutionary who led American General "Black Jack" Pershing (and a young Lieutenant named George Patton) on a merry chase all over northern Mexico. President Wilson and the U.S. Army were after Villa because he supposedly crossed the border and attacked Camp Furlong, near the town of Columbus, New Mexico, in 1916.

Some historians now believe, however, that Villa didn't know about the attack and was not there. They suspect that German emissary Franz von Papen (who much later helped bring Hitler to power) may have been behind it, in an attempt to draw Wilson's attention away from the war in Europe.

Whatever the truth, Villa is one of the great romantic and colorful heroes of Mexico, and—significantly—was once photographed with one foot up on the floorboard of an old F-head Indian V-Twin, grinning devilishly at the camera. It's this picture that Skip uses as the emblem of his company.

That first night, we decided to do a little border raid of our own, so we crossed into Juarez for dinner, taking a hotel bus to a wild, noisy place called Chihuahua Charlie's Bar & Grill.

On the way over, traffic came to a standstill. Our bus driver explained that someone had phoned in a threat to blow up the bridge at the border. "Why would someone want to blow up the bridge?" I said.

"They don't," he said, "but it forces the police to close the bridge and check for bombs. Then, the traffic backs up and they don't have time to check for drugs. Too many cars and trucks."

We finally made it to Charlie's and discovered, much to our delight, that they had a nearly inexhaustible supply of margaritas, Mexican food, and guitar music, much of it served up by lovely señoritas and great big guys in concho pants and crisscrossed ammo bandoliers. We passed around a huge Mexican hat and got our pictures taken by a canny photographer who somehow detected we were tourists.

After that rehearsal, our first day of riding took us 260 miles down the U.S. side of the Rio Grande in Texas. We went east to Cornudas, then south to Van Horn and Marfa, where the 1956 movie *Giant* was filmed, cutting southwest toward the border on Highway 67.

All of this was on a wide-open two-lane road with almost no traffic, a mixture of purple mountains, high prairie, limitless cattle ranches, swooping arroyos, and descents into broad valleys full of sweeping turns and climbs—fast, open road through a classic Western landscape, under a huge, clear West Texas sky.

Gil's K1 did not subtract from the pleasure of this first day. Six years ago, I attended BMW's introduction of the K1 in San Antonio, rode the bike for two days, and must admit that I was only partly impressed. It seemed too long and heavy for a sportbike, yet lacked the luggage or comfort to make it a good sport-tourer. The reach to the handlebars, even with my long arms, gave me a literal pain in the neck.

Gil's K1, however, had set-back blocks to bring the handlebars rearward a couple of inches, which revolutionized its comfort level. Still no luggage, but a tankbag and a rear seatpack carried enough for a solo rider (Skip's Chevy Suburban carried a little extra luggage for each of us.) Also, Gil had installed a 4-into-1 header and recalibrated the EFI, so the bike had a wonderful deep growl and perfect, crisp throttle response. It felt solid, fast (150 miles per hour), dead stable, and precise. By the end of the day, I understood why Gil had never been able to bring himself to trade the K1 in on his new RS; it has a kind of bone-deep composure and a high level of mechanical polish that makes it wear well, hour after hour.

That night, our destination was a restored adobe cattle ranch and private fort called Cibolo Creek Ranch, located four miles off Highway 67 on a dirt road. While other bikes squirmed and wobbled, the heavy, long-wheelbased K1 sliced through the dust and loose gravel like a Coast Guard cutter. A pleasant and unexpected surprise.

Cibolo Creek Ranch was built during the 1850s by pioneer/cattle baron Milton Favor, and was just recently restored by the Texas Historical Commission. The workmanship is exquisite and the care they took to get it right is remarkable. It has fortress walls, moats, stables, a big screened porch, a shaded colonnade along the guest rooms, library, music room, and an elegant Spanish-style dining room.

It also has a big outdoor firepit, where we stood around a mesquite blaze at night, warming ourselves and sipping from the agave and mescal family of fine drinks. Skip and I got into a long, complex (or so it seemed to us) discussion in which we explored moral relativism, the internal conflicts of Hegelian ethics, and which current dual-purpose bike would be best to buy.

Being one of the four "single" guys on the trip, I was assigned a roommate, and he turned out to be none other than the upbeat, irrepressible Randy Lewis, retired IndyCar driver and now president of Lewis Vineyards in Napa. A genuine fast guy: Despite never having a really first-rate ride, Lewis had managed to grid himself on the fourth row of the Indy 500 three years running, alongside the likes of Mario Andretti and Al Unser Jr.

The same speed and talent showed itself in his motorcycle riding, and I spent a good part of the trip trying to keep Randy's disappearing FZR1000 in my distant sights, while not actually killing myself. A recent convert to motorcycling, he rode faster than anyone on the trip and never put a wheel wrong. So much for genetics vs. experience.

The next day was free for local exploration and riding, so I took a solo trip down the Rio Grande toward Big Bend National Park. The river road, Highway 170 between Presidio and Terlingua, turned out to be a landmark piece of motorcycle pavement—tightly twisting, rising, and falling through the narrow river gorge of painted rock that's half badlands and half fantasy. The K1 loved it, growling and wailing, cutting up distance like a well-oiled chainsaw.

I stopped at the mining ghost town of Terlingua, home of the famous annual chili cookoff. The town itself is nothing but a bunch of fallen-down adobe walls, yellow dust, and a couple of stores. In the general store I bought myself a "Viva Terlingua" bumper sticker to put on my guitar case back home, in honor of Jerry Jeff Walker. The chili cookoff was less than a week away, and already the nearby arroyos and parks were filled with campfires giving off a heady mixture of wood smoke and simmering Texas red.

It was too late in the day to explore Big Bend Park, so I cut north through Alpine and then headed back through Marfa. I'd hoped to see the old ranch house from *Giant*, where James Dean, Rock Hudson, Elizabeth Taylor, Mercedes McCambridge, et al, had once worked their magic, but a gas station attendant told me it had been wind-damaged and then torn down. That grand two-story mansion, he told me, was "nothing but a bunch of boards nailed on telephones poles."

The next day we crossed the border at Ojinaga after a short delay in which Mexican immigration officials frowned at the mass of paperwork Skip had prepared for each bike, then stamped, notarized, embossed, signed, collated, stapled, and blessed each document as if it were the Treaty of Ghent. Young soldiers with automatic weapons looked on.

Funny how there's always an inverse proportion between the number of official documents and the effectiveness of government. You'd think bureaucrats might notice this embarrassing connection.

Free at last, we rode into Mexico.

Chihuahua!

To Mexicans, the big northern province of Chihuahua is their own Texas, the mythical West of their national imagination. It's a land of mountains, cattle ranches, fertile valleys greened by precious water, and wide-open spaces. Villa's home turf, where nearly every town was fought over, taken, and retaken about a dozen times during the revolution. Bloody ground.

Seems peaceful now, and the ride into the city of Chihuahua was our third day of astoundingly beautiful road, this time cutting through the Rio

Conchos valley, over high, windswept mountains and down into a wide basin. Two lanes, good pavement, lots of turns, no traffic. And no cops.

Chihuahua is a clean, busy town with a nice cathedral square, lots of banks, modern hotels, and restaurants. We stayed at the Palacio del Sol, right in the center of town, and had a good dinner at a small restaurant called Rincon Mexicana nearby.

From Chihuahua, we headed west through farming and ranch country and began our curving, upward climb into the Sierra Madre toward the old logging village of Creel and Mexico's famous Copper Canyon National Park. Best riding yet, in a series of great riding days.

For some reason, the name Copper Canyon (Barranca de Cobre) had suggested to me a rather desolate, dry, and dusty mining region. Not so. It's high, rugged country, but green and covered with pine forests, encompassing the largest and deepest canyon system in North America. Deeper than the Grand Canyon, it is over four times as vast. The name Copper comes not from mining, but from the color of the exposed rock. Spectacular country, almost unknown to most Americans.

The Mexicans call this area the Sierra Tarahumara because the almost inaccessible valleys and peaks are home to some 50,000 Tarahumara Indians. A shy, private people renowned for their stamina and swift running ability, they never "surrendered" or entered into any political discourse with the government of Mexico. When pressed or threatened, they just disappeared farther into the hills, thereby missing out on several revolutions, two world wars, the disco craze, both O. J. Simpson trials, and the civilizing benefits of network television.

To survive, they hunt and grow small hillside gardens, and also make beautiful baskets and other handicrafts, which they sell at tourist sites along the tortuous Chihuahua al Pacifico railroad line.

We stayed at a nice motel in Creel, parked our bikes for a day, and then took an overnight trip by bus to the high, Cliffside Hotel Mirador. We were supposed to take the train, but a landslide had closed it down for a few days. All along the line, marooned tourists had to accustom themselves to being stuck in one of the most beautiful places on earth, with only Mexican food and margaritas to survive on. Grim stories emerged of people forced to drink their own wine. Which we certainly did.

Our group included no fewer than four California vintners: Gil and Beth Nickel of Far Niente, John Trefethern of Trefethen Vinyards, Ren and Marilyn Harris of Paradigm, and Randy Lewis of Lewis Vineyards. Each of them brought a few cases of wine along and packed it in our Suburban chase car—the luggage & winemobile. If Skip had crashed, he would have drowned in cabernet sauvignon.

Fortunately he didn't, so some of our evenings are lost to history, with no reliable witnesses. I do know that Gil told at least one joke that required him to stand on the table and clutch his ankles, but telling it here would only cause problems.

So we arrived by bus, and the Hotel Mirador turned out to be, like Cibola Creek Ranch, one of the most beautiful lodges I've seen. Timber, adobe, and tile put together in a superb piece of Southwestern architecture, built into the cliffs on the rim of the canyon.

The average American conception of rural Mexico (well, mine, at least), might scarcely credit such a place existing on the Great Divide of the Mexican Sierra. But this was true of all our hotels; they were as good as—or vastly better than—most places I would stay on a bike trip in the U. S., cheapskate that I am.

My own cost on this trip, incidentally (single, with my own bike), was $1,289 for eight days of travel, covering hotels and two meals a day. Lunches, gasoline, drinks, and air travel to El Paso were on me. As the trip progressed, it seemed like a bargain.

After Copper Canyon, the trip back to El Paso felt like a downhill run toward home, but it was good riding all the way. Well, except for the border crossing. After a night at another good hotel in Casas Grandes, we crossed back into the U.S. at Palomas, which has a main street of hippo-sized ski moguls fashioned in mud. A hydrant had burst and the whole downtown was a giant mudhole.

As we slithered and bobbed up to a stoplight, I raised my faceshield and said to Gil, "This town is a disgrace! Don't they have a mayor they can run out of office?"

But we were back at the border, and border towns have ever been transient places where normal rules do not always apply, where cultures rub up against each other, generating frictional smoke and showing off their worst traits. Mexico can't control its birth rate, which always outstrips its resources, and the U.S. can't control its appetite for cheap goods—as if there could ever be such a thing—and the border towns are a product of those two facts. Improvidence meets avarice. There's a sense that no one is in charge.

This time we were waved across the border without even being stopped. We had lunch in the town of Columbus, where Pancho Villa either had or had not made his historic, ill-advised raid on the U.S. The fast ride back to El Paso on the border road would have been unremarkable except that Ken blew a rear tire on his GS BMW and managed to ride out the worst high-speed tankslapper I've ever seen. He calmly replaced his tube on the roadside with simple tools and we were on our way.

Back in El Paso, we loaded our bikes at an airport cargo dock, while across the runway Air Force One sat on the ramp. President Clinton was in town, making one of his last speeches of the 1996 presidential campaign. The bellhop at our hotel told me most of the Hilton had been filled with Secret Service agents for the whole week before Clinton's short visit, screening El Paso for the usual bad actors and dimbulbs.

Say what you will about any president, the courage to dive into crowds over and over again is almost beyond comprehension in the secure lives most of us lead. You could feel the tension in El Paso, and it hung in the hotel like a leftover ringing in the ears when a fire alarm has been turned off.

Curiously, our Napa Valley Touring Society trip through the Ozarks had taken us through election night four years earlier, when Clinton was in nearby Little Rock, awaiting the results. When Clinton runs, we ride.

After a big steak dinner at the famous Billy Crew's Steak House, during which I accidentally ordered a T-bone about the size and thickness of a window air-conditioning unit, we had many toasts and said our goodbyes. In the morning we all flew home our separate ways.

Before my own flight, I had breakfast with Skip and Ken. Over coffee, I confessed that I hadn't known what kind of bike would be best for Mexico. Dual-purpose? Pure dirt? Touring? Yet this trip had covered some of the best sportbike roads I'd ever ridden.

Skip smiled and nodded, "We do 18 rides a year down here, all over Mexico, and almost any bike works. But many people think the pavement ends at the border, and they're afraid to come down here. 'What about banditos?' is a another question we hear all the time. Half of our job is simply to dispense with anxieties. We do this mostly by taking care of the paperwork at the border crossing, and after that giving people some history and a feel for the place.

"Mexico is a remarkable country to tour," he added. "Three hundred miles from an American shopping mall, you can ride curving mountain roads through country populated by primitive Indians in loincloths. And mile for mile, dollar for dollar, these roads can match anything in the world. Once people discover this, they keep coming back. They want to go deeper into the country and see more of it."

He had that right, at least in my case.

When I got home, the driveway was drifted with snow and the right front tire on my snowblower was flat. Also, the garage door was frozen to the concrete floor and had to be broken loose with a crowbar. No big deal, really. I've learned to live with seasonal darkness and cold.

But without Mexico, I'd go crazy.

September 1997

BASIC BLACK

A Brief Social History of the Black Leather Jacket

I was asked to write this for a motorcycle gear section in Cycle World, *probably because I'm old enough to have a 35-year-old collection of the stuff stashed in my coat closet. Not all of it still fits.*

It was an embarrassing moment for me. A couple of years ago, I went out to lunch with a bunch of employees at the rock-and-roll station where my brother used to work. One of the younger DJs came with us, wearing a black leather motorcycle jacket of *The Wild One* variety. Without thinking, I asked what kind of motorcycle he had.

"Motorcycle?" he said, looking at me, blinking. "I don't have any motorcycle. Why?"

Foolish question on my part.

Non-motorcyclists take the black leather jacket for granted now, as a mere fashion accessory. Everyone from the Ramones to Madonna has appeared publicly in some version of the Brando-style "Eric von Zipper" motorcycle jacket, so that it has become as harmless a cultural cliché as carhops on roller skates or the 1957 Chevy.

We live in the age of pre-fab charisma, where mere money can buy you an artificially aged (right at the factory) Fender Stratocaster or a pre-stressed 50-mission flight jacket. Buy the stuff, share the life. And with a black leather jacket, the spurious risk-image of motorcycling can rub off on you without the inconvenience of learning which is the clutch lever or ever getting wet. Or crashing. Everyone wants a piece of the danger, but no one wants to get hurt. We want authenticity to come easy, without too much stress or conflict.

It was not always so.

There was a time in America when symbols had real meaning, and the black leather jacket was a potent one. No one dreamed of wearing a motorcycle jacket without owning a motorcycle.

Why?

Well, for one thing, wearing a black leather motorcycle jacket into the wrong bar could get you beaten up. It could also get you kicked out of school, shunned by "nice" girls, turned down for jobs, and stared at by cops with mirrored sunglasses. Style choices used to come with unpredictable and amazing consequences. Sadly, I am just old enough to have lived through this strange era.

Where did it all start? And why?

Logic certainly had a role. Leather has traditionally been—and remains—the best anti-abrasion material for motorcycle clothing. The uniquely intertwined corkscrew cells in leather will not tear or rip along a faultline as most fabrics do. Also, leather is windproof and, when lined, warm. And it's long-wearing and good-looking.

Okay, but why *black* leather?

That's easy. It's the same color as dirty chain lube, seeping Harley gear oil, old Indian wheel-bearing grease, the underside of your Triumph, and the blacktop upon which you knelt to examine the gaping connecting-rod hole in your BSA engine cases. Doesn't show the dirt, as Mom used to say. If we could breed flies and junebugs without yellow-green innards, it would be perfect.

I've looked through a lot of my old motorcycle books for the first appearance of the black leather jacket, but it's hard to tell where the tradition begins. From the earliest days of motoring and flying, people realized leather's advantages in fighting off this new form of machine-generated wind, and I have photos from the 1911 Isle of Man TT showing riders in full black leathers—often with neckties worn underneath. American racers, for the most part, wore wool jerseys and looked like rugby players.

Non-racing riders seem to have gone for natty woolen-and-tweed suits, with the occasional use of sheepskin-lined leather coats with big wool collars.

But the first photo of a street rider in the classic black leather motorcycle jacket doesn't appear—in my files—until just after WW II: The age of the restless, existential rebel hopped up on Bop music and bongo drums. Or just someone who needed a warm, practical jacket.

Typically, this was the short "Cycle Champ"–style jacket, usually of horsehide, with a bottom belt, overlapping front, snap-down collar and countless zippers—some with rabbits' feet attached. Sort of a leather Eisenhower jacket, with good-luck features.

Racers and sport riders generally shunned all of the self-snagging appurtenances and stuck with an unadorned black leather jacket with a mandarin collar, tight-fitting sleeves, and two simple zippered chest pockets. A racing-striped version of same may be seen on Peter Fonda in *Easy Rider*. This has always been my favorite type of motorcycle jacket. I still have my original Buco version, and just had a less-battered replica of it made by Bates.

Both styles were around in the 1950s, and they soon became emblematic of British Rockers, serious American riders, and various brands of rebel in the motorcycling sub-strata. Elvis had one. So did James Dean, Eddie Cochran, Gene Vincent, and Marlon Brando. (How's that for unpaid star endorsement?) And before the Beatles were cleaned up by Brian Epstein, they had 'em, too.

It didn't take Middle America long to connect these jackets with rock-and-roll, overstimulated hormones, greasy ducktails, big sideburns, loud pipes, and the sort of trouble that rode into Hollister, California, one fine day and tore up the town. Ordinary citizens had seen the photos in *Life* magazine and they were Not Happy.

You could almost say they were violently, homicidally unhappy. A wave of revulsion for all things motorcycle swept over the country, and the black leather jacket was its arch symbol.

By the time I was a freshman in high school in the early 1960s, wearing a black leather jacket was an invitation to be ostracized by all but the toughest elements in your hometown. Even the hoods in my high school quit wearing black leather jackets. They were afraid some older, unemployed biker with three teeth would kill them with the broken-off neck of a beer bottle, just on principle.

Anyway, where would they go? No café would let them in the front door, nor would anyone's parents. Nor the school. All they could do was stand on the street and draw contempt. Black leather was powerful medicine.

The country slowly got over that phobia as things loosened up in the 1960s, but when I took my first cross-country motorcycle trip in 1967, I still had to park half a block from a motel and leave that black leather Buco roadracing jacket on my bike each time I tried to get a room. Otherwise the No Vacancy light came on.

I usually took it off and folded it before I walked into restaurants, to prevent icy stares, stalled conversation, and very slow service. Or none. The movie *Easy Rider* in no way exaggerates the anti-biker/hippie/beatnik/long-hair mood of the era. It could be very chilly out there. Dangerous, even.

For the most part, we don't even have to think about this stuff anymore. It would surprise a black-clad motorcyclist to be discriminated against now—at least in any non-formal setting.

America has learned to live and let live a little better than it used to, and we can probably thank the Ramones and Madonna—and my brother's DJ friend at the radio station—for turning motorcycle jackets into a relatively benign, standard fashion item, so the rest of us can wear this practical gear in its intended place without drawing flak.

I think it has also helped that Harley-Davidson, with its charity rides and fund-raisers, has managed to portray even leather-clad bikers as basically nice people. Who'd have thought you'd ever meet the nicest people on a Low Rider?

But that's a fairly easy message to get across these days, especially to a generation of aging Rockers. Society has learned to be remarkably tolerant, now that we are them and they are us.

And Brando is 73.

November 1997

INTO THE LOW COUNTRIES

Come With Us Now Over Shining Wet Roads Through Misty Mountains and Brooding Forest to the Dutch TT at Assen, on the Fifth Annual *Cycle World* GP Euro-Tour

As a history buff, this is a trip I would love to repeat, with more time to visit the Western Front of WWI and to see more of the route my father-in-law, Fred Rumsey, followed as an infantry soldier in WWII, all places we criss-crossed on our tour. More than usual, our route seemed haunted by the overlapping layers of European and family history.

As we climbed the dark, narrow stairs that spiraled up the guard tower into the medieval castle at Bad Bentheim (which sounds, I admit, more like a mechanical problem than a castle), my wife, Barbara, said, "Can you imagine what it was like for knights to run up these stairs in full armor?"

I paused for a moment, sweating heavily, and looked down at my scuffed motorcycle boots and the creaking knee pads in my riding leathers. I hefted my black full-face helmet with its shatterproof Lexan face shield and pondered the gauntlet-like riding gloves with reinforced palms I'd stuffed inside the helmet.

"Can't imagine," I said.

Armor, I thought, is not dead, but has only taken a new and better form. We do battle with ourselves and the road now, rather than one another.

At the top of the tower, we looked out over a beautiful green valley and the slate roofs of the village below. An ancient, distinctly European view that probably hadn't changed for 600 years.

"I wish our friends back home could see this," Barb said.

I did too.

Our friends, in fact, had made a valiant attempt to appear envious when we first revealed our proposed motorcycle route from Munich to the Dutch TT at Assen, but you could see doubt in their eyes.

"Munich to Holland? Hmmmm … is there some nice country between those two places?" they'd ask politely, as if we'd proposed a vacation ride from Moline to Gary, Indiana.

"Well, we're traveling through the Black Forest to the Nurburgring race circuit in the Eifel Mountains, up the Rhine and Mosel River Valley wine country, dipping into France for a short time, then cutting through the Ardennes forest and across Holland to a motorcycle grand prix."

That helped. If you lace your description with words like "mountain" and "forest" and "wine," most people are able to imagine a good time, even if "motorcycle grand prix" has no resonance for them.

But for some of us, of course, it does.

The Dutch TT is one of those events that is supposed to transcend mere competition, falling into the "happening" category of big events. It's a place where Europeans go just to make the trip, to be part of some unsignaled packing of tents, donning of leathers, and early morning mass-awakening of engines all over the continent, and to find themselves in the company of a few trillion other like-minded motorcyclists. It's a place you are supposed to go at least once, like Mardi Gras or the Isle of Man.

So Barbara and I flew into Munich on a Sunday morning in June, watching from the window of our 747 as the sun rose weakly over a rain-soaked Europe. The only breaks in the gloomy overcast were a picture-perfect view of the entire Isle of Man, no less (lights of Douglas glowing in the early dawn like a small candle), and another clearing right over the famous GP car circuit at Zandvoort, Holland. Good omens, heaven smiling down on racetracks.

Barb and I arrived a day early so we could rest up and also walk around downtown Munich. We took the airport train to our hotel in Sauerlach, just south of Munich, then trained backed into the city.

We'd explored Munich as young marrieds back in 1973, and found that not much has changed. Except that Germans seem to be a lot more polite and laid back than they were then, now that the crusty old WWII generation is dying off and the era of radical-chic anti-Americanism has all but disappeared in Europe. Perhaps Americans have also become better guests. At any rate, people were polite and helpful everywhere we went.

Ah, Munich. Wonderful beer at the Hofbrauhaus, and a central market square of aromatic foods—roasting sausages, blue cheeses, smoked fish, pickled eels, baking breads, and pastries—all arranged around a shaded park and bustling beer garden. "I think we should rent an apartment here and move to Germany," I told Barb. "Just eat and drink for a hobby and see if we can get our weight up to around 300 pounds."

"How do Europeans stay so thin?" Barb wondered aloud.

"Bicycles," I suggested. They were everywhere.

Back at the Sauerlacher Post Hotel, our small band of brothers and sisters gradually assembled for this, the fifth-annual *CW* GP Euro-Tour, arriving by Edelweiss courtesy bus. The bus was piloted by our revered guide of former trips, Joseph "Fuzzy" (pronounced "Futzi") Hackl and a new guide named Christian Preining. Both are Austrians who speak excellent English, though Fuzzy is famous for adding colorful new idioms to the English tongue. At the morning briefing, he informed us that our easy first day's ride would be "a sheet of cake."

One of our group accused him of speaking "Germonics."

We had lots of first-timers on the tour, but also a good number of Euro-Tour vets, including a reunion group of high-spirited riding buddies from the 1995 Czech GP tour who call themselves the *Spitzbuben*, which is German for "mischievous boys." They seemed to have a lingering reputation among the Edelweiss guides as the Katzenjammer Kids of Europe, wanted by Interpol in several countries for unpaid speeding tickets, accidental wheelies, passing tour buses at the speed of light, and other crimes of gusto.

Others were from all parts of the country, but besides Barb and me, there were only two other couples: Allen Engel, a ship's captain from California and his landscape architect friend Sally Dunn; and Tom Overby, a tax lawyer from Little Rock, who brought his college-age daughter Audrey along for her first trip to Europe.

Also on the trip were *CW* Editor David Edwards and staff photographer Brian Blades, an old friend and former dirt rider who'd been brushing up on his street technique for this trip. Filling out the list was Werner Wachter, owner and founder of Edelweiss Bike Travel, a pleasant fellow of quick intelligence who looks as if he could be an Austrian ski instructor. And maybe is, for all I know.

Rain hammered against our window like lead pellets in the morning and hotel hallways were alive with riders rustling around in rain gear, sounding like 25 fat ladies in nylons and barn boots. After breakfast and a morning briefing, we walked to the bikes.

Our motorcycles were a mixture of new-generation BMWs of all types, and Suzukis, mostly 1200 Bandits. I had requested a BMW R1100RS—I've been thinking for several years about buying one (but have, so far, been too cheap), and I wanted to renew the acquaintance.

Our group left Sauerlach in clumps and batches, with a few lone riders, some following the guides, some not. The beauty of Edelweiss tours is that (a) everyone has a map and (b) your only responsibility is to arrive at the next hotel for dinner. Barb and I followed Werner (I hate turning the wrong way out of the hotel parking lot), along with David, Brian, and a few others.

Werner led us through a light misting rain through the green, lovely Barvarian hill country and farmland west of Munich on two-lane roads. Brown Swiss dairy cattle watched over split-rail fences as we passed; citizens of half-timbered villages paused in their chatting and stepped up on the curbs; men in lederhosen, Tyrolean hats, and loden-green jackets (but without accordions) regarded our silver-green BMW with approval. The Alps loomed, shrouded in swirling clouds, just to the south.

Germany has lovely roads for riding motorcycles. Smoothly paved, they curve and dip and follow the contours of the land. Villages are often no more than 7 or 8 kilometers apart, but the roads between are sparsely traveled and almost entirely unpatrolled by *Polizei*.

Germans—and Europeans in general—seem not to have developed this simmering, Puritanical disapproval of speed you find in America. Once they are out of the city, Germans simply travel at whatever logical speed is suggested by the road and the capability of their vehicles, be it 65 or 90 miles per hour. Even in slow vehicles, they don't begrudge other people who can go faster. This makes for nice riding; almost heavenly, by our standards.

On the autobahns, of course, there are no speed limits. There, I discovered our R1100RS would hit 215 kilometers per hour (about 135 miles per hour) if we sat in normal riding positions and did not go into a tuck, but the wind flow and noise were a lot more pleasant below 180 kilometers per hour, and we settled on 160 (about 100 miles per hour) as the most serene cruising speed. Which, where we live—the Land of the Free—would get us thrown in jail and our bike towed.

Following Herr Wachter across Bavaria to our evening destination of Bad Urach removed some of the map-reading strain, but even Werner was confused at times. Germany is a hard country in which to navigate. Unlike, say France, which has numbered roads, Germany depends on clusters of destination signs to point the way. You come to a sudden cross-roads, and instead of an arrow that says "Route 19," you are confronted with one small yellow sign that says…

Marktoberdorf
Klosterlechtfeld
Totenschweinhocksmitstuffin

…and another one that reads…

Pfizerknottendinkelrude
Rotenkaisersunterwarren
Bad Rainagain
Behanginwashonderseigfriedline

As you go flying past the intersection at about 120 kilometers per hour, your navigator/wife leans forward and shouts, "What did those signs say?"

Struck completely dumb in the presence of a thousand Teutonic syllables, you simply skid to a stop and put your head down on the tank and groan.

Nevertheless, we found our way. Stopped for lunch next to a spectacular eighteenth-century Rococo church called Wieskirche. There we took over a small café and dined on the famous Bavarian Weisswurst, a white veal sausage required by stern tradition to be eaten before noon, while theoretically still fresh—"even if it's been frozen and thawed," Werner explained with a wry smile.

Evening found us at an excellent hotel in Bad Urach. Bad, of course, means mineral bath or spa, so David and our mutual old touring buddy Charles Davis set out to find a mineral bath and a rubdown, which they did, arriving for dinner looking 10 or 20 years younger. We all had our evening Weissebier (everything in Bavaria is white—sausage, beer, mountains, flowers, etc.) and then filed into a grand old dining room for dinner. Someone asked a waitress what was for dinner and she replied, "Meat!"

"Meat" in southern Germany means small, tooth-resistant curls of roasted pork in a bland white gravy, with some form of potato on the side, and this substance is the main reason that Italian restaurants are more numerous in America than German restaurants: a classic case of *Fleischfurcht*, or "meat fear."

At dinner that evening, we learned that one of our group, Todd Borchart, an irrepressible character and Italian GP Euro-Tour veteran who goes by the nickname "El Chico Loco," had slid wide on a wet corner and hit the side of a truck. His bike was bent and his right leg was broken, but he was doing well at a nearby hospital.

I should say his leg was re-broken, as he'd injured the same leg in a desert dirtbike crash years ago and it had never healed properly. Word was, the German surgeons were trying to straighten out both the old and new damage.

A very long day's Wednesday ride took us across the Neckar River, on magnificently curvy roads through the heart of the *Schwartzwald*, or Black Forest, across the Rhine, into French Alsace and the vineyards of the Vosges Mountains, back into Germany and into the famous Mosel wine region for a night at Bernkastel-Kues, a name that has appeared on many empty wine bottles in my lifetime.

Barb and I rode mostly alone that second day, stopping for coffee at a café in Johanniskreuz, Germany's answer to the Rock Store, a gathering place for riders. There were a few motorcyclists at the café, but not many. Then two huge tour buses full of gray-haired German ladies arrived and swamped the place. They surrounded our table and jostled our chairs, crackling and chatting in shrill German tones. It was like a scene from Hitchcock's *The Birds*.

We left in search of oxygen. On the road, fellow tour member Peter Wylie on his Suzuki TL1000 passed us with a wave, sailing off into the distance at high speed. Five miles later, we found him standing in the road next to his bike, at the end of a 50-yard streak of rubber. As he was accelerating through the gears, his transmission had suddenly seized up solid in fourth gear, locking the rear tire. The TL had been a testbike for several German magazines, so its trans had probably seen better days.

We dragged the bike into a handy rest area and left it for the chase truck to retrieve, then Peter hitched a ride on the back of David's R1100RT. Fuzzy and Christian conjured up a new bike and Peter was back in action the next day.

Our own machine, the R1100RS, was proving itself a good choice for the trip, with just one minor glitch. It had an on/off throttle sensitivity that caused it to surge at low speed, but I soon learned to compensate by being a little more subtle with the right wrist. My only other complaint was with the saddlebags, whose multi-step, easily bent locking mechanisms were a constant source of cursing, misplaced keys, and minor frustration. (I picture their inventor now living in a madhouse, catching flies in a jar and muttering incantations to himself.) BMW had the greatest bags in the world on my old 1984 RS, then changed them. Go figure.

For all that, I'd still like to have a new RS, just for all of the things it does so well. It goes, handles, stops, and carries two people in swift, compliant comfort. Looks good, too, I think.

At yet another mind-bogglingly lovely road, we dropped down into the Mosel River Valley, passed the great and impossibly charming riverside towns of Bernkastel and Kues, then climbed through some of the world's most renowned vineyards to a modern hotel that looked like CIA headquarters, but with pink porch panels. That night we had "meat" for dinner again, but first celebrated the long day's ride with a glass of the local Weisswein (more white stuff) and an excellent Bernkastler Riesling.

People have been making—and drinking—fine wines here for at least 2,000 years, ever since nearby Trier was a Roman outpost (hundreds of Roman wine goblets have been recovered in excavations around Bernkastel), and the proconsul Ausonius sang its praises in poem, thanking Bacchus for sending him here. We did, too.

As I sipped this ancient magical potion and looked across the river at the ruins of a castle on the opposite bank, I had one of those European Moments. This is a short reverie in which you suddenly glimpse the deep, saturated oldness of Europe and are temporarily humbled at the ridiculous shortness of your own generation's moment in time.

Telelever front end? Electronic fuel injection? A blink of the eye. It's the vines that last. And those goblets. Good basic technology for the ages.

A third day of hard travelin' took us all the way to Holland, but not before we'd visited the car and motorcycle museum at the Nurburgring, followed the borders of Belgium, and had lunch in the beautiful old village of Monschau.

We sat at an outdoor café in Monschau (in a blessed calm between rainstorms) and I looked at the map. We were not far from Malmedy, Rocherath, St. Vith-Battle of the Bulge country in WWII. My father-in-law, then a young Captain Fred Rumsey, had fought his way through these very hills in 1945, losing most of his buddies on the way. His unit was given a presidential citation for destroying 78 German tanks during three days of bitter street fighting in Rocherath, just 15 miles from our lunch stop. Fred was awarded a Bronze Star for his part in the struggle. Nasty times for such beautiful country.

We hit the road again, into the teeth of yet another rainstorm.

A word about rain here: It rained every day on our trip—David Edwards would later refer to it as "The Wet Crotch GP Tour"—with only a few interludes of fleeting sun and dry road. Yet somehow it didn't matter much. Once you've gone through the cursed process of donning your rainsuit, wet-weather riding has its own restful rhythm and beauty, and the green European countryside can look quite dramatic with shafts of sunlight breaking through midnight-blue storm clouds. There's a Wagnerian wildness about it that suits the Rhineland.

How's that for cheerful?

At Emmerich, we finally breezed into Holland, crossing the Rhine into a sunlit Dutch afternoon with looming gray-white clouds from a van Ruisdale painting. After the rugged hills of Germany, Holland is almost soothingly soft; a flat, carefully stitched tablecloth of tidy villages with intricate red brickwork, sleepy canal-boat traffic, straight roads lined with shady poplars, and fields of flowers with bicycle paths cutting through them, all seen through a dreamy, moisture-laden atmosphere. In Germany, the land is the scenery; in Holland, it's that sky that dominates.

We followed two-lane roads past Arnhem, then picked up the A28 four-lane past the town of Assen to our hotel in Groningen, just to the north. We had a free day before the races, so Barb and I joined David, Brian, and Charles for an all-day train excursion into Amsterdam. The coach-class cars were almost full, so we feigned stupidity and rode in an empty first-class compartment—until the conductor checked our tickets.

"These are very lovely tickets," he said, "but, unfortunately, they are not for this first-class car," (Almost everyone in Holland speaks perfect English, which is more than you can say for the U.S.)

"Gosh-all-fish-hooks!" we said, or words to that effect, and moved.

Amsterdam, with its webbed canals and tall, vertical houses, is one of the great cities of the world, but it seems overwhelmed these days by its own reputation for tolerating almost everything. The upshot is a rather sleazy mix of amateur art, sex shops, head shops, panhandlers, backpackers, hustlers, and ladies of the night (or morning or afternoon) sitting in neon display windows. It was a good place to be for about three days when I was 21, but the city feels to me now like the landscape of *Austin Powers, International Man of Mystery*, something left over from another time. A little tired.

The museums, the scenery, and the Indonesian food were great, though. We had a fine lunch and took a canal-boat ride while Brian went to the Rijksmuseum, which Barb and I had seen on our first visit in 1973. At lunch, Barb said, "One thing I like about this place, is you don't hear all those annoying European police sirens, like you do in Munich."

"That's because nothing is illegal here," David explained. "Who would you arrest?"

Good question.

Saturday was race day, but the Friday night before was festival night in downtown Assen. Unlike Douglas at the Isle of Man, which is Bike Central, Assen has its guest park just outside the barricaded downtown, which is as charming as Disneyland's European Village, but real. Bands play on every other street corner, bungee jumpers leap from cranes, beer tents sell beer, food tents sell pretzels and sausages, and everybody walks.

Everybody: kids, grandmas, bikers, riders in full leathers, moms, young couples with prams, all circulating in a huge, swirling counter-clockwise flow through jam-packed streets. No pushing, shoving, or swaggering, just a polite, cheerful crowd out for a mass stroll. I've never seen anything quite like it. In the U.S., we seldom get an all-ages family crowd at a bike rally.

On Saturday we rode to the track, joining the flow down A28 until we were ducted into one of a dozen parking fields whose size and glittering mass of handlebars, gas tanks, and headlights almost defies description. How many bikes do you picture on Earth? Triple that number, square it, and then multiply by your age, and envision them all parked at Assen. Ever wonder where all the cowhide goes when McDonald's is done making hamburgers?

Leathers. At Assen.

We hiked around the track to our excellent grandstand seats at a fast left-hander on the back side of the circuit, with a good view of several other corners and part of the main straight. Assen is a bikes-only venue (no car races) so the seating is pleasantly close to the track, which is flat but fast and interesting.

I won't go into details on the race, except to say that the 250 GP, won by Tetsuya Harada on an Aprilia, was a barnburner, and a better race than the 500. Mick Doohan is so good on the big bikes that no one can really stay with him. Makes you long for a Schwantz, Rainey, or Lawson to keep him honest.

With the GP over, it was fast autobahn riding back toward Munich, but not before we'd hit the two-lane *Romantische Strasse* (quite literally "Romantic Road"), stayed in the lovely Rhine-side town of Andernach, and visited a couple of fine castles at Berg Eltz and Bad Bentheim. An outdoor lunch was prepared for us by Fuzzy—who is an actual chef in his other life, and always makes the best meals of the trip—at a park on the famous Lorelie Rock overlooking the Rhine.

This is where the Rhine Maidens used to sing their siren songs and lure sailors to their deaths against the rocks. I went to high school with girls like this, and I can tell you the risks are not overstated.

We later stopped again at the Nurburgring, the famous 14-mile race circuit tested in the Eifel Mountains. The track was open for anyone with the 22-deutchmark ($13)-per-lap fee. So our group lined up behind various Porsches, taxicabs full of tourists, sportbikes, and teens in hot-rodded Opels (can you imaging this happening in America?) and paid our money, just as the rain began pouring down again.

Before we pulled onto the track, Christian walked up and said, "A road-racing friend of mine recently won a race here in the rain because he didn't crash. He normally finishes 14th." He peered in through my helmet visor to see if I understood.

Message delivered. The track was indeed quite slippery in the rain—slick with oil and rubber—so we didn't exactly set any new two-up lap records, but the length and difficulty of the track, one of the most beautiful on

Earth, made its impression. With 174 corners per lap, you feel like you've been gone for a month when you finally get back to the start-finish line. And, in my case, I probably had.

Another key stop on the way home, our last night on the road, was the fabled city of Rothenburg.

The last 100 kilometers into town, Barb and I joined up with the dreaded Spitzbüben and shared a very fast, exhilarating ride on narrow valley roads along the Tauber River. It was fun, but I couldn't help thinking that if I rode the whole trip at this pace, fate would eventually catch up with us and smite us on the kneecap or elbow. Nevertheless, I arrived in Rothenberg on an adrenaline high, with virtually no cobwebs on my sidewalls or brake roters.

Rothenburg is perhaps Germany's best-preserved medieval walled city. Once reduced to a half-populated economic backwater by the predations of the Thirty Years War and the Black Plague, it was finally rediscovered in the last century. Heavily shelled during WWII, 40 percent of it had to be rebuilt again to original plans.

When you look at these beautiful old half-timbered homes and inns, exquisite cathedrals and civic buildings, and think of them being bombed and shelled, it occurs to you that the German people should have beaten Hitler to death with his own hat just for the architectural damage he brought down on the country, let alone the human suffering inflicted on the world. Centuries of hard work, artisanship, and inspiration, gone in a flash of bad temper, like a child breaking his own toys.

We took an evening tour of Rothenburg with the caped and hooded night watchman, a man whose role is as old as the medieval city. He carried a lantern and a pike and gave us a fascinating lecture as we walked through the narrow cobblestone streets and looked out over the parapets with a full moon rising.

Another European Moment: My grandfather came from Germany in 1910, and I could suddenly imagine his ancestors living this life, seeing this view from a castle wall centuries ago, the night and the watchtowers freighted with different meanings than they had now. I felt like the temporary genetic expression of something much older than myself. That, or a character in a Donovan song.

Last day. The road from Rothenburg was one of the best of the trip. We dipped, swooped, and plunged through the hills of the River Altmuhl region and then descended through the Altmuhtal Naturpark in warm sunlight and headed south to the ring road around Munich for one last good, drenching rainstorm before we pulled up at the Sauerlacher Post Hotel. End of journey.

El Chico Loco rejoined us for dinner that night, seated in a wheelchair. Seems the surgeons had not only fixed his broken leg, but repaired the botched job done by an American hospital back in the 1970s after his dirt-bike accident. He read us a hilarious account he'd written of his week in the hospital, and said he'd seen the Dutch TT on TV in the hospital lounge, sipping champagne ordered from the maternity gift shop.

Seems a German policeman came to his hospital room and served him a traffic ticket for going to fast.

"I was going *fast*," Chico told him, "but certainly not *too fast*. If I'd been going too fast, I'd be dead. All I've got is a broken leg."

The cop agreed and reduced the fine. A happy ending, all things considered.

As everyone made farewell speeches, I looked around the room and thought no two European motorcycle trips are quite alike. I've been on three Edelweiss tours now, and on every one you meet new people, cover new ground, and try to comprehend a thousand things you've never seen. A fast-moving motorcycle trip here is essentially a compression of life. It's an unrelenting succession of impressions that unwind just ahead of your front wheel and leave a single vision of the trip that is as complex and full of details as a Gothic cathedral, yet all one thing, complete in itself.

Later, you frame that picture in your mind and it stays with you as almost nothing else does. And when people ask later, "How was that ride from Munich to Holland?" you don't even know where to begin.

"Like going from Moline to Gary," you joke, "by way of the Middle Ages, with mountains and forests and wine and racetracks."

September 1998

TO RIDE A VINCENT

We Know the Vincent Black Shadow is a Beautiful Thing to Look at, But How Does the Legend Hold Up After an All-Day Ride in the Texas Hill Country? Our Editor-at-Large Heads South to Investigate

After a lifetime of trying to bum a short ride on the legendary Black Shadow, I finally got to ride one for a whole day in Texas. A year later, I sold nearly everything I owned to buy the bike in this story. Two years later, I sold the Vincent to pay off our house. Now I have a clear deed on our house, but no Vincent. This should probably be rectified.

It was the fastest bike in the world the year I was born, 1948, introduced just two weeks after my birth. I heard about it in gas-station bull sessions when I was growing up, read about it in Floyd Clymer's *Cycle* and later in *Cycle World,* and heard the legend passed by word of mouth. The Vincent Black Shadow. The fastest production motorcycle in the world. A stock one was supposed to do 125 miles per hour, at a time when most large-displacement streetbikes could barely stagger to 100. And modified Shadows went even faster. Much faster.

Look at the pictures: Rollie Free in his swimming suit and bathing cap, streaking (almost literally) across the Bonneville Salt Flats, prone on his modified, stripped-down, straight-piped Shadow-prototype of the competition Black Lightning—breaking the record for a naturally aspirated motorcycle at 150.313 miles per hour. *Life* ran the photo on October 4, 1948, and this picture and others of the record attempt have appeared over and over again in motorcycle books and magazines ever since.

"That engine was put into the frame with a whip and a chair," someone wrote, and the phrase stuck in everybody's mind. A sinister-looking black bike full of external plumbing and raised oil lines, standing out from those early B-Series engine cases like veins in a bat wing. The Black Shadow. When I was a kid it sounded menacing, like a combination of black widow spider and masked movie-matinee phantom, everything exciting and dangerous packed into one machine.

I grew up trucking all this lore around in my small, young brain. The Vincent as ultimate.

So naturally, I have lusted after Vincents these many years, both in heart and mind. I have gradually accumulated a small library of books and magazines on this illustrious marque whose history stretches from 1927, when Phillip Vincent bought the respected but insolvent HRD motorcycle company, until another insolvency closed the factory in 1955. The bikes I like best, the 1,000cc V-Twin Series B and C Rapides and Shadows, were all made after WWII.

The Rapide was the "regular" version, the Black Shadow the high-performance model, hot-rodded with higher-compression pistons, bigger Amal carbs, and hand-polished internals, good for a whopping 55 bhp—10 more than the Rapide. It also had fins on its dual 7-inch front brake drums, and, of course, black-enameled engine cases and cylinders.

The Rapide is, perhaps, more beautiful with its polished-aluminum cases, while the Shadow is . . . well, more legendary and even more romantic, if that's possible. Also about $10,000 more expensive, these days.

But I have not bought either one.

And why not?

Well, as I mentioned in a recent column, these bikes have always stayed just ahead of my income and/or frivolity level, much like the carrot on the stick dangled in front of the donkey. When Vincents were $5,000 back in the early 1980s, you could buy a brand-new 900SS Ducati for that. Now Vincents are anywhere from $15,000 to $35,000, depending upon model, history, and condition, and you can buy a Ducati 916, slightly used, for $14,000. You see the problem.

But none of this has stopped me from wanting one. I mentioned this life-long fascination to Editor David Edwards over dinner at Daytona this year (while showing him J. P. Bickerstaff's new book, *Original Vincent Motorcycle*, which now goes everywhere in my luggage or under my arm) and he asked, "Have you ever ridden one?"

"Yes," I replied. "Jay Leno kindly let me ride his Vincent Rapide about 10 years ago. We went to breakfast, riding up a winding canyon in the Hollywood hills to a café. It was a great experience, but we didn't really get out on the highway. I guess before I sell everything I own and shell out $15,000-plus for a motorcycle, I'd like to ride one for a full day on the road, spend a few hundred miles in the saddle."

David raised one eyebrow and said, "You know, I'll bet that could be arranged. We just did a story on the Rollie Free speed-record bike ("Return of a Warhorse," *CW*, January); it belongs to an avid Vincent collector named Herb Harris, in Austin, Texas. Herb has several Vincents, including a Shadow he rides on the street. He said if we ever wanted to come down to Texas and take a long ride out into the Hill Country, he'd love to have us visit."

I looked at David and grinned like a person showing off a new set of extremely white teeth.

"I'll call Herb and ask if we can do it. Probably have to wait until spring, when it's a little warmer and the bluebells are blooming in the Hill Country."

God, I love this job.

Austin, Texas, the green Hill Country, and Vincents. Three of my favorite things and places on Earth, all in one trip. As Jelly-Roll Morton used to shout while banging away on the piano, "Somebody shoot me while I'm happy!"

Nobody did, so a few months later my plane landed on a hot, sultry late-spring day in Austin, where I was met at the airport by a cheerful Herb Harris and his good friend and Vincent co-restorer, Stan Gillis. Herb owns a law firm in Austin, and Stan is a former Dallas banker who gave it up to restore motorcycles and work part-time for the law firm. *CW* photographer Jeff Allen flew in from California, we checked into a nearby hotel, and then drove to Herb's home in suburban Austin for a look at the bikes.

Herb has a nice brick home that is my idea of perfection—large garage and six motorcycles parked in the living room: three Vincents, a BSA Gold Star, and a Manx Norton, a testament to the good nature of his wife, Karen. The Rollie Free bike was being shown in England, but Herb has another famous racing Vincent in the living room, the 1949 Reg Dearden

Lightning, converted at the factory to use a Shorrock super-charger. I told Herb that if I had this room in my house, I would never go to bed. I'd just sit up all night long with a drink and look around.

The garage collection is not bad, either. Out there, he has a BMW R100RT, a 1927 Brough Superior 680, an immaculate 1965 Triumph Bonneville, an unrestored-looking 1936 Vincent HRD Comet Special 500 and—the object of our trip—a 1951 Series C Black Shadow, flawlessly restored.

And what a sight. All engine, set off with glistening black paint, gold-leaf trim, and stainless steel.

Philip Vincent and head engineer Phil Irving ("the two Phils") designed these bikes to use the engine as a stressed member. Like a modern Ducati 900SS, the triangulated swingarm pivots on huge bearings in the back of the unitized engine and transmission cases. Dual spring boxes and single hydraulic shock are up under the seat, where they push against the "UFM," or upper frame member. This is nothing but a long rectangular box that serves as the oil tank, bolted securely to the cylinder heads. There are also two friction dampers, tightenable with lovely knobs, attached to the seat stays.

The steering head bolts to the front of the UFM. Front forks are girder-type "Girdraulics" with long spring boxes behind them and a single hydraulic shock behind the headlight.

In other words, you essentially have the front and rear suspension bolted to a great big V-Twin engine, with a little help from the oil tank. Add seat and gas tank, and there's your bike. Brilliant and simple.

But the mechanical detail of the bike is anything but simple. The two Phils made everything adjustable—or "infinitely maladjustable," as Stan points out. There are tommybars and knobs everywhere. Wheels can be removed, like those of a racing bicycle, without tools, and all the footrests and levers can be adjusted to fit the rider or passenger.

The engine itself is notable for several innovations. It had a) unit construction when most bikes did not and b) rocker shafts that operate on collars on the centers of the valve stems, rather than on top, with separate upper and lower valve guides. This allows shorter pushrods for less reciprocating weight, shortens overall engine height, and keeps the valve springs high and cool in the heads. It also lowers the rocking friction of the valves against their guides.

Vincent called this a "semi-overhead cam" engine, which is something of a stretch, as a thing is either overhead or it isn't, and these aren't. But it's a clever design.

The angle between the cylinders is 50 degrees, and the heads are hemispherical, with two valves each. A magneto handles the sparks and a Miller generator powers the lighting current. And above the headlight sits one of the most famous talismans in all motorcycling, the gigantic 5-inch "Shadow clock," a 150-mile-per-hour Smiths speedometer made especially for the Black Shadow. It's the size of a saucepan—which, in fact, was exactly what the early speedos were made from. Cookwear never looked so good. Or went so fast.

I ask Herb if the bike needed much work when he bought it.

He nods wearily.

"The engine had supposedly been 'professionally rebuilt,' but it had many latent problems and needed to be rebuilt from the crankpin out. We sent it out to Dick Busby, a Vincent specialist in Culver City, California, who does all our engine work now, working with Haig Altounian. Mike Parti did the crank. We started calling Busby 'Bad News Dick,' because every time he called he had bad news about the engine: 'Your timing gears look like they've been under water for three years!' That king of thing."

Gradually, it got done, though. The tank was repainted by Wayne Griffith in Los Angeles, and the original "loaf of bread" seat was restored to neat tautness by Michael Maestas in Sylmar, California. Herb and Stan did most of the assembly.

The Shadow, Herb says, was originally sold to Indian Sales Corp., USA (chassis number 5708), shipped in December of 1950 and sold in 1951. Its ownership lineage was lost after that, but Herb bought it in 1995 from a collector in Dallas. "He got rid of it when it spit him off," Herb says. "He went through a puddle that turned out to be more than a puddle. It was three feet deep. The bike somersaulted and bent the front wheel, but there was no other real damage. Those forks are made of forged-aluminum alloy, manufactured for Vincent by the Bristol Aircraft Company, and they are extremely strong."

"We restored it to pretty original and stock specifications," Stan says, adding that the only non-standard touches are 8.5:1 "Kempalloid" pistons, replacing the original 7.3:1 pistons, and a 21-inch front tire from a Lightning rather than the stock 20-incher. Also, it has a Ducati 900SS dry clutch, from the current generation.

I pull in the lever, which feels about like my Ducati's. "Is this an easier clutch to operate?" I ask.

"No, the stock one actually has a lighter pull and is nicer to use, but the Ducati clutch is easier to clean if the engine breathes oil on it through the bearing seals, which occasionally happens," explains Stan.

So, riding would come in the morning, but first dinner.

Herb and Stan took us out to the Oasis, a great Tex-Mex restaurant built on a series of porches overlooking Lake Travis, like a big treehouse 1,000 feet above the lake. Over dinner, I learned that Stan and Herb have been riding since high school and, between them, have owned, restored, broken, or patched up just about every motorcycle ever made: BMWs, BSAs, Ducatis, Harleys, Hondas, Kawasakis, Laverdas, Nortons, Triumphs, etc. Motorcycle guys of wide focus, lifelong and hopeless, which we now know to be the best kind of person. They've got the disease.

In the morning we had a Mexican breakfast at the famous Cisco's Café in east Austin, under paintings of Willie Nelson and Texas humorist Hondo Crouch, of Luckenbach fame, then headed back to Herb's garage.

I put on my jacket, got my helmet ready, and Herb gave me the cold-starting drill:

1. Turn on fuel tap—or both of them, if you plan to go 70 miles per hour or more.
2. Tickle front carb float chamber for 3 seconds.
3. Tickle rear chamber briefly, just until it admits fuel.
4. Kick engine over with compression release in.
5. Say small prayer.
6. Pull in compression release and kick firmly, releasing lever halfway through stroke.
7. Repeat again and again. (The bike tries to start on first kick, and actually lights off and runs on Herb's fourth kick.)
8. Open oil cap in center of tank and see that oil is returning. If it is, you are ready to ride.

Herb warns me it takes a while—at least 15 miles of riding—for the engine oil to be really warm, so the first few miles should be moderate.

I straddle the Shadow and listen to the engine's deep, steady idle. It's remarkably free of rattles and gear noise, yet I have read that Vincent Twins normally sound like "a gas stove being dragged over cobblestones" at idle.

"They all come out different," Stan tells me, "no matter how you build them. This one is quiet. Dick did a nice job, shimming everything."

I pull in the Ducati dry clutch (which, inexplicably, doesn't rattle as it does on my 900SS), click the right-side gear lever firmly up for the first of four gears in the famously stout Vincent-made box, and we are off. Herb is leading on his BMW R100RT, and Jeff, Stan, and Herb's son Brian follow us in a minivan.

As soon as we are rolling on the highway, memories of Leno's bike come back to me. You sit close to the tank on the Vincent, with a short reach to the semi-flat bars. The bars, pegs, and controls are set up for Herb, who is 6-foot-4, but they fit me (6'1") exactly right. This is just about the ideal sportriding position for me, similar in layout to a 400F Honda or Ducati Monster. It is what I call the "alert Airedale" riding position—canted forward slightly onto moderately narrow, flat bars, feet just slightly back, head up.

A car pulls out on the highway in front of us and I get my first real surprise from the Vincent: The brakes work. Light, two-fingered pressure on the front lever hauls it down fast from 70 to 45 miles per hour, though the rear drum is only fair. The front brakes feel almost modern, unless you have a really long, howling stop on the highway, and then they begin to fade a bit at the very end of the stop. In any case, they are vastly better than any of the mid-1960s drum-braked Triumphs I've owned.

Handling, too, is surprisingly modern: Quick in slow corners, with a very slight tendency to fall into really slow turns (just above walking speed, as in a parking lot), and dead stable in fast sweepers, without a sign of headshake or fork deflection over bumps.

The bike loves to tick along at 70-80 miles per hour in an effortless all-day canter. I've heard so much about Vincents with a "hinge in the middle" that I'm ready for anything, but there's no hinge anywhere on this bike. It's solid as a brick, unfazed by switchbacks, dips, roller-coaster hilltops, and fast sweepers of bumpy mid-speed corners. Not a bobble all day, and this is surprise number two. It is, honestly, one of the nicest-handling bikes I've ridden, neutral and instinctive on turn-in and lean. Grip is good, too, with the 21-inch Avon Speedmaster II front and 19-inch Avon Super Venom rear tires.

In both acceleration and handling, it's eerily close to the 1979 Guzzi 1000SP I recently bought, but lighter on the bars and a little more exciting and sharp in its upper-end rush. The road-feel also reminds me somewhat of a Ducati 750GT; it's got that same easy gait, but with a shorter and more nimble chassis. Performance is far from eyeball-flattening, but the engine pulls hard from almost any rpm and builds speed quickly. There's no tach, and little temptation to buzz the muscular Twin—peak power occurs at 5,700 rpm—even though it's quite smooth at the upper end.

Sound from the engine is a rich, full thunder, but mellow and never headache-loud. It's a lot quieter than the twin Contis on my old bevel-drive 900SS Ducati. The exhaust note is satisfying, but not quite comparable to anything else. You can't say it's like a Harley or a Ducati; as Stan says, it just sounds like a Vincent.

We stop at the little village of Driftwood to pose the bike in front of an old general store that is now a working silversmith's shop. Texas flag flying, old gas pump out front. I lean on a porch pillar to get my picture taken next to the bike and say, "How is a Vincent owner supposed to stand?"

Herb shouts, "Look superior!"

Next we head for Lime Creek Road, Austin's version of the Angeles Crest Highway, a wonderful winding river road full of dips, ess-bends, and whoop-dee-doo rises. Great fun. The Vincent actually runs up the back of the BMW in many corners, even though Herb is riding fast and smoothly. The Vincent is simply lighter, lower, and easier to manage. It doesn't have to be wrestled as much as the tall, fairing-equipped BMW.

Ride? The forks and rear suspension are remarkably supple over small bumps, but they can deliver a pretty good jolt to the spine in a large dip or pothole because there's not much travel. Over the rough stuff, you learn to ride in the equestrian mode, standing up slightly in the stirrups and light in the saddle.

Vincent and Irving hated telescopic forks because of their inherent stiction and brake dive, and insisted on girder forks after most others had abandoned them. On these roads, the men are largely vindicated in their shared opinion. Only the most recent telescopic forks (and BMW's Telelever suspension) feel as responsive over minor, pattering bumps or as settled under braking.

We turn out onto a long, empty stretch of road and Herb hustles the BMW up to about 80 miles per hour. I stay with him easily on the Vincent and then decide to open it up and pass. I hammer forward to 95 miles per hour and breeze past, still accelerating steadily before I have to shut it off for a blind hill. There's lots left at 95, but I decide that's fast enough on a hot Texas afternoon (102 degrees) with a 47-year-old British classic that doesn't belong to me.

Herb is laughing when we stop at a gas station for cold drinks. "What a wonderful sound that thing makes going by at speed! I never get to hear it from another bike!"

It amazes me how easy the Vincent is to ride in the company of a relatively modern, big-bore motorcycle. Other than high maintenance and the archaic (but useful) rear stand, there's no real penalty for the bike's 50-year-old design.

Over lunch (okay, candy bars and Gatorade) I tell Herb and Stan I've been reading for years what evil handlers Vincents are supposed to be, how non-existent their brakes, how disappointing their supposedly legendary performance, etc. It's become practically a journalistic convention to ride Vincents and then try to take them down a notch, to destroy the myth. "It's obviously not a Honda CBR900RR or a Yamaha R1 in performance, but it's certainly a magnificent bike by any standard," says Stan. "And, for its age, it's spectacular."

"A lot of people want to hate Vincents," Herb says "In fact they love to hate Vincents. I guess the bikes were on a pedestal for so long, and so few people actually owned and rode them, that it was comforting to believe they weren't all that good."

"You have to remember, too," Stan adds, "that the Vincent is a very complex bike, and if you work on one and don't know what you're doing, you can really mess it up. A badly assembled Vincent is a disaster."

"Handling is absolutely no problem," Herb says, "if the swingarm pre-load is correct and you keep the tire pressures right. Also, you can't have the front end adjusted to its side-car position, which a surprising number of people have done by accident. You have to get everything right, and then they're really nice to ride."

Stan grins and adds, "We've developed a saying while restoring Vincents: 'These bikes are monuments to unlimited funds, talent and perseverance.' You can get them right, but it does take dedication."

At the end of the day, when we rumble back into Herb's driveway, we've covered just over 200 miles of hard riding on a very hot day. In that time, the only problem was a shift lever that loosened lightly on its shaft, and that was quickly snugged up with a wrench. Also, the clutch got just a bit grabby when I turned around (over and over again) in the road for photos. I killed the engine twice while maneuvering, but both times started it with a single kick. Otherwise, the bike had been flawless.

Back in the dark air-conditioned coolness of Herb's living room/museum, we finish off the afternoon talking about the bikes. I put a question to Herb, one that has been much on my mind.

"It seems to me there are an awful lot of disaster stories out there about Vincents with engine trouble, like the problems your own bike had when you bought it. We know that Vincents are *great* motorcycles, in the sense of being legendary, but do you think they are *good* motorcycles? Are they honest?"

Herb nods, as if he's heard the question before.

"I think they are. The Vincent repays your efforts, and that makes it honest. And I like the special reward that comes from owning such a bike. Vincent achieved great things; it was on the absolute edge of the performance envelope, the highest performance of the post-war era.

"Also," he adds, "the materials used throughout the bike are absolutely first-rate. They used the best of everything they could find and cut no corners on quality. Every piece on the bike is nicely designed and beautifully made out of superior materials."

"No disillusionment after restoring these Vincents?"

Herb Harris smiles and shakes his head. "No. I'm always testing romance against the reality with motorcycles, and with Vincents the spell has not been broken."

Nor for me. I still want one.

October 1998

ANCIENT ITALY, NEW DUCATI

What Better Way to Venture Forth into the Alps Than on a Lotus Tour with Ducati's New 900SS?

Two of my favorite things in life are Italy and Ducatis. I have two Ducatis, so all that remains is to figure out how to spend more time in Italy.

Riding through the Alps a few years ago, our intrepid group of thirsty sportbike riders stopped at a scenic little outdoor café in St. Moritz. The place looked inviting not only because the sun was shining down warmly upon its many Campari umbrellas, but because there were at least a dozen Ducati 916s parked nearby and the tables were crowded with people in full riding leathers. Our kind of place.

We sat down, ordered our usual non-alcoholic-hyper-alertness beverages (any variety of concentrated Italian coffee that is less than 4 percent water) and soon discovered that our fellow motorcyclists were American. "I'm Burt Richmond of Lotus Tours," a friendly, bearded gentleman said, extending his hand, "from Chicago."

Chatting with Burt, I learned he was the official Ducati agent for Americans who take overseas delivery of their bikes. "We pick them up at the factory in Bologna," he explained, "take a one-week ride through northern Italy and the Alps, and then ship the bikes back to the U.S., to the new owner's nearest Ducati dealership. You ought to come on one of our tours," he said, grinning. "We have a lot of fun."

I've kept in touch with Burt (who keeps a warehouse-sized collection/museum of bikes in downtown Chicago), and this summer finally found the time and incentive to take him up on his offer. He called me up and said, "If you come along on our northern Italy tour next month, the Ducati factory will loan you a bike to ride—the new 900SS."

As a person who has owned three of the old bevel-drive 900SS models (one of which I still have) and two of the new generation 900SSs, the allure of trying out the third iteration of this famous line was as irresistible as a plate of *lingua bollito* served by, say, Isabella Rossellini. Having some sort of vested interest in the progress of the 900SS family, I was duty-bound and genetically programmed to go.

Bologna is a lovely city from the air, with an ancient walled center of red-tiled roofs on cathedrals and towers separated by narrow streets and broad plazas. The more modern neighborhoods spread outward along the main roads, like spokes on a wheel. The Ducati factory is in *Borgo Panigale*, an industrial district just southwest of the city.

Our group of 11, arriving at different times and airports, bussed or cabbed into central Bologna to the Hotel Orlogio (Clock Hotel) and went out for a late dinner at a nearby restaurant. Interesting group: a mixture of experienced riders with long Ducati ownership history, and a few others new to either Ducati, street riding, or both. Ducati, like Harley, seem to have done a good job of drawing new recruits into the web of its legend.

All males, this time. A father-and-son duo, Jim and "Bingo" Gubelmann from New Jersey, the latter taking the trip as a high school graduation present. Jim runs a vintage racing team called "Tropical Gangsters" for a hobby, and used to race Triumphs himself. His nephew, Wyeth Gubelmann, will join us later in the tour.

Two dentist riding buddies from Marin County, California, Serge Glasunov and Ai (actual name) "Streak" Streaker, both with 916s at home, riding rented bikes, a new 900SS and an ST2. Two guys, an affable investment banker from Chicago named Jamie Adler and a pipe manufacturer from Florida named Billy Fine, both on ST2s, having their first-ever Ducati rides.

Lotus Tours (1634 N. Sedgwick, Chicago, IL 60614; 312/951- 0031) likes to sell you a bike for factory pickup, but the company can also arrange rentals from a Bologna agency. As a third alternative, you can buy a Ducati in Italy and then leave it in Europe, at Lotus' Nice, France, headquarters, where it will be stored and maintained, at a cost of $420 per year, poised for your occasional use. One of the members of our tour, an executive from Connecticut named Perry Lewis, does just that.

If you don't buy a new Ducati, the cost of a Lotus tour is $4,575 for an eight-day trip on the least expensive rental bike, a BMW F650, with an extra $400 charged for a private, unshared room. Upgrades in rental bikes cost $154 for a BMW R850R, $157 for a Ducati Monster 600, $309 for a 900SS, and $452 for an ST2 (Ducati 916s and 748s are not rented; body damage is too expensive if they fall down).

Buying a bike (sold at suggested manufacturer's retail), rather than renting, saves you $600 off the price of the tour. Crating and shipping back to the States is free, but you pay setup and delivery fees at the dealership, as well as the usual state taxes and licensing.

In other words, basic cost of the tour with a shared, two-person room if you buy a Ducati is $3,995. If you elect to rent an ST2, for instance, and have a private room, it can cost as much as $5,439. Breakfasts and dinners are paid for; you buy your own drinks, gasoline, and lunches.

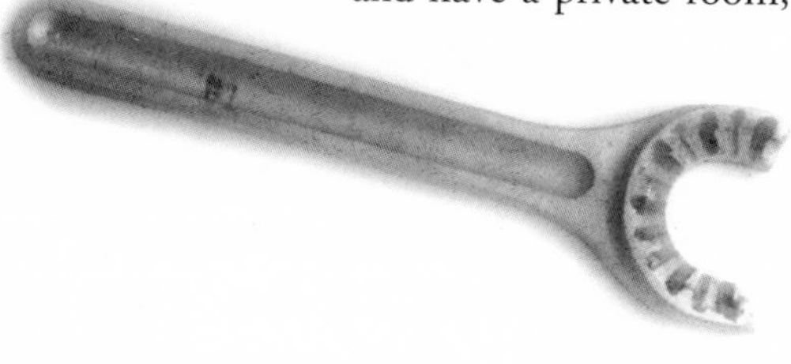

As guided tours go, Lotus is among the most expensive, but Richmond is unapologetic. He likes good food and good hotels, and likes to travel with people who are willing to pay a little extra for first-rate accommodations. Which, as I would soon discover, we would surely have.

Friday of our trip was what I call a "transport day," picking up the bikes and hitting the autostrada to get out of the city and within next-day striking distance of the Alps. While waiting for some of our bikes to be readied, we took a tour of the brand-new Ducati Museum, which is a truly impressive display of all the important factory racing bikes, set in a huge, circular room with a helmet-shaped auditorium in the center. The great Singles, the Paul Smart Imola 750SS, one of the Hailwood Isle of Man bikes, the latest generation of World Superbike champions—they're all there, beautifully lighted and displayed.

There's also a gift shop, where you can buy way too many stickers, posters, and T-shirts, which you will have to carry around for the rest of the week—or at least store on the Lotus Tours baggage van, which follows the group, cheerfully absorbing our excesses.

Late in the afternoon, factory workers brought my new yellow 900SS around from the prep area, and we were on our way, headed north to our hotel in Bassano de Grappa.

Initial impressions, in the parking lot and on the road:

First, the styling. The elegant and classical simplicity of the old 900SS has given way to a more aggressively styled set of body panels, with more swoop and fluidity of line, overtones of the Supermono. Part of the lower fairing is rounded outward to cover two new air ducts that feed air to the cooling fins of the rear cylinder. The bottom of the fairing features a flamboyant, forward-thrusting tusk with shark-gill louvers.

People seem to either love the new body or hate it. I told Ducati Marketing Director Andrew Whitney that I personally know six owners of the old 900SS, none of whom is thinking of buying a new one because they like the looks of the old one better. He said the new design may appeal to a different group of buyers and, in any case, Ducati is swamped with orders for the new bikes, based only on early photographs released to the European press. He also said, "Ride the bike and live with it a while before you make up your mind."

And ride we did. My first long, fast run up the autostrada left me with mixed impressions. Gone is the relaxed, all-day GT-bike seating and handlebar position of the old 900SS. The clip-on bars have been dropped a good two inches and are farther forward, putting the rider into an uncompromising race-bike position. After 45 minutes on the four-lane, my hands and wrists were asleep from carrying the full weight of my upper body, and my neck had a crick in it. On the plus side, the seat is significantly more comfortable than the old one (which had to be replaced instantly with a Corbin product), and suspension compliance is much improved.

The steel-tube trellis frame under the new bodywork doesn't look much different, but subtle and useful changes have been made. Wheelbase has been reduced to 54.9 inches from 55.5, rake angle has been steepened 1 degree, trail reduced .1-inch, sharing its dimensions and design with the 916.

At the rear, the single Showa shock now has a longer stroke, and is set up with more sag to give the rear tire a better "reach" under heavy braking and weight transfer. On the road, both ends of the bike feel less stiff and jittery, more compliant over bumps, and better planted in corners, more civilized in general.

Another immediate and obvious improvement is a new front master cylinder with a different bore ratio. Instead of that slightly vague, crush-your-own-fingers gooshiness of the old 900SS, the new one feels, well, normal (at last!), with excellent sensitivity at the lever and superb stopping power. The new-generation Brembo calipers and rotors, shared with the ST2 and 916, have wider mounting points for more stiffness, higher polish on the pistons for freer movement, and revised hydraulic channels. Big improvement.

By the time we got to our hotel in Mussolente (which everyone naturally called "Mussolini," beginning our "mispronunciation of the day" tradition), I was pretty pleased with everything except the bike's riding position. The next day, ascending into the spectacular white stone spires of the Dolomites, would tell. Into the curvy stuff.

Ever upward we climbed into cooler, cloudier weather on serpentine roads into the mountains, with small glaciers perched in the cols and valleys. Amazingly smooth pavement, switchbacks, fast uphill sweepers, and Alpine vistas ever opening before you like the architecture of a vast and mighty Creation. Americans tend to remember the Alps as a small, compact geographic zone, compressed by memory into a sort of Disneyland riding park. But they aren't small. They are mighty mountains, and they seem to go on forever.

Whenever I ride elsewhere—California, New England, the Blue Ridge, and so on—I tell myself, "This is just as good as the Alps." Sometimes it is, but only for a few minutes or a few hours at a time. The Alps go on and on, all day, and for days thereafter. Weeks, if you wish. The scenery and roads are simply too grand to comprehend with a small human brain—or at least with my small human brain. Others may have better luck.

I ended up riding mostly with Serge and Streak, our two dentist pals from California, and they were both fast, smooth riders, the kind who keep your antennae humming, eyes wide open, and your standards up. Perry Lewis, another fine rider, joined us on a few days, and so did young Bingo Gubelmann, who had never ridden on the street before this trip but was growing smoother and faster, showing remarkably good judgment in traffic. Ah, the adaptability of youth.

There in the mountains, pressing on quickly, the new 900SS came into its own. Simply stated, it's a much better sportbike than its predecessor. It turns in easier and more quickly, soaks up bumps better, brakes harder with more control, can be trail-braked into a corner with less upset, and changes direction faster. Essentially, it feels about 20 percent improved in every functional category. The 900SS has been, in effect, more "Honda-ized" in a positive sense. It feels more refined, smoother of touch, less stiff-legged and harsh.

Even the riding position, which is so awful on the open road, comes into its own in the mountains. The weight shifts and body motion of fast riding takes the strain (and your mind) off your hands and wrists, and the bike becomes a useful tool for disposing of corners effortlessly.

Part of the 900SS's smoother personality comes from its new Marelli fuel injection, replacing the twin 38mm Mikunis, and a few other engine modifications. It has new cams with longer duration, a redesigned shift drum, and a higher output alternator (520 watt vs. the old 350 watt). Peak horsepower arrives at 7,800 rpm, 800 higher than before, and there's more of it.

Torque delivery is more seamless, with a little less sense of upper midrange rush, but the biggest and most helpful change is a smoother running engine at low rpm — as when cruising through a village or riding around town. The old bike was always a little unhappy and lumpy below 4,000 rpm, chugging and chinking along as if loading and unloading its drivechain in stops and starts. The new one is smooth and tractable at low rpm, almost like an inboard marine engine by comparison, burbling serenely away beneath you. The exhaust note is somewhat subdued but it sounds better to me than the stock pipes on the old bike, less like a lawnmower, with more fullness and mellowness of tone.

At one point on our trip, we stopped at a café a few thousand feet below Bernina Pass, and I parked my low 900SS next to an older, white-framed 900SS like the one I used to own. The owner, a Swiss rider, asked (using his English-speaking girlfriend as a translator) if he might take a ride on the new bike.

"Sure," I said, "if I can take a ride on yours." So we traded bikes and headed up to the pass. The instant contrast took away a little of my rosecolored nostalgia for my old bike; the early 900SS was more comfortable and (I still believe) more beautiful, but nowhere near as quick and agile—or as effortless to ride—on the demanding mountain roads. I was suddenly quite content to be on the new bike for the remainder of the trip.

The Swiss rider came back ecstatic and said, according to his girlfriend, "Super! Better for the sportriding!" He was right, of course. All the changes have made the new 900SS an almost ideal Alpine companion, flowing along the mountain road, blasting past the occasional tour bus, or cruising through the picture-postcard villages of the Tyrol. Of which we did plenty.

Burt Richmond does not mess around when he designs a route, and we hit virtually every major pass in the Alps: Timmelsjoch Pass, Stelvio, and Bernina, plus a trip over the famous Grossglockner Pass in which we felt our way along in the fog and missed seeing the Grossglockner glacier, mistaking it for a different one. Ignorance is bliss.

Lotus Tours also delivers on its promise of better hotels for the extra expense, and they got better and better as the trip progressed. We stayed at a fifteenth-century castle at Kitzbuhel, the spectacular Castle Labers in the wine country around Merano, and then a final descent out of Switzerland back into Italy, down to the shores of Lago de Garda, where we stayed at the famous Villa Cortine Palace Hotel (which really is a palace) out on the tip of a peninsula at Sirmione.

To reach this hotel, we had to cross bridges over two different moats, the latter with a genuine drawbridge, iron gate, and tower for pouring down hot oil upon invaders (perhaps an all-season 10W-50). I told Burt, who has had his Chicago dwellings twice burgled, he should take note. "We're coming to this in American cities," I explained. "The moat and drawbridge are the wave of the future."

Food? It's hard to get a bad meal in Italy, and we never succeeded in finding one. Even the Austrians and the Swiss prepared wonderful dinners for us in sumptuous surroundings. Management of trip details and minor problems was also excellent. Richmond is one of those born tour leaders; he can keep 30 facts in his head simultaneously, successfully operate telephones in three languages, tell jokes, stay calm, arrange flights, gently twist the arms of hotel managers when need be, and ride his faithful yellow 907ie as fast or slow as anyone on the tour cares to go. He was assisted in all this by the equally capable David Hessel, who swapped luggage-van driving duties with Burt every other day and also photographed our trip.

And, as usual, we had a great bunch of guys to travel with. I looked around the table at our typically hilarious farewell dinner and thought of that old saying about the pioneers and cowboys who settled the Old West: "The faint of heart never left, and the fools perished along the way."

Motorcycle tours have a little of that same filtration process built into them. Only folks with a sense of adventure and the ability to keep it on two wheels for a week ever sign up for these trips, and they are by nature a lively bunch.

One rider in our group, Billy Fine, the owner of a small pipe manufacturing plant in St. Petersburg, had never ridden a Ducati before, never been to Italy, and had only ridden a Yamaha XT350 on the street. Yet he found a Ducati dealer ("all my friends had Harleys, but I wanted something different"), signed up for European delivery of a silver ST2, bought himself an airline ticket to Italy, and took an Italian cab to our hotel in downtown Bologna. He loved the bike, rode well, and had the time of his life. Not, in other words, among the faint of heart who never left. It's these impulses, acted upon, that make such trips fun.

And, in conclusion, the new 900SS? Nine steps forward and two steps back, is how I would characterize it. The bike's styling did not grow on me much as the week progressed, nor did its more severe riding position on the first and last long days of autostrada disposal. The classic Grand Touring character of the old bike is gone. But in its place is a real sportbike whose sporting function has been improved in almost every way. Its revised chassis and engine are living proof that time marches on, and after nearly a decade of the old 900SS, it was time to refine the old girl.

Ducati perhaps believes—or hopes—the new ST2 sport-tourer will draw those riders who hope to cover long miles on a Ducati, freeing the new 900SS to concentrate on twisting roads and shorter rides, bringing it more in line with the latest generation of Japanese and European sport bikes. This may be a smart move. Time will tell.

June 2000

SIDECAR IN BAJA

Riding an Old-Time Idea into the Land that Time Forgot

This is the only trip where I've left with a human for a passenger and returned with a dog.

"The best thing about Baja," photographer Jeff Allen said just before our trip, "is that the U.S. doesn't own it. Otherwise, it would be ruined."

Not everyone who visits this half-wild 1,000-mile peninsula appended to the bottom of California *norte* would agree. But I do. I know exactly what he means.

When you cruise down the freeways of Southern California, it sometimes seems our culture has evolved into nothing more than an opportunity to shop. You pass hundreds of car dealerships, chain restaurants, and malls, repeated every few miles like microchips on a computer board. There's a growing sameness that numbs the mind. Mine, anyway.

South of the border, things are different.

Predictability falls away and you re-enter an older version of the world in which life is a place where anything can happen. Architecture seems to have been built without the benefit of a straight edge, cars have more dents, and street-smart dogs trot along and cross the highway. (Some fail.) No restaurant looks like any other, and the food seems homemade. There's dust and smoke in the air and the sunlight looks different, like a memory of the Old West on fading Kodachrome.

Personally, I love the place. I first explored Baja, California, almost 20 years ago, on a series of off-road motorcycle trips. Wanting to see more, I took a three-week Jeep trip in 1986 with my buddy Pat Donnelly, driving a CJ-7 all the way to the tip of Baja on dirt roads and trails. We camped in open army cots under the stars and drank tequila around campfires on balmy desert nights.

After that, I took my wife, Barbara, down to explore Baja in the same spirit that you introduce two good friends who have never met, and we camped at the El Marmol ghost town built around an old onyx mine. All good times, but I hadn't been back for 10 years.

So when Beau Pacheco, former editor of *Big Twin*, now heading up Harley content for *Cycle World*'s special-publications department, called me in the depths of February and asked if I would like to get out of the Wisconsin winter for a week and ride a new Harley with a sidecar down into Baja, I almost laughed out loud at the sheer musicality of those words: "Harley" . . . "Sidecar" . . . "Baja."

He might have thrown "margaritas" and "sunshine" and "enchiladas" in there, but he didn't have to. Some things are implied.

One word that did catch me a little off-guard, however, was *sidecar*.

When Beau phoned, I had actually been in the act of examining the new 2000 Harley-Davidson sales brochure, which shows an FLHTCUI Ultra Classic with Sidecar, complete, as part of the current product line. Price? A heady $30,000.

It looked like fun, but my experience in driving one of these rigs was pretty limited. I'd driven one briefly about 18 years ago—just long enough to find out how weird they can be when you have no idea what you're doing. And to learn they handle better with some weight in the car.

"Will anyone be riding with me?" I asked.

"My son Travis, who's a captain in the Air Force, is on leave right now and he'd like to go along. Jeff Allen and I will take the company van down with all Jeff's camera equipment and meet you guys along the way for pictures. Travis speaks fluent Spanish. Also, he fits in the sidecar better than I do."

Perfect.

A week later I was standing at the *CW* office in Newport Beach, helmet in hand, at 4:30 A.M. I shook hands with Travis, a friendly, easygoing guy (always a plus around amateur sidecar pilots), and asked if he would mind letting me do the first leg of the trip alone. The idea was that if I survived all the way to El Rosario without killing myself—or others—I would then be unofficially qualified to "give rides."

Travis didn't seem to mind this suggestion at all. So with my duffel bag and a few gallons of drinking water in the sidecar for ballast, we lurched and weaved onto the road early on a foggy, misty morning.

A sidecar, of course, is not like any other vehicle. It doesn't—as some have suggested—exist halfway between a motorcycle and a car; it's simply a Third Way. It lacks all the saving dynamic virtues of both bikes and cars, so driving one ("riding" seems an inadequate verb) is an art form unto itself.

In right turns, the car feels as though it wants to lift and flip over on you, while the motorcycle itself leans and groans vertiginously outward in defiance of all sound motorcycling instinct. In left turns . . . well, it doesn't want to turn left. It prefers to go straight and can be made to change its mind only through brute force on the handlebars. Until you get used to it, both motions set off primitive alarm bells in your brain that Something Is Going Wrong, inducing the occasional cold sweat.

In straight-line cruising, inertia and wind want to hold the car back, so you have to keep a steady pressure on the right bar to hold it straight. In hard downhill braking, the car wants to circle the bike, unless you use plenty of rear brake—which, on the Harley, is linked to a nicely effective disc brake on the outer wheel of the car.

In other words, it's more work than riding a motorcycle. But once you get used to the rig, you begin to relax and it becomes fun. It's simply a unique and refined skill, like flying an airplane, or playing the dulcimer with a sledgehammer.

After a sunrise blast through the growing commuter traffic of San Diego, we were waved through the border station into Tijuana, town of tacky hillside dwellings and business signs in lively Aztec shades of purple and yellow and red. We swung along the coast and took the *cuota*, or toll road, down toward Ensenada, the excellent four-lane highway following seacoast cliffs with spectacular views of the crashing surf.

We cruised through the port town of Ensenada, a favorite old weekend haunt for Barb and me when we lived in California. We'd come down to eat grilled garlic shrimp, have a few margaritas, and walk around at night in the sea breeze.

The first time we came here the thing that impressed me most was the dignified reserve of the merchants in the shops. In so many of the world's tourist marketplaces—Tangiers or New Delhi, for instance—people get in your face and haggle loud and hard. But Mexicans leave you alone until you decide to buy something and then they will, perhaps, bargain quietly. In Ensenada, it's generally the Americans who seem loud.

Once you get away from the turmoil of the border towns, there is an Old World politeness and modest serenity to the culture that forces you to slow down a bit yourself. It's one of the reasons I like Baja. People are calm and friendly. Even the children are nice.

South of Ensenada you climb into the spine of mountains that defines the whole peninsula and then descend into a valley of agricultural towns—Santo Tomas, Colonet, Camalu—sprawled along the highway in strips. These are not tourist places, but hard-working towns that smell like diesel and herbicides, with trash scattered everywhere.

In America, we tend to gather all our trash in one place and then bury it. In this part of Mexico they produce much less trash, but they prefer to spread it out in a wide grid, so there is at least one empty bleach bottle, beer can, or plastic bag about every 6 inches. It's all a part of what Jeff Allen calls the STDP, or "Strategic Trash Distribution Program."

But as you head south in Baja, the towns seem to get neater, cleaner, and more charming, and by the time you get to El Rosario, 217 miles south of the border, things are looking good.

We got fuel in El Rosario at a Pemex station, at 22 pesos (about $2) per gallon. Some stations have both 93- and 87-octane unleaded, but most have just the 87, which is not exactly rocket fuel. It is, in fact, a carefully formulated mixture of dishwater and special knock enhancers. Within minutes, my Ultra Glide was pinging like a steel-drum band I once heard in Jamaica. I had to go light on the throttle and shift down a gear to keep it happy, especially on hills—and with a passenger.

Yes, having survived 200 miles of freeway and mountain roads without hitting armco or oncoming trucks, the Reign of Terror was apparently over and the sidecar was open for business. I moved all baggage to the saddlebags and Travis folded himself into the sidecar—a reasonably comfortable press fit.

Travis was heavier than my luggage, so the car handled better in right turns, but wanted to understeer a little more turning left. Otherwise there wasn't much change, except for added uphill pinging.

And there were plenty of hills. South of El Rosario, the road cuts inland, winding through the heart of the central mountains and into some of the most beautiful and surreal landscape on Earth. It's a 100-mile-long band of genuine Sonoran desert strewn with huge boulders, giant saguaro cactus, and the magical "Boojum" trees of Baja.

Known to the locals as *cirio* (or candle) trees, these strange plants look like colossal inverted carrots, with a single small flower on the tip, like the bow in Zippy's hair. Assuming fantastic shapes, they can grow to be 20 feet tall or more, and they exist nowhere else on the planet. A Baja trademark.

When you camp here at night, the Boojum trees actually seem to move in the moonlight, taking small steps toward your campfire. No paranoia in my family.

Despite the poor gas, the Harley Twin Cam 88 did remarkably well at hauling a loaded sidecar through the central mountains—better than the Evo motor on my old Road King would have done. The Twin Cammer revs smoothly to its 5,500-rpm redline, so you can lean on it a little bit when you want to move out into traffic, or pass a truck before an uphill curve. It's not scintillating, but just fast enough.

In truth, the sidecar has a strange "retro-izing" effect on the Electra Glide. The side forces add a few creaks, groans, and rattles that Harleys haven't had for years, and also slow the bike down to about late-Shovelhead performance levels. Add a little more transmission clunkiness from the sidecar load and the Ultra Glide seems almost backdated to the old FLH Heritage I rode up the coast in 1982. But somehow it all fits with the sidecar theme, an idea that comes to us more through a sense of nostalgia than cold logic.

With the sun setting, we gassed up at Guerrero Negro, then slanted southeast across high desert and dropped down into a sudden green valley that hides one of Baja's most charming old colonial towns, San Ignacio.

Built around a quiet, shaded square with a large and well-preserved mission church, the town is literally an oasis, a well-watered grove of palm and date trees that looks more like the Biblical Nile than the desert southwest.

We got in late, checking into a nice motel called La Pinta, with an interior courtyard built around a pool. There, we hooked up with Beau and Jeff, who had just arrived in the van. We were a little hungry (*i.e.*, starting to admire roadkill), but it was just after 9 P.M. and the hotel manager informed us that all the local restaurants were closed. "But wait," she said, "let me make one phone call."

Miraculously, a restaurant called Rice & Beans, just down the road, agreed to fire up its kitchen again for us and turn the lights back on. We had our best meal of the trip, while the owner, an upbeat entrepreneur named Ricardo Romo Cota, joined us.

Ricardo's hospitality turned us into loyal customers, and we ate nearly all our meals there for the next two days. Ricardo's fine margaritas didn't hurt our loyalty, either, and seemed to enhance our sense of cosmic oneness with the mild desert evenings.

We spent a day of rest and exploration in San Ignacio, touring the church, checking out the stores (full of real goods, not just souvenirs), and hiking around the hills near the town. We stood on a ridge overlooking the mission square and Jeff said, "Except for the occasional car or motorcycle that rolls through town, I'll bet this place doesn't look any different than it did 300 years ago."

Walking down to the shady plaza, we found Beau and Travis sitting on a park bench, smoking cigars and looking pensively at the mission church. Beau said, "This church was built in 1733 . . . think of the weddings . . . "

Nothing like a little dose of permanence to calm the mind and lower the heart rate. Time doesn't quite stand still in Baja, but you have the feeling here that clocks are ticking at a much slower rate than our own, and that eras somehow seamlessly overlap. Even now, Pancho Villa could come riding into San Ignacio on his own famous old Indian and nothing would look out of place.

Late that afternoon, we ended up giving local children rides around the square, their faces almost wild with joy. The same little girl and boy kept turning up over and over again for another ride. Funny, but we never would have done this in the U.S., not without the nervous parents standing by and giving permission. Lawsuits, you know. In small-town Mexico, the kids are still free to be children.

Before we left San Ignacio, Beau gave me a ride in the sidecar, so I could see what it was like. No wonder the kids didn't want to get out. If you can trust the person driving the motorcycle, a sidecar is the place to be. It's like a cross between a carnival ride and a low-flying biplane, but with a perspective on space and speed you never get from either. It's addicting.

The next morning, I came outside and found Beau in a heated argument with the hotel manager. Seems Beau had heard a dog crying piteously somewhere and discovered a wriggling cement sack in the back of a pickup truck. He untied the bag and found a small puppy inside with large paws and big, brown eyes.

It turned out the pup was about to be "disappeared" because there were too many stray dogs in the neighborhood. Beau told the manager what he thought of people who toss small dogs into rivers, and announced he would take the mutt home with him. Which he did.

This, Travis sagely pointed out, was the exact fulfillment of the term "lucky dog."

Before leaving, we had our mandatory dose of *huevos con chorizo* and then headed north on a sunny, windy day. Mileage had not been great, even under calm conditions (25 miles per gallon or so), and it sank to about 20 miles per gallon with a stiff headwind. With the Electra Glide's 5-gallon tank, I flat ran out of gas after 110 miles and coasted into a Pemex station with the engine sputtering to a stop.

By late afternoon we rolled into our motel at Catavina. This little town isn't much more than a few houses, a nice motel, and a closed-down gas station. We had to buy fuel from an enterprising old gent who was selling the stuff from 5-gallon jerrycans out of the back of his battered pickup, at a 50-cent markup.

Catavina may not be much of a town, but it's nestled in the most beautiful part of northern Baja, and the surrounding countryside looks like a vast rock garden of giant cacti and pure white desert sand. At night we took a desert moonlight cigar-smoking hike and found ourselves under the pure industrial-diamond black sky of Baja. You could clearly see the Milky Way, and about a thousand more stars than you can near the ambient light of civilization.

This brilliant display set off a deep discussion in which we all revealed how little we know about the constellations. Without the Big Dipper to lean on, we'd have been out of luck. The problem is, Orion's Belt doesn't mean much to us any more, as a visual symbol. What we need is a constellation called Sonny Barger's Panhead, or maybe Cassiopeia's Barcalounger. Something modern.

Our last day on the road, we motored north into growing clouds and patches of drizzle. The Ultra bat-wing fairing and lowers kept most of the moisture off, so I didn't have to break out the rainsuit. Travis reported weather protection in the sidecar was pretty good as well, except for a little wind buffeting at the sides of his head.

In Ensenada we found a vet who could give Beau's new dog the necessary shots and certificates, but he was still worried the U.S. Customs agents might take her away for some reason, or put her in quarantine. As a smuggling experiment, we tried putting the dog in the dark, carpeted baggage compartment behind the seat in the sidecar and starting the engine, just to see if she could relax in there. She immediately started yelping, quite audibly, over all the engine noise.

"It won't work," I told Beau. "They're gonna wonder why our sidecar is howling."

In the end, we needn't have worried. Traffic was backed up at the Tijuana border station for an hour, and the overloaded customs officials waved Beau and Jeff's van through without question, complete with dog. These poor guys had their hands full; the border is out of control.

It was early evening when we got back to the office in Newport Beach. The Harley was still running like a clock and much happier on American unleaded. It had been a long day in the saddle, but I wasn't really tired. Between the wide fairing, cushy seat, comfortable bars, and well-located floorboards, the Ultra Classic is, hands down, the most comfortable place I have ever spent four days seated.

Also, I'd gotten used to the sidecar. The learning curve was over; the tension was gone. By the time we got home, its presence was not much more novel than the right half of your car when you're driving. I still cornered a little slower, but I did it automatically rather than experimentally.

It got easy. And fun.

Also, you can drive off steep road shoulders or through sand and gravel without thinking about it, and you don't have to put your foot down when you stop. In slow traffic, that's more of a luxury than you'd think. You get spoiled.

I'd still rather ride a plain motorcycle, without sidecar, on most trips. But if I had any incentive to have one at all—a bum leg, extra kids, beer keg duty, a passenger who's not comfortable on the rear seat, etc.—I'd be perfectly happy to travel with a sidecar.

There's more to it than just roads and maps and reaching your destination. It's a kind of time travel, really.

Especially in Baja.

Section II

THE COLUMNS

February 1989

COMMON THREADS

Only a few weeks ago I introduced myself to a new neighbor on the block, a guy named Bill Dunlap. I have to confess that the main reason I walked up and talked to Bill was that he happened to have a 1974 Norton 850 Commando parked in front of his house. He came over to look at my Triumph, and naturally we got sitting around the garage, talking and having a few beers. In the course of conversation it turned out that in addition to a weakness for British bikes, we have other remarkable similarities in taste. It seems we are both blues fans—and own exactly the same models of electric guitars—and that we have also owned identical kinds of cars and are both fascinated with flying, and so on.

It would be almost eerie, except that it's happened before. When I met my friend Russ Lyon a few years ago, I discovered that, at the time, both our garages contained a Jaguar E-Type, a Ducati 900SS, and a Triumph Bonneville. When Russ and his wife Sandy invited Barb and me for dinner, I also found that their book collection was nearly an exact duplicate of our own. Furthermore, we had similar political outlooks and even went camping in the same part of the Anza-Borrego Desert every year. It was weird.

Since then, it's happened over and over again. I even get occasional letters from readers who seem to share my tastes (such as they are) so exactly that we could almost be linked together by common brain waves, like the identical-thinking children in *The Village of the Damned.* It seems to me there's some sort of Pythagorian logic at work here: If you like A and B, then it follows that you must also like C and D, but not necessarily X and

Y. The common root here (A), seems to be British bikes. They are the acid test, and the key to the whole syndrome.

If you really like motorcycles from England, you belong to a kind of separate race, a splinter society of individuals who may look and talk almost like normal humans, but were, for all we know, put here by aliens to colonize the planet for some yet undisclosed purpose. Perhaps to increase intergalactic sales of Oil-Dri. Maybe we arrived in pods, like the humanoids in *The Invasion of the Body Snatchers*. Maybe our mothers were frightened by Clydesdales. Who knows. The important thing is, we're here.

The sad part is, there are probably people out there who are honest-to-God British bike buffs and don't even know it yet. They may just be getting started in motorcycling and haven't learned the real truth about themselves. Still, the Force is with them, latent though it may be.

To help those people discover whether or not they are destined to mature into real British bike fanatics, I've put together the following psychological exam, based on years of personal research and nearly six weeks spent in Psych 101 before I dropped the course like a hot cylinder head. Read each question carefully and answer honestly:

1. You wake in the night to find your house on fire. Before you escape from the flames, there is time to rescue only one possession. You take: (a) the wedding pictures; (b) a Ming vase; (c) a cardboard box containing an old set of worn-out Amal Monobloc carbs and a Velocette tank badge.

2. You walk into a bar and the bartender says, "What'll it be?" Your answer is: (a) a Perrier with a twist of lemon; (b) a nice glass of white wine; (c) a pint of Guinness stout, "and leave the head on it."

3. The drink you chose in the question above should be served: (a) ice cold; (b) chilled; (c) about room temperature, assuming it's a cold, rainy day and the room is unheated except for an inefficient gas-log fireplace.

4. Your favorite airplane is the: (a) Cessna Citation; (b) Beech Bonanza; (c) de Havilland Gypsy Moth.

5. A radio station calls and says you've won free tickets for any one of the following concerts. Which one do you choose: (a) Madonna; (b) Michael Jackson; (c) John Mayall.

6. Coming out of a theater at night you find it's pouring rain. You say to yourself, "Damn! I should have brought: (a) my umbrella; (b) cab fare; (c) a full set of waxed cotton thornproofs with Derri boots and a bottle of Rain-X for my split-lens Climax goggles."

7. You arrive home cold and soaking wet because your thornproofs need re-waxing. Your first thought is to have: (a) a hot cup of cocoa; (b) a furnace installed; (c) a pint of Guinness, served at room temperature, of course.

8. Of the following three, the most inspirational public figure of the twentieth century would be: (a) Mahatma Gandhi; (b) Dr. Albert Schweitzer; (c) Mike Hailwood.

9. The car you would most like to drive on a winter cross-country trip is: (a) a BMW 750I; (b) a Mercedes 300E; (c) an MG-TC with canvas side-curtains.

10. Your worst recurring nightmare is: (a) being left behind at a train station; (b) falling down an endless elevator shaft; (c) coming out of a movie theater in the pouring rain and realizing you've got to ride home on a 1967 Triumph with Energy Transfer ignition made by Lucas and you've forgotten your waxed cotton thornproofs and even if you do get home, the place is unheated except for an inefficient gas-log fireplace and you're out of Guinness.

11. The baddest, meanest name for a big, fast V-Twin motorcycle is the: (a) Suzuki Intruder; (b) Kawasaki Vulcan; (c) Vincent Black Shadow.

12. Which of the following seafoods sounds best: (a) lobster Thermidor; (b) Alaskan salmon in white wine sauce; (c) fish & chips with malt vinegar, served in a piece of old newspaper.

13. The perfect island paradise for a honeymoon or that romantic get-away vacation would be: (a) Hawaii; (b) Tahiti; (c) the Isle of Man.

That should about cover it. If you so much as thought of picking C for even one of the answers, you should probably start looking for an old British bike. Nothing else will do.

August 1989

FIRST IMPRESSIONS

In the opening scene of the movie we find ourselves looking down on a motorcycle parked in front of a garage or shed, on a paved driveway. The motorcycle has a chrome-plated tank, in the old English fashion, and is bristling with rods and levers and interesting hardware. The apparent owner, a young blond fellow, is methodically, almost lovingly, tending to the motorcycle. He wipes off real or imaginary smudges with a rag and carefully adds oil to the side tank from an antique-looking oil container. We aren't told the time of day, but from the sunlight it looks like early morning, and there is a relaxed aspect to the man's movement that makes us think it might be a Sunday. When the motorcycle is ready, he sets several of the levers, just so, and lowers a set of round government-surplus-looking goggles over his eyes. A boot makes a sharp stab at the kickstarter, and the engine, a big V-Twin, fires to life. The camera shows us a brief glimpse of the engine. It has the initials JAP on its polished cases.

Now the bike is moving through a village, around a road-repair crew and then onto an open country lane. The rider shifts up through the gears, going faster and faster, with that big V-Twin making glorious music. There's a shot of the rider, grinning to himself as patches of sunlight flicker rapidly across his face. The trees on both sides of the road are beginning to blur into a golden-green haze and the rider's head bobs erratically with the motorcycle's stiff suspension. The bike and rider are really moving now, and the narrow pavement is flowing by at an impressive rate. Suddenly there are children on bicycles in the road, the rider brakes and swerves, and we see a shot of the motorcycle, riderless, hurtling over a ditch, then lying on its side in a hedgerow. Wrecked.

The movie, of course, is *Lawrence of Arabia*, and the blond fellow was a young, newly discovered Peter O'Toole, playing Lawrence himself. The motorcycle was a Brough Superior with an engine supplied by J.A. Prestwich. The movie was made in 1962, and I first saw it when I was a highly impressionable 14 years of age. Twenty-seven years ago.

When it was announced several months ago that *Lawrence of Arabia* was returning to the big screen, re-edited, expanded, and better than ever, I started a daily vigil, watching the newspapers to see when the movie would open. I, for one, planned to be there on the first night, seated front and center with a large supply of popcorn and Junior Mints.

Besides being a magnificent piece of cinema in its own right, Sir David Lean's *Lawrence* was one of two powerful influences that caused me, way back in 1962, to suddenly turn my back on years of folk wisdom and parental advice and take up the sport of motorcycling. The entire movie was memorable, but it was those opening few minutes of footage that stayed with me when I walked out of the theater, slightly dazed.

What, of all things on Earth, I thought while riding my bicycle home from the movie, could possibly be more perfect than to have a motorcycle, and to wheel it out of a garage early on a sunny morning, wipe it off with a rag, check the oil, ride quietly through town to warm it up, then go hurtling down an empty country road, listening to the engine and feeling the wind in your face?

The answer, of course, was that nothing could be more perfect. Nothing. On that day, a general curiosity about motorcycles was solidified into a genuine passion. I was hooked.

Just to make sure the hook was in good and deep, fate stepped in with a second tug of the monofilament about one week later. I found myself hitchhiking, without much success, to a junkyard in the nearby town of New Lisbon, Wisconsin. (I used to spend a lot of my spare time wandering around junkyards, sitting in old cars, smoking cigarettes, avoiding mud wasps, etc.) I'd been standing by the highway for some time when two full-dress Harleys came thundering by. To my amazement, the front rider signaled a stop and pulled over. I ran up to the bike and an older man in a white T-shirt and a yacht-captain's hat grinned and said, "Hop on."

I climbed on the back of a huge sprung saddle with fringe and conchos and we roared on down the road. I remember looking over the guy's shoulder at the speedometer and noting that we were going 80 miles an hour. The whole ride was a crazy overload of sounds and sensations, too much to take in. What struck me about it, though, was the absolute sense of freedom. I looked around myself at the Harley and thought, *With one of these, you could go anywhere.* On that big motorcycle, the open road seemed to beckon endlessly as it never had when I rode in a car.

I never made it to the junkyard that day. The two Harleys stopped at the New Lisbon Harley-Davidson shop to see about some parts or service, and I spent the rest of the afternoon hovering around the edges of the hardcore bike crowd who hung out there, listening to their talk and trying to learn something about motorcycles. It was the beginning of a habit that persists to this day. While other people are out shopping at the mall, I'm usually hanging around a motorcycle shop.

A few years ago my friend John Oakey asked how I got interested in bikes and I told him this story about going to the movie and then hitching my first ride on the Harley. He laughed and said, "Jeez. I saw *Lawrence of Arabia* that same year and vowed that I would *never* ride a motorcycle. The guy got *killed*, for God's sake!"

I just shrugged. "A fluke," I said. "Bad timing."

There's no accounting for what grabs people's attention and what doesn't. But Sir David Lean and the friendly guy on the Harley certainly captured mine. If there is such a thing as compound interest on a good idea, I owe them both more than I could possibly repay.

December 1989

THE MUSEUM OF PREHISTORIC HELMETS

I have this dream occasionally that my wife Barbara and I will turn up missing and the police will come to our house to look for clues. After picking the lock or prying the door open with a crowbar, the chief detective and his assistant will wander around our house for a few minutes, hands thrust deep into their trench coat pockets, saying nothing. Then, finally, one of them will speak.

"What do you make of it, Bob?"

"I dunno. You tell me."

"Strangest thing I've ever seen. Helmets everywhere."

"Pretty sick."

We've all got our weaknesses, and one of mine is that I've probably got a few more motorcycle helmets around the house than I actually need for my own protection. There are four or five lined up on top of the bookcase, like so many beer steins in a Heidelberg fencing club, and at least one or two more lurking in every closet in the house.

Some of these helmets are perfectly modern things that I use daily, while others represent either a refusal to dispose of the past or a suspicion that I might someday need one for some kind of Halloween costume. (For the same reason, I've kept my Army uniform and a paisley shirt that looks like something from a *Monkees* rerun.) At any rate, there are too many helmets.

After trying to clean out my den room and closet this weekend, I decided I should do one of two things: Either (A) give most of my helmets away to needy children in the neighborhood, or (B) get a grant from the

Smithsonian to open a Helmet Wing of the Science and Technology Museum, or at least have them erect a small display called "Twenty-Four Years of Progress in Head Protection, 1965–1989."

I like the museum idea better than the notion of giving them away. A nice little display at the Smithsonian would get most of the helmets out of my den, but I could still visit them. They could be organized in the order acquired, as follows:

Exhibit A: We'd have an empty pedestal here, a memorial to the Missing Helmet. My first helmet was a Bell TX500, white in color, bought in 1965. I paid $38 for it, shunning the $19 metalflake discount-store variety, because I was sure it was the last helmet I would ever need to buy. It was stolen off a parcel rack in the men's restroom of the Chemistry Building at the University of Wisconsin in Madison while I stood nearby, helpless, in the vicinity of a tall porcelain fixture. The guy who stole it looked like a cross between Corporal Klinger (without the cocktail dress) and Dustin Hoffman as Ratso Rizzo. If you see a guy who looks like this, wearing a TX500, call me collect.

Exhibit B: Bell TX500, replacement for the above helmet, only I still have this one. It's a beautifully made helmet with soft earpads of genuine leather and a 1968 Snell sticker inside. I painted it dark blue once, Dan Gurney fashion, but then my roommate borrowed it to ride his Triumph to Chicago and threw it through a plaster-and-lath wall after a fight with a girlfriend, scratching the paint, so I changed it back to white. I thought this helmet was cool at the time, but it looks dated and tight-fitting now, with the effect that the wearer's head appears to have been shrunken by pygmies. I continued to wear it occasionally, until just a few years ago, when then-*CW* Executive Editor John Ulrich told me I looked like a nerd. I checked in the mirror and saw he was correct. Now the helmet sits on a shelf.

Exhibit C: One Everoak brand helmet, white in color, with the reassuring legend "Manufactured to British Standard" stitched into its red silk lining. This is without a doubt the oldest helmet I own, though I have no idea what year it was manufactured because it was thrown in free with a used Honda CB160 I once bought. It has a genuine cork inner shell, and the outer shell is made of some semi-flexible substance that looks like canvas impregnated with glue. I used to call this helmet "the Dive-Bomber" because its pudding-bowl shape required that the accident victim arc through the air with a certain amount of precision and land directly on top of his head. Otherwise, it was useless. My roommate Barry wore the trusty Everoak Dive-Bomber to a campus anti-war demonstration to protect his head from nightstick-wielding riot police. As I recall, the police caught right on to this little trick and poked him in the stomach. Not that the helmet would have done any good.

Exhibit D: A 1975 Bell Star. We're getting into the modern era here. This was the first popular full-face helmet. I hated these things when they first came out because I thought they made you look like a propane tank with eyes, but I later grew to like them. Especially after I crashed my Box Stock KZ550 at Riverside. Without that chin piece, I'd still be eating oatmeal through a straw. This helmet has a big streak of Turn Seven blacktop embedded in its shell. It did its job, leaving me without so much as a headache, so I retired it and bought a newer version of same.

Exhibit E: A Bell RT, open-faced, blue in color. This was my dirt helmet, until a spinning back tire tossed up a piece of Mojave Desert, which I cleverly caught in my mouth like a dog going after a Milk-Bone. Now, for desert riding, I wear . . .

Exhibit F: A Bell Moto III, with chin protector.

I suppose I'd better cut the museum donations off there, or I'll end up with only three or four helmets for everyday use. Which would be almost as bad as having only three or four motorcycle jackets.

Which brings up another terrific idea for a museum display . . .

January 1990

HIGH FINANCE

Novelist D. H. Lawrence once asked how it was possible that so many young Englishmen were able to leave the green, pastoral beauty of their farms to work in the coal mines, living deep underground for all their daylight hours. His answer?

Motorbikes.

Young men wanted motorbikes, he said, so they could return to their villages and farms, take their girlfriends for a ride, and generally Be Somebody.

Personally, I never worked in a coal mine to get money for a motorcycle, but I did plenty of other odd things. So did my friend Denny Berg.

Denny owns a motorcycle shop called Time Machine, only a couple of blocks from my office. I've been spending a lot of time over there lately, partly because it's a good place to hang out in the presence of Gold Stars, Harley XRs, Royal Enfield Interceptors, and other treasures that are being restored with meticulous care, and partly because Denny is building my Triumph engine.

The last Triumph engine I built myself inexplicably burned a quart of oil every hundred miles—on the left cylinder only. Two re-rings and a rehoning later, it improved slightly. But then I was always hearing Sounds.

This time I decided to set aside an engine fund and let a true expert lay his hands upon the venerable Twin. Denny used to build flat-track Triumphs for fast guys like Eddie Lawson and Dick Lewis, so he knows where these engines fail, and why. The goal here is a long-lived Triumph engine that doesn't have to come back out of the frame for the foreseeable future, or the rest of my life, whichever comes first.

Other than watching the engine progress, the best part of hanging around the shop is just talking about bikes. Even though Denny is a few years younger than I am (like, it seems, most of the human race), we seem to have lived parallel lives in our early motorcycling, both having owned a succession of small-bore Japanese bikes.

When I dropped by the last Saturday, we got to talking about these early motorcycles, and the subject turned to the various financial hoops we jumped through to get our hands on them.

Denny told me that in order to buy his first bike—a Honda Sport 50—he took a job at a grocery store as a carry-out boy and put in long hours to pay for the bike. This income was later supplemented with snow-shoveling, a paper route, and working in a butcher shop.

In my own case, that first bike was a Bridgestone Sport 50, and in order to convince my doubting parents that I deserved this luxury, I had to agree to take on a second summer job. I was already working at my dad's printing shop, where I could usually be found running a hand-fed press, printing infinite millions of pink lunch tickets for the local school. Unfortunately, the proceeds from that job were slated for the dreaded College Fund. If I wanted something as frivolous as a motorbike, they informed me, I could find extra work, after hours.

Father Bernard Schrieber stepped in at that moment (*Deus ex machina*) and offered me a job mowing the St. Patrick's Catholic Cemetery, evenings and Saturdays.

Father Schrieber took me out to the cemetery, opened the equipment shed and said, "If you like machinery, you're going to love this. It's called a Turtle." He dragged out a big green mower with no wheels and a shape that really did look like a huge sea turtle with a 5-horsepower Wisconsin engine resting on its back. "It works on the hovercraft principle," he said. "You start it up, engage the clutch, and it hovers on a cushion of air created by its own blade. No wheels needed."

It really was a remarkable machine. You could swing its considerable bulk around effortlessly, like a floor buffer on waxed tile. I was in business.

The Turtle and I hovered religiously among the tombstones evenings and Saturdays (no Sundays: this is Church work, lad) through the summer and into the fall. Gradually, I paid off the $275 loan on my

Bridgestone 50, at roughly $25 per month, including the exorbitant 6-percent interest charge.

It was actually a pretty nice job. I was out of doors, got to ride my Bridgestone up through the green hills to the cemetery after dinner each evening, and when I was done mowing I would put the Turtle away, lean back against a tombstone, light up one of the Luckies I had hidden in the shed, and gaze upon my new motorcycle as the sun went down on the new-mown grass with my hometown in the distance. Then, there was the pleasure of the ride home, with evening coolness descending into the low valleys, and a stop at the A&W root-beer stand for a cool one.

The only disconcerting part of these rides home was that there was something slightly odd about shutting down a lawn mower with a big four-stroke Single, and then firing up a motorcycle with a 50cc fan-cooled two-stroke that would have been right at home on a lawn mower. I felt, as Kurt Vonnegut would later say, that some terrible mistake had been made. Bigger bikes with Turtle-quality engines would come later, along with larger loans.

But then, as now, motorcycles were a powerful incentive to find a job. Or even two jobs. In fact, I've often thought that in order to end the high youth-unemployment rate, the government need only develop a powerful psychological campaign to interest the young in small, affordable bikes.

Denny and I are living proof that a 16-year-old will do anything—mow anything, shovel anything, carry anything, or (dare I say it?) print anything—to get the money to for a motorcycle.

Nothing ever changes. We simply dream of better coal mines and faster motorbikes.

April 1991

STAYING HUNGRY

Last summer, while wandering around the pits at Blackhawk Farms during a WERA race weekend, I had one of those rare watershed moments of actual life-change cognition. I was standing there, gazing fondly upon a TZ250 Yamaha and thinking about how I'd always wanted to try racing a 250 GP bike but never had, when suddenly the bike's rider appeared. He climbed on the TZ, did a running bump start, and the little Yamaha ripped to life.

As he headed out onto the track, I suddenly realized that he was a fairly thin and fit-looking guy—what Alan Girdler would call a bird-legged kid—just as I was (or imagined I was) back when I was last roadracing, eight years ago. Since then, I'd put on a little weight, gradually eating and drinking my way from 165 to about 177 pounds. Not exactly Orson Wellesian, but not wasting away, either. I watched that Yamaha accelerate out onto the track and realized that, for the first time in my life, I felt too large and heavy to contemplate racing anything as small and refined as a 250 GP bike.

Not that you have to be anorexically thin to race motorcycles—people of all sizes and shapes have flourished in the sport—but I firmly believe that somewhere in your mind you have to at least *think* of yourself as a kind of lean wolf in order to ride well. And, at that moment, I felt more like a well-fed brown bear about to hibernate for the winter. I stood along the fence, slightly ill at ease, wondering if my old leathers would even fit me anymore.

Only a few months later, I had a chance to find out. The Ducati people invited a group of journalists to Italy, for a road tour and track session with the 1991 bikes.

"Bring your leathers," the invitation said.

So I reached into the back recesses of the closet and dragged out my green-and-yellow "desert lizard" leathers, former bane of *CW* cover photographers everywhere, curse of the comparison-test group photo. I tried them on, and naturally, they had shrunk quite a bit during those eight long years of storage. They were fine in the legs and a little tight in the waist, but in the shoulders and upper chest I felt as though I'd grabbed the wrong jacket leaving a party, accidentally nabbing Willie Shoemaker's favorite sport coat. Shoulders and chest were suffocatingly tight. What we had here was desert-lizard sausage.

When I went to Italy, the old leathers stayed behind. I took my all-purpose Aerostitch suit, which I figured would have good knee and elbow padding for the track, as well as warmth and weather protection for the touring portion of the trip. It worked fine on both counts, though I felt a little clumsy and overpadded on our track testing day, wearing jeans and a sweater under the touring suit. On a racetrack, there's really no substitute for the confidence and freedom of movement you get with a good-fitting set of leathers.

More significantly, there's no substitute for a general sense of physical minimalism when you're trying to crawl around a racebike. Even riding the Raymond Roche 888 Superbike (at 320 pounds and 135 horsepower, the most magnificent, torquey, powerful, laser-sharp motorcycle I've ever ridden), I felt miscast. There's a philosophical incompatibility between titanium bolts, magnesium castings, Kevlar swingarms, and too much dinner. It wasn't just featherweight 250 roadracers I'd outgrown; it was any light, agile racebike, regardless of displacement. Something had to be done.

Saturday night I got home from Italy and drove back to the farm.

Sunday morning I got up early, went to the closet, and got out my running shoes and sweats. I did some calisthenics, lifted a few weights, and 10 minutes later, I was huffing down a country road watching the sun come up over the corn stubble and taking in the cold, clear air.

That was five weeks ago, and somehow I've managed to drag myself out there for a run nearly every morning (except in the aftermath of a couple of notable parties where the margarita blender was running flat out). So far, so good.

I've also been reading the rule books, looking at bikes, and considering the possibility of un-retiring from roadracing this coming summer. I've given thought to any number of classes, both vintage and modern, ranging from a Clubman-class 500 Single to a new Ducati Twin. AMA's Twin Sport class also has a lot of appeal. Time and finances will tell.

In the meantime, I'm ordering a new set of leathers. Okay, they'll be just a little larger than the old ones (we have to be realistic here), but I'll try to be down to fighting weight when I order them, and then stick with it.

Leathers are not cheap, so unless you have money to burn, there's a certain permanence to the size you settle upon. I'm approaching the purchase like an insect choosing his exo-skeleton for life: No room for expansion. The individual inside the leathers will have to adapt.

The motivation for wanting to race again is not entirely clear. I certainly don't have dreams of pursuing titles or climbing the ladder of racebike sophistication. And I'm not sure, this time around, if I'm getting in shape to race, or racing as an excuse to stay in shape.

I guess mostly I'd just like to have fun and sharpen my riding skills, while remaining the sort of person who can look at a 250 GP bike and see a potential partner in crime, or at least a mechanical extension of my own sensibilities.

Not all of our role models have to be human.

May 1991

HIBERNATION

Just last week I returned from a mid-winter visit to partly sunny California, where some of our old friends asked how we're handling the cold weather and attendant cabin fever of the Midwestern winter. I've told them we manage to keep busy, what with oiling the muskrat traps, cleaning the Winchester, heating beans on the woodstove, re-reading the Sears catalog, and glancing restlessly out the window for signs of spring.

Just kidding, of course. I've actually been looking forward to winter and I'm glad it's here. Our new garage/workshop is done, the furnace is running and I have, at last count, a car and two motorcycles to restore. If winter lasts for nine years, I still won't be done by spring. The only real threat from bad weather is that it might keep the UPS or Federal Express trucks from delivering those nifty boxes of bearings and gaskets. A day in which I don't have to sign for Lotus, BMW, or Norton parts seems strangely empty now.

Anyway, parts are flowing in daily and all three projects are, to varying degrees, under way. And not only am I enduring winter successfully, but I thought it would never come.

I realize that's an odd thing for a motorcyclist to say, but the sentiment more or less follows the lyrical wisdom of the old Peter Seeger/Byrds song, which rightly noted that for every thing there is a season. Spring, summer, and fall were a time for riding and neglecting all but the simplest maintenance on my small collection of bikes, and winter is the season for changing oil, adjusting chains and valves, polishing chrome, replacing tires, and figuring out why the twist grip on the BMW feels as though I'm reeling in a 40-pound muskie instead of flipping two small butterfly valves.

Not only do I have plenty to do until spring, but I sometimes find myself overwhelmed with the myriad possibilities, suffering from a condition that has recently been called "option paralysis." This is a malady where you have so many things to do that you can't focus on any one task, so you end up (in my case) sitting on a workbench, staring happily at your bikes, sipping on a Guinness, and listening to Bonnie Raitt and John Lee Hooker on the garage boombox.

This is not a bad thing in itself, but it raises the specter of spring arriving with bikes only half ready to be ridden. I still picture them, poised like a row of battle-ready fighter planes, waiting to take off at the first sign of warm weather, then to be ridden like crazy all summer without guilt or mechanical hassles.

So far, I've gotten quite a bit of the work done, but not nearly as much as I'd expected. It may take a mid-winter thaw, the first real breath of spring, to drive me into that manic state of preparedness. In the meantime, even the dreaded option paralysis isn't quite as bad as it sounds. In the arsenal against motorcyclist cabin fever, there is yet another weapon nearly as powerful as overdue motorcycle maintenance.

Videos.

On those evenings when I don't really feel like getting my hands dirty and would probably secretly like to be going for a ride, I shut off the garage lights, come into the house, turn on the VCR, and tune in to the vicarious world of the motorcycle video.

I have a revolving group of favorites, some rented—like *On Any Sunday,* parts I and II—and various racing videos borrowed from friends. And last year I finally broke down and bought two eminently re-watchable films I couldn't do without. One is Honda's *V-Four Victory*, the other is the Duke/Videovision Broadcast tape of the 1989 Australian Bike Grand Prix.

Am I overstating the case, or is the 1989 Australian GP simply the best roadrace of any kind that has ever occurred on the face of the Earth?

Obviously, I haven't seen every race, but I've been watching car and motorcycle racing of all kinds for at least 30 years, and this is the best I've seen. It has all the right ingredients: close competition, endless passing and repassing, high speeds, a beautiful setting, visible riding genius among all of the close pack of front-runners, and unbelievable displays of courage and tenacity. I can watch it again and again, mesmerized.

When guests come to visit, my first question when they walk through the door is, "Would you like a drink?" And immediately on the heels of that question, I say, "How would you like to see the 1989 Australian Bike GP?"

If they warm up to that film, of course, they automatically get subjected to the superb *V-Four Victory.*

This is essentially a Honda PR film whose core is an on-bike camera segment of Joey Dunlop doing a full 37-mile lap of the Isle of Man TT course, flying between the hedgerows and trees, through villages, in and out of light and shadow, at speeds up to 180 miles per hour. If you get bored watching this film, you need a new set of optic nerves. And if you watch it often enough, you can actually begin to understand Dunlop's impenetrable northern-Irish accent, bested only by the Enigma Code for its ability to confound translation.

My favorite part of the film is where the narrator asks Dunlop if he has the whole course perfectly memorized, and Joey says, no, he simply remembers where he is on the circuit because, "there's bits of the course I like and there's bits I don't like."

I sometimes feel the same way about winter. But with movies like this one, old motorcycles to fix, good blues on the tape player, and the random bottle of dark Irish stout, I have a hard time remembering exactly which bits I don't like.

July 1991

SOONER IS BETTER THAN LATER

All through the cold and windy spring I'd secretly been priding myself that I hadn't come down with the flu, while all those around me had caved in. "Must be my iron constitution," says I, "or perhaps good clean living . . . "

Last Monday, of course, it hit me like a runaway freight train. My knees buckled, chills broke out, and I crawled off to bed. I remember hardly anything of the next three days, except having a vague longing for comic books and dreaming that I was watching Rocky & Bullwinkle cartoons with Vicks Vap-O-Rub all over my chest. Essentially, out of it.

On Friday, I awoke with a fond memory of wearing real clothes—with shoes and everything—and walking upright. After pondering that Nirvanic ideal for a few hours, I hove myself out of bed and decided I'd try it. Join the human race again, live a little. So I got up, dressed, shuffled downstairs, and made coffee.

Then I stepped outside, onto the porch, and was hit with something even more powerful than the flu: warm air.

It was eerie. The air outside was actually warmer than it was in the house, for the first time since . . . since when? September? The thermometer outside the kitchen door read 72 degrees. An almost tropical south wind was raking through the brown winter grass and the barely budding trees. The last of the glacier on the north side of our garage was melting audibly and trickling into the soft sod. The air smelled of damp leaves and dead mice the cats had caught all winter; a rich aroma of thawing barnyards was carried on the breeze from nearby farms; music to the nose. It was that rarest of things, a Gift Day in early spring, a summer-warm day that comes as an accident from the forceful advance of a warm front out of New Orleans up the Mississippi River Valley, where it temporarily outflanks the usual Canadian cold air off the plains of Saskatchewan, like one of Jeb Stuart's Confederate cavalry raids, probing the North behind the lines.

And like the cavalry raid, you know it can't last. The warm air will soon have to skedaddle back to where it belongs for another few weeks, content to have adventured so far north and lived.

When you get a day like this, free and unsolicited, it's time to ride. Malingering with the flu is no excuse. Patriotic men and women report to their motorcycles at once.

So, I put on some boots and a sweater, dug my leather jacket out of the closet, dusted off my helmet, and made for the garage. There, I peeled away the foam insulation strip that sealed the bottom of the big doors and swung them open for the first time since early December. Warm, moist air rushed in and immediately formed a damp haze on chrome and cold metal.

I would just take one quick ride, I decided, a ceremonial spin out of sheer duty, and then back to bed. The Triumph 650 Trophy, with its non-battery ignition, beckoned because I knew it would be easy to start. And it was. Third kick on stale gas and it was idling. I looked in the oil reservoir to ascertain that oil was pumping, eyeballed both tires for sidewall deflection (accurate within 30 psi), and then motored out the open doors into the false summer day.

Oh, Lordy, riding again. I did a 14-mile loop on my favorite county roads, then stopped at the Cooksville general store for gas. It was so warm you could ride with your jacket unzipped. It really was like summer. No sting to the air.

Naturally, when I got back to my garage, I didn't stop there. I started charging batteries, checking oil levels and tire pressures on the rest of my minor museum of weird bikes and, one-by-one, rode them into town for gas. Two of the bikes I bump-started, an effort that left me a little weak in the knees, but I ended the afternoon with a glorious long ride on the Duck, during which I nearly threw it away in a fast corner with a winter's accumulation of sand and gravel, but never mind that. I rode along reveling in the warm sun and cadence of the big Twin, alternately having chills and breaking out in sweats.

I'll pay for this later, I thought. *But I don't care.*

The next day, of course, I was sick as a dog. I felt dizzy and beaten up, as though I'd been thrown downstairs maybe 20 or 30 times during the night by a gang of Chinese opium dealers from Shanghai after I'd failed to pay my expensive bar tab. I did manage to get dressed, however, and come downstairs to sleep on the sofa.

At noon I woke up enough to realize the sky was black as night and there was a terrific thunderstorm in progress. Wind buffeted the house, but it finally calmed down and I went back to sleep.

Later that afternoon, Barb came home from work and said several tornado funnels had touched down within a few miles of our house. Four farms were destroyed just over the hill behind our place, and one man was killed. Another man survived in his basement by holding onto a drain pipe as his whole house was lifted away into the sky.

Today the weather is cold, dark, and windy; 30 degrees with snow flurries. The fields are still scattered with uprooted trees and small pieces of houses and barns. And garages.

Ancient people used to look for signs and messages in the weather, making much of these strange and restless days of spring. And in my own primitive way, I too have found a message in the events of this week.

When you feel like playing hooky, play it. When the sun is shining, go for a ride. If you need a motorcycle, just buy it. Sooner is better than later.

December 1991

GOODBYE, MR. HONDA

Mr. Soichiro Honda is no longer with us. I read in the papers he died on August 5th in Tokyo.

The story said he was born in 1906, that he was 84 years old. That's eight years older than my father. Is this possible?

The overlap of generations—and the effect of one generation on another—is a strange thing. Those of us who think of ourselves as America's post-war baby boomers are, on the average, a good 40 years younger than Soichiro Honda was, and yet somehow I can't help believing he really belongs to our generation. Before anyone else does, I think we should claim him for our own.

The simple fact is that his genius and his years of accumulated know-how really came into full bloom just about the time many of us became speed-crazed teenagers. (Or, in the case of the Honda 50, merely motion-crazed teenagers.) The invasion of Honda's small, well-engineered and inexpensive motorcycles dovetailed perfectly with our coming of age and filled a great vacuum that no one else seemed to have noticed.

Many of us, now approaching our mid-40s, were already hanging around motorcycle shops and lusting after Harleys and Triumphs before we ever heard the name Honda. We wanted bikes badly, but our options were limited. Big bikes were out of the question, financially and parentally speaking (and boy, did they speak), but the traditional motorcycle companies just didn't offer much in the way of cheap, small-bore equipment.

So we high school kids were largely stuck with such choices as (1) Whizzer conversion kits for old Schwinns; (2) mini-bike kits with go-kart wheels and lawn-mower engines; (3) used Harley Hummers with piston rattle; or (4) Cushman scooters with variable belt drive and styling borrowed from an ice-cream delivery truck.

Contraptions, in other words. Mostly cantankerous little devices that hugged the shoulder of the road while smoking heavily, balking at hills, and burning out their tiny centrifugal clutches, if they were lucky enough to have them.

Then, suddenly, there were Hondas. Word spread like wildfire, and so did the bikes, all through the early Sixties.

The price range was $245 to $700 *new*, depending on the model. Most models (other than the 50cc step-through) had slick, four-speed transmissions hidden inside engine cases, where they couldn't even snag your pants cuff and leave grease marks. Electricity actually reached the headlight, which in turn lit the road. Performance, per cc, was amazing. A Honda Super 90 would go about 60 on the highway while getting around 100 miles per gallon. The CB160 was quicker than most of the old 250 British Singles and cost less. The 305 Super Hawk was a giant killer. What's more, these bikes looked good. Someone in Japan understood. Goodbye, Cushman.

Until Hondas arrived, motorcycle technology seemed to have lagged well behind modern standards for cars and aircraft. It was assumed, for reasons I will never understand, that motorcycles had to be wrenched upon constantly, that they were destined to leak oil and vibrate excessively, scattering parts and vaporizing light filaments.

Perhaps I'm painting too bleak a picture of the pre-Honda era, as there were many fine and relatively refined bikes made earlier, but the majority of 1950s motorcycles had what seemed to me a World War I aircraft flavor to their mechanical innards—and outards. ("Advance the spark, Biggles! We've a Hun on our tail.")

My own first bike was not a Honda. After a brief fling with a semi-functional James/Villiers 150, I bought a Bridgestone Sport 50, mainly because we had a local dealer. A good little bike, but it was a two-stroke and had the usual oil-mix/plug-range hassles.

Shortly thereafter, I got a Honda Super 90 and decided I was a four-stroke kind of a guy. After that, I owned 10 more Hondas of progressively larger displacement, sampling other brands of Japanese bikes only when they, too, converted to four-stroke engines. (My old Yamaha RD350 being the only stray.)

Through all those years of Honda ownership, the company—or maybe the old man himself—always seemed to know exactly what I wanted next, before the thought was fully formed in my head. Or, more likely, Mr. Honda simply built what he knew was right, and his ideas made sense when I saw them. In any case, I always felt as if I had a friend in Japan, a kindred spirit who could interpret mechanically what I could not express.

I never met Soichiro Honda. I know him only from his upbeat, candid autobiography, his life's work, and from his portrait, which has hung on the wall above my desk for years, right next to that of Ducati's Dr. Taglioni. Like Taglioni, Honda belongs to that small pantheon of engineers who managed to bring both irrepressible character and expertise with them to the drafting table.

You have to have owned a motorcycle designed by an individual (or worse, a committee) where one of those two traits is missing to appreciate what we've lost.

What else can I say? Mr. Honda's bikes took me across Canada, through college, off to visit my girlfriend on a summer of weekends, around the track on my first season of roadracing, down Highway 61 to New Orleans, across the Mojave Desert, up Pike's Peak, touring with my new bride, and on a mad autumn dash to the USGP at Watkins Glen. And back. Always back.

Eleven bikes, and none of them ever let me down. Not once.

Thank you, Mr. Honda. They were good times, all.

May 1994

THAT CRITICAL FIRST RIDE

True story. When my boyhood friend Pat Donnelly was in his early teens, he was invited to a birthday party on the family farm of his classmate, Conrad Shaker. Conrad had a horse and saddled him up so all the kids at the party could take a ride. Pat, who had never been on a horse before, climbed into the saddle and gave the horse a gentle prod with his heels. The horse took exactly two steps forward, exhaled loudly, fell over on its side, and died.

Pat, who was wearing a brand-new pair of extremely cool engineer boots just like James Dean's in *Rebel Without a Cause*, had his leg and boot trapped under the horse, but both were eventually extricated with minimal damage. The party was over. Pat gave up on horses, and two years later bought his first motorcycle.

Usually it works the other way around.

A more typical first-ride story comes from my good friend Lyman Lyons, who grew up in Louisiana. A buddy of Lyman's had saved up all his paper-route money for several years and bought himself a new scooter, a Cushman Eagle. The friend insisted Lyman "take a spin" and Lyman complied with a display that only the masterful Buster Keaton could have orchestrated. He whacked open the throttle, froze at the controls (forgetting which way to twist the grip), rocketed across several front lawns, and finally blasted through a thick hedge, which probably saved his life by slowing him down before he hit the inevitable trees.

The brilliance of this physical comedy was lost on the Cushman owner, who quietly examined the crushed front fender and bent fork, and simply said, "My scooter . . . " over and over again.

Lyman, needless to say, did not rush right down to the Cushman dealer and plunk money down on his own two-wheeled fun machine. He was somewhat abashed and never really recovered his full measure of youthful enthusiasm for scooters—or motorcycles.

I have now lived long enough to have heard at least a hundred of these first-ride disaster stories, and I'm sorry to say that most of them involve motorcycles rather than horses.

Tell a group of people at a party you ride a motorcycle and at least one person in the crowd can produce a richly detailed, moment-by-moment account of catastrophe on a first bike ride. Usually the tale is quite similar to Lyman's, and ends in a vow never to ride again, or to "stick to four wheels."

As nearly as I can tell, a typical sequence of events in most of these mishaps seems to be: (1) surprise at the abruptness or speed of forward motion combined with a poor sense of twist-grip modulation; (2) growing panic in realizing that the technique for stopping safely has not been adequately rehearsed; and (3) a total loss of steering control as the unnatural instinct to countersteer is replaced, through terror, by an attempt to physically turn the handlebars in the direction you want to go (which is effective only at very low speed) causing the rider to hit the very object he or she had hoped to avoid.

When you think how many times this has happened to first-time motorcycle riders, and how many of them have gone away dazed and confused, the world-wide effect on motorcycle ownership has to be phenomenal. A few minutes of simple training might have eliminated many of these accidents, and a course from the Motorcycle Safety Foundation would prevent just about all of them.

Those first few rides are clearly the most dangerous—as are the first few months of riding—so I'm all in favor of as much training as possible.

And yet . . . when I listen to these stories, there is a side of me that says perhaps not everyone is cut out to be a motorcyclist. My own first ride, for instance, was not a lot better than Lyman's, yet the effect was quite different.

I was trying to buy an old Harley 45 from a guy who ran a local gas station. I was 15 and could not legally ride on the street, so he let me take it for a short ride in the pasture behind the station. I chuffed around successfully for a while, mastering (?) the foot clutch and tank shift, and all was well until I returned to the station. I looked down at the clutch pedal as I came to a stop and ran into a bunch of trash barrels full of scrap metal and old oil filters. The bike and barrels tipped over with lots of noise, but no real damage. I quickly scrambled up and got the bike on its stand, just as the owner came around the corner, wearing a flipped-up arc welder's mask.

"No problem," I said. "Just bumped into some cans."

He scowled and went back to work, welding.

A week later, when I turned up with the money ($100) he told me he'd decided to keep the bike. So I made a down payment on a brand-new Bridgestone Sport 50.

Strangely, it never occurred to me to shy away from motorcycling because I'd dumped the Harley on its side. I would no more have given up the idea of owning a motorcycle than Lyman—who is a good baseball player—would have given up baseball because he struck out his first time at bat. The incident was a small setback, but not a trauma. All the defense mechanisms in my brain closed ranks, made their excuses, and the event was quickly paved over, seamlessly, almost as if it had never happened.

The difference here, of course, is simply a matter of commitment. Lyman was merely curious, while I was absolutely fanatical. I had to have a bike, and nothing else would do. Most of us will accept a lot of hard knocks to fulfill some personal dream, but are turned away rather quickly if we take a bruising in pursuit of a merely marginal interest.

Maybe that first ride is just a filter, a means to separate those of us who have to ride motorcycles—or horses—from those who don't.

September 1994

RIDING HOME

There must be a temperature/sunlight sensor built into the brain of every motorcyclist who lives for the Sunday-morning ride. How else to explain the events of last weekend, when I awoke for no good reason at 6:30 A.M., rather than snoozing on to 8:00 or 9:00, as usual?

Perhaps I sensed warmth and light radiating through the walls of the house. After a long, hard winter, there is probably a biological mechanism that kicks in—the same one that awakens hibernating bears or tells snakes it's time to crawl out from under a rock and lie in the sun.

Anyway, I awoke as if a switch had been thrown, and was on my feet and making coffee in minutes. The house was empty, Barb had gone to Chicago for the weekend to visit her sister. I walked outside and looked at the thermometer on our porch. Sixty-seven degrees.

A perfect morning.

I did not walk down the driveway to get the Sunday paper. Instead, I went back in the house, put on boots and riding gear, and emerged minutes later to wheel my new black ZX-11 out of the garage. Ready to ride, before seven o'clock in the morning. Amazing.

But where to go?

My friend John Jaeger has said that the angels give us only 10 or 11 days like this in a lifetime—days when clear weather intersects with a weekend morning on which we find ourselves with no responsibilities, duties, promises, or appointments.

You don't want to waste a day like this, so I sat down on the porch swing with my Wisconsin state map and considered the options. Some theme was needed, some destination or goal, rather than just a vague meandering.

I looked at the front cover of the map, and there was a picture of our governor, Tommy Thompson, with his wife. I looked at the picture and thought about it.

Tommy and I grew up together in the same small Wisconsin town of Elroy, population 1,503. He was five or six years ahead of me in school—one of the older, cool guys when I was just a wee slip of a nerd—but we often found ourselves in the same anarchic neighborhood football games, or serving mass as altar boys at the same church services. A long time ago. In Elroy.

That's where I would go: Elroy. I would ride home. Hadn't been there in several years, my family long since moved away. It was 100 miles northwest, in the beautiful, hilly Wisconsin Uplands; 150 miles if you took the good roads, the empty ones with red barns, one-lane bridges, and no cops; roads with names like P or WW.

The map went back in my tankbag. Visor down, ZX warmed up, we were on the road. What a morning. Angels, indeed.

Fast running until the intersection with Highway 14, frequented by the cars with the funny blue and red lights. Slow down. The ZX hardly comprehends the difference between 55 and 95 miles per hour. At any speed under 100 miles per hour, it growls along like a half-sleeping giant and doesn't know its own strength.

After crossing the Wisconsin River at Sauk City, I turn off the main highway and back onto the intricate gray network of country roads. No motorhomes, no state patrol cars; just the occasional country church to watch for, people spilling out into the bright sunlight, blinking, shaking hands. White shirts, white dresses. White apple blossoms. Spring.

Through Leland, Lime Ridge, and Cazenovia, then into Hillsboro. We played these guys in basketball and football. Big Bohemian guys. Tough. Out of town on F and toward Elroy on WW and O.

Suddenly I come over a ridge, and there it is. Church steeple, cemetery, hillside of houses, Main Street. After a stop at the cemetery to visit family graves, I ease down the steepness of Academy Street past the house I grew up in, at 309, and stop for a look. After a decade of falling-down neglect, someone has fixed it up, and there's a For Sale sign in the yard. But all the trees are gone. The once green-shaded house is baking in the sun like a bald head.

How about that; I outlived the shade trees my dad and I planted, and the huge elms that were already there.

I ride to the other end of town, where my parents built a small ranch-style house when I was in high school. New and convenient, but not so much character. Nice neighbors, though, and we had some good times there.

Late afternoon, and time to head home. The shadows are growing long; it's getting cooler.

Before heading south, I take one last loop over a favorite road. People here call it the Ridge Road, but its official name is County P. It's 8 miles of wonderful, scenic, convoluted blacktop that follows a topographical spine between Elroy and another small town called Kendall, just to the north.

When I lived here, it was my standard motorcycle and sport-car road. My measuring stick for the way things handled, my own small-town Angeles Crest Highway. I rode Bridgestones, Hondas, and Triumphs here—and drove a Triumph sports car, a TR-3. And my dad's 1966 Mustang. I knew every curve and how fast it could be taken. Still do.

Threading over it with the ZX, I find the road is still as familiar as the lines in my own hand—or, lately, the lines in my own face. Even the tar patches seem to be in the same place. A good old glove of a road.

Downshifting for the familiar city limits of Kendall, I find myself thinking about the famous Thomas Wolfe admonition that you can't go home again.

True enough, I guess, in some respects.

But when I lived here, home was more than an old house that now has a For Sale sign in the yard and no trees to shade the lawn. It was also a place where I looked out the window and dreamed of having the freedom to ride motorcycles through these ridges and hills, on days just like this one.

On a motorcycle, on these roads, I am always home.

December 1994

SAVING FOR A VINCENT

Yesterday evening I rode my Norton into the big city, stopped at my favorite bookstore/coffee shop and found—lo and behold—a new Vincent book that I didn't already own.

This one is the *Illustrated Vincent Motorcycle Buyer's Guide* by Zachary Miller. The cover photo shows a gorgeous 1952 Series C Black Shadow against a background of fiery red autumn trees.

Why not just hold me up at gunpoint?

My overstressed Visa card came out so fast I'm sure it left flashburns on my wallet and a faint smell of burnt cowhide and melted plastic in the store. I bought the book, slipped it into my tankbag (along with the collected poems of Seamus Heaney; try 'em!), and thundered home for a read.

Just what I needed: a sixth book on Vincents. I have five already, occupying a special place on the bookshelf near my favorite reading chair, segregated from all other forms of literature so I can find them easily. My dad's old Speed Graphic press camera is one of the bookends and the other is a bottle of scotch. When all else in life fails, what you do is pour yourself a glass of dark, smoky Lagavulin single malt, pull out a Vincent book, and read. Or just look at the pictures.

I have to look at the pictures, of course, because I have no Vincent.

Over the years, there has generally been a direct relationship between the books on my library shelf and the motorcycles that have found their way into my garage. For instance, I have a lot of Ducati books (Alan Cathcart and Mick Walker should soon be able to retire, just on my own prodigality), and, since about 1980, I've almost always had a Ducati in the garage.

Same with Norton and Triumph; lots of books, bikes to match. The books seem to be a symptom of imminent purchase, like a touch of fever just before you come down with the flu. Read the book, go weak in the knees, break out in a sweat, and buy the bike. That's how it works. Only Vincents have been the exception to this pattern. Why?

Well, I suppose, because they cost too much. Always have. Ever since the 1960s, when I first discovered and became enamored of these machines, they have been just out of reach, like a carrot on a stick.

When I was in college, a decent used Vincent (some oil leakage, a touch of clutch trouble, intermittent headlight somewhat dim) cost about $1,400. This was only a little more than the price of a brand-new Triumph Bonneville.

Which would you buy? Magnificent old crock or new masterpiece? I couldn't afford either one, so the question (like everything else then) was academic. My room, board, and tuition for all of 1966 totaled $1,500, toward which I earned $1,300 that year, working a good union job on a railroad section crew shoveling gravel for $3.28 an hour. My parents did not advise the purchase of a Vincent Black Shadow, nor a Triumph. In fact, they were not pleased when I bought a used Honda CB160 for $200.

Zoom ahead to 1980, the year I got my first journalism job at *Cycle World* and we moved to California. Used Shadows and Rapides were in the $4,500 to $5,500 range (with some oil leakage, a touch of clutch trouble, intermittent headlight somewhat dim), while a brand-new black-and-gold Ducati 900SS Desmo—the absolute class of the modern motorcycle world—cost about $5,200. Which would you buy? I couldn't afford either one.

Two years later, I bought a very nice used Ducati 900SS for $3,500. A modern Vincent, in a way, more usable and capable, but still not a direct replacement. A different kind of magic.

And here we are in 1994.

As nearly as I can tell, decent Vincent Rapides and Shadows (now mostly restored, with less oil leakage, not so much clutch trouble, and slightly brighter headlights) are selling in the $14,000-$24,000 range. And a new Ducati 916 is about $15,000. And I can't afford either one.

Okay, here's the thing. I *could* afford one. I could, that is, if a Vincent were all I wanted in life and I had been saving for one these many years, making regular sacrifices. But I have other hobbies. I race a car, I buy CDs, I have a weakness for vintage guitars and amplifiers, I eat pizza, drink Lagavulin, and make house payments. I blow money on Vincent books.

So every time a Vincent comes up for sale in *Hemmings* or Buzz Walneck's *Classic Cycle Trader*, I am caught flat-footed. I'll see what appears to be a nice Rapide for $16,000, look in my checkbook, and see that I have just enough to make the upcoming loan payment on some newer, more practical bike I already own.

Just like the old days. The price of the bike is always slightly out of line with the possible joy it might bring, and its high cost threatens to displace too many other pleasures and necessities. My income has gone upward over the years, but the price of Vincents seems to have progressed at the same pace. The stick that holds the carrot, adjusted for inflation, remains exactly the same length. Call it perpetual out-of-reachness.

But, I've been thinking.

Maybe the time has come to start saving for a Vincent. When I was in college I had a slotted coffee can marked "Triumph Fund." Maybe I should set up a metaphorical coffee can account at the bank, marked "Vincent Fund." Maybe if I saved half the money, it would be worth springing for a loan.

Maybe if I didn't get distracted for a couple of years buying a lot of other frivolous stuff, I could think about buying a restored Vincent, or getting a basket case and rebuilding it myself.

Think I'll start now. This week. Today. It may seem a little late in life to start saving, but it seems to be my destiny to own one of these bikes. If it were not preordained, why would I have so many books?

January 1995

DUCKS UNLIMITED

The comedian Charlie Ferguson, who used to read the news on the old *Hee-Haw* TV show, would sometimes open his broadcast with, "And now for the news: It's the same news we had yesterday, but today it happened to a different bunch of people."

An accurate view of world affairs, no doubt, but I've noticed that most of the news around here seems to happen to exactly the same people, over and over again. At least where Ducatis are concerned.

Take my friend Bruce Finlayson. Bruce is a former roadracer who ran a Ducati 250 back in the 1960s and went on to race Hondas, Triumph Triples, and Yamahas, later owning a wide variety of interesting streetbikes. But five or six years ago, he sold off a few of his modern bikes, took a stride backward into history, and bought himself another Ducati, a 1974 750GT. He'd no sooner restored that to perfection than he picked up a very nice 1977 900SS.

This is where I came in. I met Bruce when Barb and I moved from California back to Wisconsin in 1990, bringing with us my own 1977 900SS.

Bruce and I did some ridings together, yet within two years we had both sold our desmo Ducks. Bruce found he was riding the old 750GT more, and he wanted a traveling bike, so he sold off the 900SS to buy a clean, used BMW R100RS. I, on the other hand, had fallen hard for the new-generation 900SS and sold my old one to justify the purchase.

In both cases, the line of reasoning was this: (A) We do not ride these bikes very often or for very many miles because they are neither comfortable nor very practical; (B) they can quickly be turned into ready cash; (C) we want to try something new; and (D) life is short.

And last year, following almost this same line of would-be logic, I sold my new-generation 900SS. I wanted to try something completely different, a fast, comfortable, mile-eating ZX-11 for my all-day solo rides into the back country. I was also in the grips of a reductionist phase, and had it in mind that perhaps I was headed for the ownership of just one all-purpose, do-everything road bike.

Bruce, too, was trying to cut back his moderate collection to just two bikes. "Fewer insurance bills," we told ourselves, "fewer license plates and oil changes. Simplify!"

That worked for a while. Then we went to a monthly meeting of the Slimy Crud Motorcycle Gang and explained this ingenious plan of life simplification to a fellow Crud, Stu Evans. He nodded and said, "I recently considered selling off all my bikes to buy a new BMW R1100RS. But then realized it has never been my goal to own just one motorcycle."

Hoo jeez. That got me thinking. Any maybe Bruce, too.

How else to explain the events of the past four weeks?

First, Bruce ran across a terrific deal on an immaculate, low mileage tri-colored 1985 Ducati 750 F1A and brought it home from Pennsylvania. We had a big bike-welcoming party, drank some good Italian *rosso,* and filled Bruce's garage with clouds of fashionably pungent cigar smoke.

Almost simultaneously, Bruce told me about a Ducati 250 Mach 1 project bike for sale in Chicago (see recent lengthy column) and I found myself hauling *that* home. We had another bike-welcoming party in which Barolo flowed like Chianti, or vice versa, and cigar smoke filled the workshop.

Then, only two weeks ago, I found myself standing in the showroom of Bob Barr's local Kawasaki/Ducati shop (again), staring at a red, full-fairing 1995 Ducati 900SS SP. Almost like my old bike, but with a silver/gold frame, some carbon-fiber pieces, better brakes, and a slightly better seat.

I sat on the SP rocking it back and forth. Lord, how I missed having a light, narrow, 400-pound sportbike with the front tire feeding crystal-clear messages through the clip-ons into the palms of my hands. A bike I could load into my own van (Daytona-bound) without the help of two men and a small boy. Comfort be damned.

Averting my eyes from the lovely, costly 916 standing nearby, I casually inquired what kind of ZX-11 trade might land a new 900SS SP in my garage.

A very good trade, as it turned out. Same monthly payments, but a few more of 'em.

So, another Ducati 900SS landed in my garage last week. Another Crudfest transpired, with no fewer than four bottles of Italian red, many beers, and enough cigar smoke to cast a Fellini-like haze of unreality on the whole proceedings. Milinov sang *La forza del destino* on the boom box. *Destino*, indeed. *Forza*, indeed.

Okay, are we done? No.

Yesterday Bruce called and—get this—told me he'd run across a deal on a rather tattered but complete 1974 Ducati 750SS in Chicago. The bike had been in a storage shed for 20 years, but with one carb and the valve covers off.

Unbelievable. The Holy Grail of bevel-drive desmo Twins. "Are you going to buy it?" I asked, naively.

"It's in my garage," Bruce said. "I used my income tax escrow fund."

More wine and smoke.

If one more person buys a Ducati this winter, I'll have to check in the Betty Ford Center and dry out for a week.

Four Ducatis in four weeks, new and old. Huge mountains of debt.

Did I mention that these bikes are slightly impractical and mildly uncomfortable? So why do we keep coming back to them?

I guess because they are beautiful, light, and uncompromised in their purpose. And, for reasons we can scarcely understand, they touch off celebrations and parties, as if they'd been born rather than bought.

We don't need them. But then we don't need red wine, pungent cigar smoke, or Italian opera, either.

What we need is to have our heads examined.

July 1996

TRIUMPH DEFERMENT

It was, so far, the coldest night of the year, said the TV weatherperson: 27 below zero, with a wind-chill index of 55 below, for those of us who like to torture ourselves.

Nevertheless, I climbed into my Ford van and hit the starter. It cranked over with a slow groan of protest, but fired right up. Good old modern fuel injection.

It was a terrible night to be out, with wind sweeping dry snow across the road in headlit clouds of instant snow blindness, but I was on a mission from God: buying back my old 1968 Triumph 500 Tiger Competition.

A few years ago my friend Brian Slark, who was then a vintage motorcycle dealer/restorer in St. Louis, called and said he'd run across a good, restorable, low-mileage 1968 Triumph T100-C, the high-pipe, street-scrambler model for which I have always had a weakness. A little weather-beaten, he said, with gawd-awful gold-metalflake paint on the tank and sidecovers, but mechanically excellent and otherwise correct.

So, of course, I drove down to St. Louis and took it off his hands. Once home, I polished the bike up a bit, but managed not to launch into a major restoration. The bike ran so nicely I didn't want to take it off the road. I rode it around all autumn, ignoring its cosmetic flaws, even if the paint job made me feel like I should be wearing bell-bottoms.

Came winter, and I decided a new, reliable van was in order, so I did a major garage cleaning and reluctantly sold the nice little T100-C. It went to a local businessman named Joe Robertson, who said he would probably do a full restoration.

I had all but forgotten about the Triumph when my friend Jeff Weaver, an old riding buddy of Robertson's, mentioned that Joe had ridden the bike only twice and then parked it in his garage. It had been sitting there for two years, on semi-flat tires in his unheated garage, gathering dust.

Now, I don't know about you, but images like this weigh heavily on my imagination and make sleep difficult. It's like hearing that Michelle Pfeiffer is cold and homeless, camped in your front yard. A selfless, charitable act of rescue is called for almost immediately.

So, I called Joe and bugged the poor guy for about two weeks until he finally admitted he probably wouldn't get around to restoring the bike and agreed to sell it back to me.

"I'll be right over," I said. Hence my precipitous drive on the coldest night of the year.

The bike was a little dusty, but none the worse for wear. Still gold, still complete. A slightly tarnished gem.

When I got it back into my own lavishly heated garage, I cleaned and polished for about two hours, then mixed up a small blenderful of margaritas, sat back in my bike-appreciation garage rocking chair, and stayed up until about three in the morning, soaking it all in.

Everyone has a bike, I suppose, that represents unrequited love—the bike you wanted but couldn't have at some awkward, poverty-stricken time of life—and the 1968 Triumph T100-C is exactly that bike for me.

One Saturday in the spring of 1968, my college roommate, Pat Donnelly, talked his dad into driving us to a Triumph shop in the town of Richland Center, Wisconsin, where a "Triumph Blowout Sale" was in progress.

When we got there, the dealer had two identical high-pipe Hi-Fi Aquamarine Green T100-Cs parked outside in front of the showroom. Perfection.

While Pat and I ogled the bikes, Pat's dad, who is the Bargainer from Hell, went to work on the dealer. After about 45 minutes of relentless hammering, he somehow got the dealer to agree to sell the matching pair of bikes for $1,800. Nine hundred each!

How he did this, I don't know. There was a healthy demand for Triumph 500s in 1968, and they normally sold for around $1,100. At any rate, Pat and I were elated. We'd both been unloading Coca-Cola trucks at night to save for Triumphs, and this was a huge price break. Pat's dad told him he could take out a student load for the balance (we had each saved about $450), so all we needed to cinch the deal was my parents' permission for me to do the same.

My parents did not say, "No way in Hell!" because they didn't use that kind of language. But that was the message. "Forget it," they said. "You aren't buying any $900 motorcycle while you're still in college. You can pay for your room, board, and tuition."

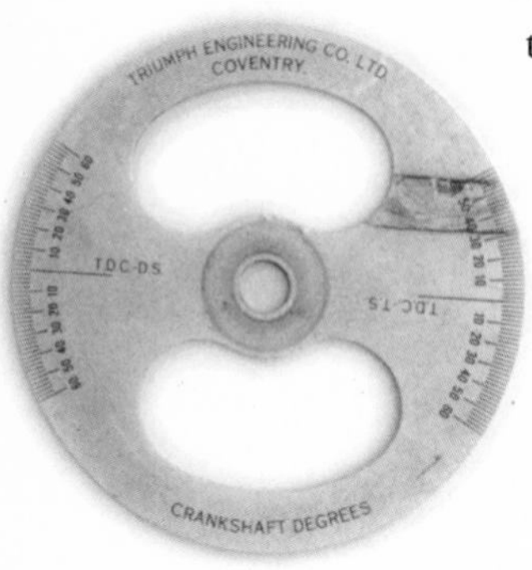

"I already did," I pointed out, "working on the railroad section crew last summer."

"Then you can buy more of your books and clothing," they replied. "Besides, you've already got a motorcycle."

Yeah. My old Honda CB160. Not the same.

In retrospect, I suppose this sounded like a huge amount of money then—like a kid coming home from college today and telling his folks he needs a new Ducati Monster, on sale for only $7,999. But I was not a happy young man.

I could see the whole golden summer stretching out in front of me while I rode that beautiful green Triumph everywhere—in a dream that was now melting like April snow. I can honestly say I have never wanted any material object so badly in my life, before or since.

The denial of this request to take out a $450 loan had a great deal to do with my quitting college later that year and joining the Army. I had suddenly lost my taste for being somebody's 20-year-old kid.

All of this passed before me as I sat in the garage the other night and stared at the T100-C. For three hours or so, hardly moving.

People occasionally ask what it is we see when we spend long periods of time contemplating an old motorcycle. Sometimes you can't even begin to explain.

September 1996

MINIBIKE FLASHBACK

A couple of weeks ago, I was riding into the big city from our deeply rural home when I came upon a stretch of road with cars parked on both sides. Turned out it was a yard sale. I hit the kill button on my yet-unrestored metal-flake-orange eyesore Triumph 500 and climbed off for a look.

It was late in the day, so the sale looked pretty much cleaned out, the remains being mostly mid-1970s Partridge Family synthetic clothing and pieces of furniture with at least one bad leg. What caught my eye, however, was a minibike. Apparently just purchased by a farmer and his son, it was being loaded into the back of a pickup. The kid was beaming.

The minibike had no discernible brand name, but was of the standard early-1960s variety: double-loop frame (rusty), rectangular upholstered seat (duct-taped), go-kart wheels and treaded tires, small chrome headlight, canister-shaped lawnmower gas tank, yellow Clinton "Wasp" two-stroke engine with pull cord dangling.

I hate to admit it, but I found myself staring at the minibike with almost the same drop-jawed fascination and wonder as the kid for whom it had apparently been purchased. If this father and son had not been there to buy the slightly tired machine, I would doubtless have bought it myself, after about 0.5 seconds of careful contemplation.

Minibikes of this design are powerful touchstones of my own teen years. They fit into that same class of memorabilia as my Dave Sisler–model baseball glove, which is sitting right here on my bookshelf, or the Boy's Model 67A single-shot Winchester .22 that (to my wife's eternal amazement) has hung on some wall of every house in which we have lived.

Honda 50s and other small Japanese bikes and scooters are generally given the lion's share of the credit for ushering in the motorcycle mania that struck America in the early 1960s, so it's easy to forget that minibikes also played a part.

The very genesis of this magazine is tied to them.

CW's early Editor/Publisher Joe Parkhurst ran *Karting World* during the first boom years of that sport, a magazine that featured much advertising for, and the occasional road test of, minibikes.

Later, following my own (and my mechanically minded pals') unfolding metamorphosis away from karts and into the more legally roadable world of minibikes and motorcycles, Parkhurst moved to *Cycle World* magazine. He simply recognized what one sociologist has called the latest "mini-virus." Minibikes were an interim idea whose time had come.

They were to motorcycles what the go-kart was to a sports car; the irreducible minimum, easily produced. Frame, engine, wheels, gas tank, brought together with an appealing shop-class-project simplicity. You looked at them and said, "Of course. Why didn't we do this before?"

Typical of my entire youth, my own parents were not drawn in by minibikes, nor did they want me spending $125 of my lawn-mowing "college fund" on a diminutive and probably dangerous motorbike. So, of course, I had to build my own.

And so I did, and quite successfully for once.

I took a cast-off boy's 26-inch bicycle frame to a local welding shop and had a flat steel motor-mount plate welded into the bottom of the front loop, and a piece of water pipe welded across the rear seat stay, to hold ball bearings for a reduction shaft (I had built enough stationary, belt-smoking go-karts to understand the need for low gearing).

The engine, a 1.5-horsepower Briggs & Stratton four-stroke washing-machine engine (yes, rural people used to have gasoline-powered washing machines), was borrowed from my dad's cement mixer and drove a V-belt off its 2-inch pulley back to a 12-inch pulley on the reduction shaft. To the other end of the shaft was welded a small bicycle sprocket that drove a large bicycle sprocket bolted to a 12-inch pneumatic wheelbarrow tire and wheel at the rear. I had a matching wheel at the front. A lawnmower gas tank was slung from the crossbar by metal straps.

No clutch. No brakes. You bump-started it and relied on compression braking to slow down. No twistgrip. A push-pull cable from a lawnmower operated the throttle.

This contraption worked perfectly the very first time I tried it. With its super-low gearing, top speed was only 15 miles per hour, but it would climb steep embankments like a burro. No brakes were needed; closed-throttle compression almost threw you over the handlebar. Fuel mileage was phenomenal. I could ride virtually all day on the 1-quart gas tank by leaning out the mixture for load conditions as I rode, turning a jet on its primitive carburetor.

One grand, green summer, I rode this thing all over Juneau and Monroe Counties on unpatrolled country roads. (My parents required that I remove the V-belt and push it out of town before riding, but were otherwise more amused than disapproving.) I put hundreds of miles on the minibike, even packing a knapsack and spending the weekend with my school friends, the Volzka brothers, who lived on a remote farm.

I doubt I've enjoyed any subsequent motorcycle ride more than I did those carefree summer minibike trips when I was 14, wandering the western Wisconsin landscape of red barns, shaded lanes, and indolently watchful dairy herds. It was my first real taste of freedom. I could go anywhere, for once, without pedalling, and—more important—without asking.

A great machine.

Someday, perhaps, I'll buy a commercially built one, with real brakes and a centrifugal clutch. Like the minibike at the garage sale. That kid was mighty lucky I didn't get there a few minutes earlier.

But I'm glad I didn't. Judging from the look on his face, I'd say it's his summer. In bike ownership, we should always concede to the larger, more powerful dream.

November 1996

THE RIGHT MAP FOR THE BIKE

With certain motorcycles, there is a defining moment when you know you are going to have to buy one, sooner or later. A gear suddenly locks to its shaft and the two spin as one, idea and destiny together.

That happened to me when I was at the Harley-Davidson plant in York, Pennsylvania, last fall doing a story for *Big Twin* magazine, our all-Harleys sister publication. I spent an entire Sunday sitting down at the end of the motorcycle assembly line, interviewing H-D workers who build, ride, and modify their own Harleys.

The assembly line had been shut down for the weekend on Saturday at noon, and the last bike on the conveyer was a Mystic Green and black Road King, missing only a few bits of hardware to be complete.

All day long I looked at the thing, letting it soak into my brain, much the way a strong sauerbraten marinade works on chuck roast. Between interviews I would walk over and stand by it. By the end of the afternoon, a welder named Kevin "Smokey" Barley said, "I believe you better buy one of those."

And I said, "I believe I will."

Returning home, I ordered one from my local dealer, a gentleman named Al Decker who, with his wife Mary, has run a Harley dealership for 50 years. The bike is supposed to be here in about three weeks, theoretically.

I bought essentially the same motorcycle from Al four years ago, a 1992 FLHS. Not much different from the current Road King, except that it had a plastic instrument pod left over from the 1970s and the optional "pillow-look" touring seat with little puckered buttons all over it. On the positive side, it had a better handlebar, a stock luggage rack, and was $4,000 cheaper.

But the Road King is more like the bike I was looking for in the first place, a functional, modern antique with a slightly closer resemblance to an early Hydra-Glide Panhead, the standard by which I judge all American Twins. Anyway, the FLHS is gone; the King is coming.

Quite a few of my sportriding buddies, of course, have suggested any number of desirable bikes I might buy for the same price—a fine collection of them, even. But nearly all duplicate in some way the sporting virtues of my Ducati 900SS or my old Triumph 500. Which I already have.

What I miss having is a bike at the other end of the spectrum. A motorcycle for carrying two people and luggage across the vastness of America while exuding a certain historical charm and making great mortar-like thuds of combustion. The motorcycle equivalent of a Stearman biplane, if you will. For my money, nothing fills this bill better than a H-D Twin. Still.

Especially if you tweak about 20 more bhp out of its engine aftermarket-wise, which I'm fixin' to do *toot-sweet* upon delivery.

Anyway, I've noticed an interesting change in my life since I ordered the Road King: I've found myself looking at a whole different set of maps.

Big ones. National maps, with large, distant places like Kansas and New Mexico on them. It's been a while.

Before taking a Sunday-morning ride on my Triumph 500, I tend to get out small maps. Usually from my highly detailed DeLorme Atlas of county maps, with lots of thin gray roads named Shady Hollow Lane or Dogbite Ridge. Short-range stuff.

I know people like our friend Ted Simon in *Jupiter's Travels* went around the world on a Triumph 500, and there's no reason not to if you don't object to the extravagant consumption of pistons. But in my own mind, the Triumph T100-C was made for trails, farm roads, and local exploration. Its agile, lightweight talents are wasted on the big open highway; the meter is always running toward rebuild time.

On Ducati rides, a state map comes into play. On top of the Ducati's tank bag I have a Wisconsin map, usually folded to one quadrant or another. If I get up early enough on the weekend, I'll usually plan a trip of several hundred miles. As with the Triumph, you can obviously ride a 900SS farther than that, especially with a Corbin seat. In fact, I'm planning to take mine to Sturgis next week.

Still, when you look at a 900SS in your garage, you don't think of cross-country travel. That's not what it's for. You *can* ride across Texas, but you don't *dream* of riding across Texas.

And the Road King?

Here, all the state borders come tumbling down. The fine focus goes away (along with a little finesse) and you roll a big map of North America across the dining room table, like a Persian rug merchant showing his wares.

Suddenly you would pay good money and use valuable vacation time to ride to Texas, and then go all the way across it, just for fun. Visit your good friends in Blanco and Archer City, then drop down to Big Bend Park and maybe take in the Terlingua Chili Cookoff. No problem. America is at your feet.

As it should be. Most motorcycles, after all, have evolved to work best on their native roads.

Triumph 500s, for instance, may have won the Jack Pine Enduro here in the U.S., but I always feel they were actually built for a quick spin down a country lane between two small villages in the Cotswolds. Or a run to the pub.

Ducatis can cover a lot of ground anywhere, but they seem happiest in those pockets of the U.S. that most resemble the twisting mountain roads of Emilia Romagna or the open sweepers of Tuscany. It's what they were born to do.

And Harleys? To me, they seem to have been built with the Great Plains and deserts in mind . . . the American West. Big Sky bikes.

Thudding down some long, lonesome highway in Nebraska or Wyoming, you can easily imagine that Bill Harley long ago took one good look at the map of America, let out a low whistle, and said, "We're going to need bigger pistons. Two of 'em, with a slow, lazy heartbeat."

February 1997

OF DOGS AND DEER

According to historians, much of the original road system in the U.S. was based on Indian footpaths, which in turn followed ancient game trails. Makes sense to me. Who better than a deer or a pedestrian to find the most sensible path through the wilderness?

Only in recent times has the concept of a frontage road to Wal-Mart overwhelmed the natural logic of the shallow river portage, the unbroken ridgeline of the low-elevation mountain pass. But it seems the roads we really like as motorcyclists still follow the old deer trail/Indian tradition of ribbons draped over the land rather than barging through it.

While these roads have their charm, they do present two small problems to the modern rider: 1) A motorcycle travels a lot faster than a person in moccasins; and 2) the deer have not left.

Indeed, the deer are thriving. In his book, *Wildlife in America*, Peter Mathiessen says the deer population in the U.S. is now far greater than it was in the day of Daniel Boone, thanks to a ready supply of field corn and a dearth of predators. Deer, in fact, fare much better in the garden-rich environment of suburban America than they do in the lonely north woods. This year we had a record herd in Wisconsin, 1.7 million.

If you don't believe it, ask my friend Bruce Finlayson.

This past summer, he was on a motorcycle ride at dusk with a bunch of our fellow suspects in the Slimey Crud Motorcycle Gang, cruising a county road not far from Madison, Wisconsin. Suddenly, a large white-tail launched itself out of the foliage and landed dead-center in front of his beautifully restored Ducati 750 GT, which was traveling 60–65 miles per hour.

According to eyewitness reports from the five guys who were following, Bruce flew over the top of the deer and tumbled like a rag doll a considerable distance down the road, where his motorcycle slid into him. The deer was killed, and Bruce was unconscious, with a broken collarbone.

From a nearby farmhouse an ambulance was called, but when it arrived Bruce's blood pressure was dropping and his heart rate was irregular, so the paramedics called a Med-Flight helicopter. By the time the helicopter got there, Bruce had regained consciousness and was making about as much sense as usual, objecting to the medics cutting his nice old Bates jacket off with surgical scissors.

Thanks to the miracle of modern health-care economics, Bruce was pronounced fit to return home after only three hours at a Madison hospital, with a sling on his arm and a prescription for pain-killers.

He's better now, but for weeks he felt pretty battered and beaten up, discovering new bruises every day. His bike needs the fork straightened, paint, and a few random parts, but is entirely fixable. His helmet did its work but is ruined, with a broken shell and blacktop scars in seven distinct spots. It looks like a cracked eggshell.

A few days after the accident, when Bruce was back up and on his feet, I thought we should celebrate the resurrection of the body with a sacramental wine, so of course I took him a bottle of Stag's Leap cabernet. Bruce laughed as only a person with bruised ribs can laugh.

That same week, a woman who works with my wife Barbara said her brother hit a deer with his Harley-Davidson (no helmet), spent all night lying in a ditch, and was undergoing jaw and facial-bone reconstruction, among other things.

Two weeks later, I was on a ride to the famous Dickeyville Hillclimb with the same bunch of Cruds who had witnessed Bruce's accident when a dog the size of a Bultaco Metralla ran in front of my 900SS while I was idly gazing hard right at a beautiful new log home along the road. I never saw the dog until I'd missed it by inches. For the benefit of my co-riders, I grabbed at my heart and put my head down on the tank.

Sheer unvarnished dumb luck. If the dog had been a microsecond slower or the bike had arrived a tick sooner, I'd have had my own Med-Flight ride, and Bruce would have been bringing me a bottle of Red Dog ale.

Mike Puls, who was right behind me, suggested Bruce and I co-write a book called *Of Deer and Dogs*.

Since then, I've done two smoking emergency stops for deer at night while returning to our rural home from Madison, both of them on Old Stage Road. Which, incidentally, is another of those ancient Indian trails, modernized to a stagecoach road in the 1830s and now a fine blacktop motorcycle road. Except for deer.

And they are everywhere this year. There's almost no defense for them after dark, other than doddering slow speed. They appear and disappear like wraiths at night, unpredictable as shooting stars or the sudden swoop of an owl.

I haven't yet given up riding at night, but I've certainly slowed. When I ride Old Stage Road at night now, I tend to cruise in the 45–50 miles per hour range, chuffing along in third gear.

I try to get out of that old café racer mode and tell myself I'm on a scenic cruise through a game park, which is almost the truth. I haven't made an evening trip yet this year without seeing at least one deer, three cats, the random dog, a couple of possums, and a raccoon or two.

Most of these animals, I'm afraid, are still looking for wolves or humans in moccasins. Nothing in their long evolution has prepared them for the sudden appearance of a fast-moving quartz-halogen headlight from Italy.

Nor in ours, apparently. Our only real advantage in the game of survival seems to be that, like those Indians of yore, we use our trails for trade as well as travel.

Bruce, for instance, had a $400 helmet from Japan and a leather jacket from California, and the deer didn't. But for those two small distinctions, they would both have departed our gene pool on the same day.

March 1997

HOW MANY BIKES DO YOU REALLY NEED?

On a recent tour of Northern Mexico with Pancho Villa Moto-Tours, a bunch of us were sitting around a cantina one night, chasing down the day's road dust with a few margaritas, when one of the basic questions of motorcycling came up: Exactly how many bikes does a person really need, anyway?

Several of us who had spent more time thinking about this problem then is really decorous in a world filled with plagues and social injustice, quickly reached a consensus.

"Five," we said confidently.

Those at the table without enough bikes were mystified. "Why five?"

You've got to love it when people ask you questions like this. Makes the brain fizz warmly like a 6-volt battery on full charge and encourages the tongue to speak fond, familiar phrases. The tavern industry owes its very life to these profound puzzles. "Hey Bob, what's the best deer rifle?"

Stand back.

Anyway, after several hours of thoughtful discussion that would have done justice to the First Continental Congress if they'd all been on their third margarita, we finally thrashed out the following categories. Everybody, we decided, needs:

1. A sportbike.

Yep, say what you want about your sport-tourers, your dual-sport bikes with sticky street tires or your "Harleys that don't handle too bad," there is still nothing like a light, quick bike of roadracing heritage whose single purpose in life is to turn in quickly, grip a corner tenaciously, and spit you out the other side like a watermelon seed.

This bike for me is my Ducati 900SS, but it could just as easily be any of a dozen others. If you are a practicing roadracer, of course, any racing bike fills the bill.

2. A sport-touring bike.

If you love to ride, sometimes you've got to go places with luggage, and maybe even a spouse or close friend. A pure sportbike won't do here. You could use a big comfortable touring rig, but the best part of every trip is usually the mountains—Ozarks, Rockies, Alleghenies, etc. And if you don't want to spend the rest of your life staring at trout decals on the back door of a motorhome, a fast sport-tourer is the only answer.

Incidentally, I don't own a sport-tourer right now. I tell people I'm "between bikes," but I'm actually between money.

3. A dirtbike.

This can be a pure motorcrosser, an enduro bike, a dual-sporter, or a big-bore "adventure tourer." Whatever the choice, it should be a bike that does not force you to stop in sheer terror (or go down like a poleaxed moose) when the pavement ends.

A dirt road is a terrible thing to waste, and there are a lot of them out there.

The closest thing I have to a dirtbike right now is my high-pipe 1968 Triumph T100-C, which works OK if you don't push it too hard, but something more modern and durable is doubtless in the offing.

4. A great big hog of some kind.

Not everybody is afflicted with the desire for this kind of bike, but I am. That's why I bought my Road King. There are days when I don't want to put on body armor, tuck in behind a noisy windscreen, and assume the position. I'm just not in the mood.

I want to thud along behind a big windshield, grinning like a fool at the peaceful, passing world. I want to pick up a bag of dog food and a six-pack of Negra Modelo (now *that's* a meal!) on the way home and throw it all in the cavernous saddlebags. Or ride to Florida.

This bike doesn't have to be a Harley; almost any bike will do, ridden in the right spirit of benign detachment and relaxation. It helps, though, if the bike has useful luggage space and wind protection. What we are describing here, essentially, is a car you can't use in a snowstorm.

5. An Old Crock.

Vincent Black Shadow, Honda CB160, Indian Chief, Suzuki X-6 Hustler, Henderson Four, you name it. It has to be a bike from your lost youth or from an era in which you wish you'd lived, symbolic of something important to you, or just beautiful in itself. It should remind you simultaneously of how far we've come and how much we've lost.

If there is one category in which many of us have too many bikes, it is this one, as it obviously lends itself for collecting. For instance, I presently have two bikes in this category, and I'd probably have a bunch more if I had the money or garage space.

Which leads to a whole other philosophical quandary: Can a person actually have too many bikes?

For me, the answer is yes.

I appreciate large, museum-like collections managed by others but I can't handle them myself. I've had as many as seven motorcycles at one time, and I've found that beyond a count of five they start becoming slightly invisible. My appreciation level and riding time are spread too thin, like German troops on the Russian front. Also, I can't keep up with the insurance, batteries, and oil changes.

On the flipside, is it okay to have fewer than five bikes?

Well, by careful mixing and matching of traits, it does seem possible to live with fewer than five motorcycles for a while, as I am doing right now, without actually ceasing to respire. And then there's money.

Many times—during periods of student life, unemployment, moving, or scraping up cash for a house down payment—I've had as few as one or two bikes. For a few months after I got out of the Army one winter, I had none.

But these are not ideal circumstances, and it is perfection for which we are striving here.

Nope. I think our search for truth in the cantinas of Mexico was right on the money. Five is the magic number.

En Cuervo veritas.

April 1997

CHEESY CIRCUMSTANCES

Last summer, my neighbor Chris Beebe saw an ad in the paper that said (I am quoting here from memory), "Three BSA 650s for sale, one good runner in nice condition, two parts bikes; $1,000 takes it all."

Now Chris is not a die-hard BSA fan, but the deal seemed too good to pass up, so he made the call. The bikes sounded promising. The owner, who said he was riding the "good" BSA every day, lived about 20 miles out of town. Chris took the afternoon off work and drove out for a look.

When he got there, he found a sort of BSA graveyard in the front yard of a farmhouse. Scattered around were a frame and partially disassembled engine, a few buckets full of old BSA engine parts, and another frame with a complete engine in it. The latter was missing its seat, fenders, and lights. It had a non-BSA tank and a homemade exhaust system. Chris assumed this was one of the parts bikes.

But no.

The owner explained that this was the "good one" and the other scattered parts comprised the two parts bikes.

Chris looked around the yard perplexed. "You said over the phone you had a complete bike, but it looks like you don't quite have a whole BSA here . . . "

The owner grinned slyly and said, "Got you here, didn't it?"

Not being a violent man, and not having a large rocket-propelled grenade launcher on his shoulder, Chris simply shook his head and walked away. He got in his car and drove home.

When he told me this story later, Chris confessed that, for all his anger, he still looked back at those three partial bikes on the front lawn and felt bad for leaving them behind.

"I wanted to rescue them" he said, "just to get 'em away from that guy and out of that yard full of trash."

We'll ignore for a moment that the BSAs *were* the yard full of trash; there was in Chris's voice the same note of pathos you hear when a Humane Society worker fails to separate a mistreated dog from its abusive owner.

I knew exactly how he felt. It seems that at least half the old motorcycles I've bought in my own lifetime have been acquired under what my friend Jeff Craig once so aptly called "cheesy circumstances."

The moral urge to lift a motorcycle out of a sordid or unhappy environment is often as powerful as the actual need to own and ride the thing.

My first Triumph, for instance, was bought from an otherwise very nice fellow whose only real crime was that he'd leaned his beat-up 1967 Bonneville against a barn and had then neglected to put it indoors for the winter. I somehow spotted the bike while driving out in the country, even though the only piece I could see was a handlebar end sticking out of a snowdrift.

Being a good Limey archaeologist, I immediately glimpsed that backswept, bird-wing curve of the handlebar, along with the chromed ball-end brake lever, and surmised that we had a Triumph under the snow.

I had very little money at the time, but I had to buy this bike. You simply cannot leave a complete Triumph Bonneville stuck in a snowdrift all winter. The rules of civilization require you to take it home.

While it's always nice to rescue a bike from an unpleasant owner or slow death by exposure, there is yet another whole class of cheesy circumstance that falls under the heading of Basic Aesthetic Nightmare.

This is where you find the Vincent Black Shadow that's been painted metalflake lavender and are forced to buy the thing just so you can repaint it. Or maybe it's a Honda 400F with a great big Windjammer fairing held on by rusty pipe-strapping material. Or virtually any motorcycle with a seat reupholstered in white vinyl and red piping.

Whatever the travesty, real or imagined, few forces of nature are more powerful than the urge to rip someone else's custom accessories off a bike and toss them over your shoulder.

My freshman year in college I bought a Honda Super-90, partly because I needed transportation, and partly because the bike had German "iron cross" decals all over the tank, sidecovers, and fenders.

When I went to pick up the bike, I took along a razor blade and a damp cloth. I handed over the check, shook hands with the former owner, started the Honda, and rode around the corner. There, I immediately got off, crouched beside the bike, and removed all the German crosses.

What relief. It felt, in some small way, like the liberation of Paris. Lowering one flag and raising another; a change of command.

Is it possible the seller was so clever that he put those decals on his otherwise pristine silver Honda as a sales tool? I doubt it, but he might just as well have, in my case.

I used to think that the best way to sell a motorcycle was to clean it and polish the chrome, put it back to stock condition, and display it in a spotless corner of your garage, as if to verify its place as the centerpiece of your life, which it had usually been.

But maybe I'm wrong. Maybe it's the snowdrift, the rusted luggage rack, the iron cross, and the surly-owner approach that work best. The will to rescue and reform may be stronger than our admiration for a clean and well-kept bike.

Perhaps the ideal newspaper ad should read: "Ugly troll with bad temper wishes to sell tangerine orange AJS-7R lying on side in yard, frozen in mud."

I know I'd call, and Chris probably would too. For some of us, there's a very small distinction between an effective classified ad and a ransom note.

July 1997

SWORDS OF DAMOCLES

Last weekend a man from Chicago came to buy my 1987 Reynard Formula Continental racing car. This is an open-wheeled single-seater with a Ford 2-liter ohc engine, and, although it's a wonderful-handling car in good condition, I have decided to sell it because a) it is no longer competitive in SCCA national races and b) I want to take a summer off racing and heal the financial wounds of having one too many projects stuffed into my garage.

The fellow who bought my car has been racing a Bug-Eye Sprite for 21 years and said he has always wanted to try racing a formula car and, having just turned 45, has decided to do it. He doesn't mind that my car is slightly dated, because he wants to try the class before spending more money.

But enough about cars (this is a bike magazine, no?) and onto the point.

While the gentleman from Chicago was looking at the car in my workshop, his wife had tea with my wife Barbara in our house, and they had a chance to talk. It came to light during their chat that my car buyer's motivation actually ran a little deeper than he let on.

Seems a close friend of his, also 45 years old, had a sudden unforeseen heart attack last year. He's recovered completely, but this was a real eye-opener for all concerned. It drove home that old basic lesson that Life is Short.

"Since then, my husband has been trying all kinds of things he's never done," Barb was told. "He's always wanted to race an open-wheeled formula car, so he decided that right now was the best time to do it."

Reflecting on this later, I thought it was both sobering and a little amusing (if such serious matters can ever be said to be amusing) that so many of us who love cars, motorcycles, airplanes, etc., nearly always react to a life crisis in terms of a coveted machine—or an untaken adventure with a machine.

Chest pains? Quick, call your Ducati dealer and see if that 916 is still unsold! Tornado miss your house by a few hundred yards? Might as well buy a new XR and do Baja off-road, all the way down to Cabo. Time's a-wastin'!

I personally had a small medical scare a couple of years ago, nothing but a wee dark spot on my shoulder. They caught this one in plenty of time with several sessions of minor surgery, but on my way out of the doctor's office I happened to remark that it was a good thing I'd stopped in to have it looked at.

"Yes," said the doctor, almost casually. "If you'd let it go a few months longer, you'd probably be dead within the year." He looked into my eyes searchingly to see if I understood the significance of this near miss.

I did.

That afternoon, with the doctor's words resonating in my head, I drove out to Decker Harley-Davidson and ordered a new Electra-Glide Sport. I'd been staring at the brochures for months, but hadn't been able to convince myself to take out a loan and spend all that money. I'd always wanted to take an Electra-Glide on an extended, easy-cruising tour of the greater Southwest, and that very summer Barb and I did just that. Seemed like the right time.

On a similar but more serious note, former *CW* contributor Steve Thompson discovered he had a life-threatening brain tumor a few years back. It was successfully operated on, and he responded to his new lease on life by competing at the Isle of Man for the first time, and writing us a wonderful story—one of the best I ever read—about his adventures there. It was a thing he had always wanted to do, but had left undone.

I've heard many versions of this story over the years, though some are more subtle and subliminal than others. And some are retroactive.

Yours truly, for instance, has hardly ever been without some form of late-1960s Triumph in the garage. I like the way these bikes look and sound, but there's a little more to it than that. Part of their appeal lies in the fact that these are the bikes I most lusted after during the time I was in Vietnam. And every time I look at one now, it reminds me I'm back. There's a little reward built into every Triumph, a little private celebration.

I suppose people who don't care about motorcycles find some other way of handling these curve balls life throws at us. Maybe a new set of gardening tools, a deluxe bowling ball, or a trip to the Yucatán. Or, if they are of a non-materialistic bent, they may find renewed interest in some spiritual aspect of life, or merely be reminded of how much their families and friends mean to them, or how pointless it is to cause dissension in this short passage of time.

Nearly all of us, I imagine, have at least some of the higher, thoughtful stuff built into us. But what seems to distinguish motorcycle buffs from your average reflective citizen is the tendency to express personal philosophy and spiritual outlook with machinery. I don't believe I've ever had a watershed change of life or perspective that was not marked by the acquisition (or rejection) of a motorcycle.

When we want to simplify, we get a simpler bike. Or sell off a few we don't need. In celebration of some success, we tend to indulge ourselves. And after a close shave of some sort, we go for those bikes—and rides—we've been putting off for too long. Danger, perceived or real, has a great way of concentrating the mind and cleansing it of trivial matters. That mythical sword hanging over us by a single hair makes us realize what's important.

Years ago, there was a famous Gahan Wilson cartoon in *Playboy* magazine. It showed two golfers on a putting green, with a huge nuclear mushroom cloud rising over the city in the background. "Might as well play through," one golfer says to the other. "The shock wave won't get here for at least three minutes."

It's a golf joke, but most of us can easily identify with the concept. I suppose if a mushroom cloud suddenly appeared over a nearby city, my first impulse might be to run out and shop for a Vincent. Quickly.

November 1997

FOR RICHER AND EVEN POORER

Over the past 26 years, I would estimate that upwards of 100 people have said to me, "I'm surprised your wife lets you have a motorcycle."

This statement is occasionally made by men, but most often, I'm sorry to say, by rather well-dressed, conservative women whose husbands stand in the background looking as if they've been hit across the side of the head with a 2x4. More than once.

Aside from the dismal connotations of the word "lets" in a marriage, I always find this statement more amusing than offensive. Why?

Well, for one thing, my wife Barbara had her own motorcycle when I met her—a Benelli 150—but there's more to it than that.

Let me explain, begging your patience here for a short tale.

Late one winter afternoon in 1973, an old Econoline van with ladders on the top dropped me off at the corner near my house in Madison, Wisconsin. My fancy new journalism degree had failed to get me a writing job anywhere in town, so I had taken up the rain gutter and downspout trade.

Our crew had been out on the rooftops all day, installing rain gutters on a new housing project in the town of Sun Prairie, which had much more prairie than sun, and a stiff north wind raking across the plains. "Nothing between us and the North Pole but a barb-wire fence," as the radio weatherman said. We wore hooded parkas on the job, but were pretty well frozen.

I crunched through the snow to our place on Chandler Street, where Barb and I rented the top floor of an older house. Yellow light shone warmly from the upstairs windows, meaning Barb was already home. She had a "real job" (*i.e.* in her chosen profession), working as a physical therapist at the nearby Madison General Hospital.

On the way in, I noticed an old red Chevy pickup truck parked in front of our house, with a camper on the back. The camper was one of those homemade deals, with a roof of real wood shingles. It looked like a trapper's cabin on wheels.

While Barb and I made dinner, I mentioned there was a strange truck out front. Barb was silent for a moment, then said, "I know. I borrowed it from someone at work. We have to use it to pick up your birthday present tomorrow." She smiled cryptically.

That night a blizzard hit, and I lay awake listening to the wind and snow howl against our windows, wondering what kind of gift required a truck. Our only car was a rusted-out 1968 VW Beetle with almost no cargo space, so the gift could be just about anything larger than a necktie.

Toolbox? I needed a good toolbox. I was still storing my tools, at that point, in something that looked like a fishing tackle box. And smelled like it, too. Maybe we were going to Sears for a new Craftsman tool chest that didn't reek of bluegills.

I hoped she hadn't spent too much. We didn't have much money. It was a time of "justs." I was just out of the Army, we were just married, and I had just finished my last few semesters of college. Barb was still paying off her student loans.

How poor were we?

We were so poor I didn't even have a motorcycle. My parents had sold my Honda CB160 when I was in Vietnam. I'd been trying to save for a bike, but had made very little progress—almost none, actually—what with rent and groceries. My Bell 500TX helmet and Buco leather jacket hung in the closet like silent remonstrance.

In the morning it was still snowing and drifting, but we shoveled our way to the truck, then shoveled out the truck as the first snowplows went by. I got behind the wheel of the pickup and said, "Where to?"

"Take Highway 18 out of town."

Hmmm. Not the way to Sears. Too bad.

Spinning our tires and drift-busting down the highway, we pressed on through the dark morning, half blind from blowing snow. Past the outskirts of the city, through the towns of Verona and Mt. Horeb. Whatever we were picking up was *way* out of town.

When we passed Dodgeville, 37 miles from Madison, I was advised to press on, westward. Suddenly, I knew where we were going.

"We're headed for Prairie du Chien," I said.

Barb smiled.

Prairie du Chien, a Mississippi river town, was famous (among guys like me) for having a large-volume Honda dealership called Stark's Sporting Goods, which undersold nearly all other Honda dealers. It was, perhaps, not very loyal for buyers to go out of town to buy bikes, but at Stark's you might pay $869 for, say, the new Honda CB350 I'd been lusting after, when the same bike was $969 everywhere else. And you have to remember that $100 in those pre-inflationary, post-student times meant as much to most of us as $1,000 might now. Huge difference.

As we slid into the drifted main street of Prairie du Chien and headed down toward the river bridge, Barb said, "Why don't you park over there?"

Sure enough. Stark's. A red Honda sign glowed in a dim halo of light.

Inside, mixed with fishing lures, hip boots, rifles, and shotguns, were rows of new 1973 Hondas. And one of them, pulled out from the row, had a tag on the handlebars that said "SOLD: Egan."

It was a Honda CB350—first year with the disc brake—in a beautiful dark green.

I looked at Barb, who was watching my face to see if she'd done the right thing.

"How did you do this?" I asked quietly.

"I saved a little every month in the credit union at work."

Back in business, after three years without a bike. Reborn.

Almost 10 years later, Barb bought me yet another motorcycle for my birthday. An elaborate set of clues led me to a gleaming black Kawasaki KZ1000 MKII parked in our neighbor's garage. Another quiet wish fulfilled, unexpectedly.

Anyway, when someone says, "I'm surprised your wife lets you have a motorcycle," I never get annoyed. I just reflect for a few fond moments and reply, "Yes, I am too. Every time."

February 1998

THE GREAT DYLAN CRASH

Just last week I found myself on a cross-country trip in my ancient 356 Porsche, driving along the southern edge of the Catskill Mountains in New York, right through the famous village of Woodstock. Sharing the driving with me for a few days of the trip was my old motorcycle touring buddy, Mike Cecchini, from Bethesda, Maryland.

Woodstock, of course, is best known for the great rock festival of 1969, which actually took place on a farm near Bethel, New York, about 35 miles away. The Woodstock title stuck, however, because (a) that's where the festival was originally planned to be; and (b) the name had a certain magic.

Why magic?

Well, mainly because Bob Dylan lived there, having discovered the place while visiting the country retreat of his manager, Albert Grossman.

Also, Dylan's backup band (who later named themselves, simply, The Band), rented a little pink-shingled house nearby, a place they christened "Big Pink," composing the songs there for their first album: *Music from Big Pink*. With The Band and Dylan in town, lots of other musicians moved into the area, so the place became a kind of counterculture hotbed.

But, besides its abundance of famous residents, Woodstock was also known for another event in pop-culture lore: The Dylan motorcycle crash.

As every reasonably hip high school and college student knew in those days, Bob rode a Triumph. He was pictured on the cover of his *Highway 61 Revisited* album in a Triumph T-shirt, and he'd been photographed sitting astride his Triumph 500. I still have this photo in a book, and the bike looks to me (on close inspection with a magnifying glass) to be a

1964 Speed Tiger T100SR. Or maybe a 1963. In any case, you can see that the left front fork is drooling oil from the upper seal, just as my own 1968 Triumph 500 is doing at this very moment. Nice to know nothing ever changes.

I was working that summer on a railroad section crew, just about to start my freshman year at the University of Wisconsin, when news came over the radio of Dylan's crash on July 29, 1966. My friends and I were both stunned and not surprised at all, in equal measure. This, after all, was the Age of Disasters. Assassinations, the war in Vietnam, race riots, drug overdoses, and motorcycle crashes seemed to be claiming lives of the famous and non-famous at a rate almost too fast to calculate. None of us, in fact, thought we would live to be very old.

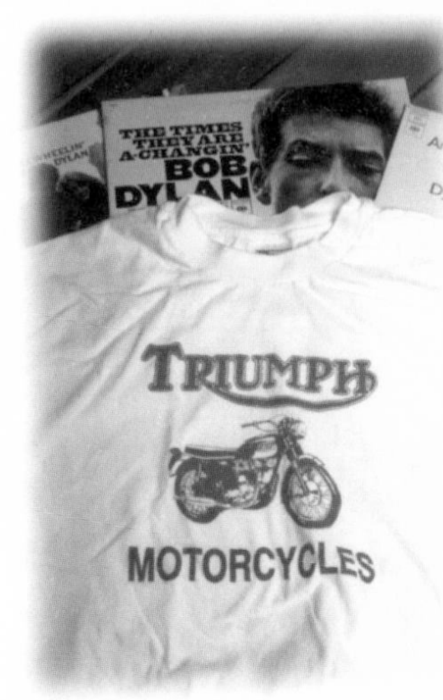

Still, Dylan's motorcycle accident was sad news. I think I can say without contradiction that he was simply *the* man, the music legend of the era. He was held in the same high artistic regard as the Beatles, but with all of it poured into a single individual. If nothing else, he wrote more songs that I took the trouble to learn on my own guitar than any other songwriter before or since.

Anyway, he crashed his motorcycle, and the underground rumor mill went wild: Dylan is paralyzed; Dylan is so badly disfigured he will never appear in public again; Dylan has a head injury and cannot speak, etc., etc.

Then in 1968, he came out with a new album, *John Wesley Harding*, and we all examined his photo on the cover for signs of damage. Scars? Stitches? He appeared to be standing upright under his own power. The album sounded good. Apparently he was okay.

The accident is still somewhat shrouded in mystery, but biographers seem to agree that he indeed had a motorcycle accident, locking up his back brake while swinging into a corner just south of Zena Road, about a mile east of Woodstock, where the road takes a tight S-bend near the site of an old mill. Some visitors to his home reported him wearing an arm sling and a neckbrace. In any case, the accident seems not to have been too terrible, and it appears Dylan used the mishap as an opportunity to quit touring for a while, stay at home with his family, and get some much-needed rest.

So, against this background, Mike and I came driving into Woodstock on Highway 212, on a late fall afternoon, 31 years later, and there, just out of town, was Zena Road. We turned off and, sure enough, found a severe S-curve just past the site of an old mill. I got out and walked around in the late afternoon sunlight.

Bad curve, all right. Beautiful spot, right next to the mill creek, with yellow autumn leaves falling lazily onto the water and whirling downstream. But easily a place where you could go in a little too fast. Maybe brake too hard too late, lose confidence, fail to countersteer, or just plain run out of traction. I walked through the corner and thought, *Yes, I could crash here myself. No problem.*

Mike, who is not so steeped in rock lore as I, smoked a cigarette patiently and leaned on the car, soaking up the sun rays while I walked around. I hoped he didn't mind the little detour, my dragging him here for some kind of quiet contemplation of historical vibes and private meaning. He kindly left me alone and said nothing, as he had two days before, when we visited the Vietnam War Memorial.

Hard to explain what brings us to these places. What are we looking for? My friend George Allez has visited at least three times the Iowa baseball diamond where *Field of Dreams* was filmed. He can't explain the allure, but every time he drives west, he stops there for a while and just takes it all in, as though the ghost of Shoeless Joe might still walk out of the cornfield.

We all have our own ghosts, I guess, and we like to pay them homage. Triumphs and the songs of Bob Dylan meant a lot to me at the time of his crash, and they still do. So it was just a place I had to go, to see for myself, as if to visit an incident from my own past at which I had somehow failed to be present. Such is the power of music—and motorcycles—to move us around in time. Pure transportation.

After a while, we got back in the Porsche and drove off in search of Big Pink. As we headed up the road, a line from a Band song ran through my head: "If I thought it'd do any good, I'd stand on the rock where Moses stood. . . . "

December 1998

THE NEARLY LOST ART OF THE KICKSTART

I should have been pull-starting the Homelite rather than kickstarting a motorcycle on Saturday morning, removing the box elder that fell on three sections of wood fence in our yard last week. One of the unheralded joys of living in the country is that you become a nearly full-time unpaid forest ranger. Chainsaws-R-Us.

Anyway, I averted my eyes from this fresh disaster of mixed branches and pine kindling because they were not quite completely blocking the driveway and went straight to the garage for an early-morning ride. The weather was too nice to ignore. After a hot, rainy summer, the mood change of autumn is upon us in Wisconsin. The sun is still warm, but the air has that spring-water-cold edge to it, with fields turning pale gold, squash vines blackening in gardens, and the sky a brilliant Battle-of-Britain blue.

Speaking of battles—and Britain—I was about to face up to the sometimes daunting task of kickstarting my Vincent, with its antique Amal carbs that have separate float bowls sticking out like Sherlock Holmes' pipe. I've had this bike for more than a month now, and I ride it every day, if possible. But sometimes it starts sooner, and sometimes later. On Saturday morning, it was later.

I played with throttle openings, carb ticklers, piston position, and varieties of compression-release synchronization with my lusty great kicks of the long lever, but to no avail.

First my helmet came off, then the jacket and gloves. A few minutes later I was soaked in sweat, splayed in my corner of the garage chair like a boxer after eight bad rounds, slamming down a Diet Mountain Dew, panting and staring at the bike with glassy eyes. Nothing I've ever done, except rock climbing, is as exhausting, per minute, as kickstarting a reluctant bike.

"You've got one more chance," I said, approaching the bike again, "and then I'm taking the Guzzi." I gave the Shadow one more fast kick with the throttle wide open and it started running instantly. Perfect tickover. Must have been a little flooded.

I put my stuff back on and took off for what was possibly the best ride of the year; 140 miles of backroads, farms, and forests reeled in with the twistgrip on a day so perfect it should have been bronzed. All that kicking vindicated.

Anyway, I am finally getting better with the Vincent. First, I took the seeping cork seals out of the petcocks and boiled them in water to swell them up (the first symptom of British bike ownership is cork boiling—an ancient Druidic ritual), then I took the old Amals apart this week and stared at the internals laid out in a cake pan like an oracle divining owl entrails, put them back on the bike with the float caps off, admitted fuel, and finally realized that the ticklers are extremely sensitive. They need just the slightest touch, not the fuel-drowning gush that my Triumph requires to light up. Anyway, I'm moving closer to Oneness here. It's fun dialing this stuff in.

Strangely, I realized the other day that of the four motorcycles I now own, three have no electric starters—only the 1979 Guzzi has an electric leg and no lever. My Triumph 500 nearly always starts first kick (unless the battery is touching the seat pan again), and the 1981 Ducati 900SS usually takes just a couple of prods while I figure out how much pumping of the Dell'Ortos it likes.

The last "modern" bike I owned with both kick and electric starting was my 1981 Kawasaki KA1000MKII. In fact, the very presence of that vestigial appendage was one of the reasons I chose this particular bike over several others.

This was exactly the period during which motorcycle engineers began saying to themselves (or each other), "Hey, wait a minute. Cars don't have hand cranks any more, so why are we putting kickstart levers on our bikes? More weight, more cost, more parts to wear out. Another oil seal to go bad. Let's leave 'em off and see what happens."

All very well, except most cars are driven daily. Motorcycles more often sit for days, weeks, or months between rides. And some of them (BMWs and my Guzzi SP come to mind) have electric clocks ticking away. Also, their batteries are relatively small. A recipe for trouble? Sometimes.

My Kawasaki battery went semi-flat within a year—lost its will to live during the rainy winter months back in California—but I didn't care. I simply kickstarted the bike for another two years before I got around to replacing it. As long as internal continuity was not broken, the bike worked.

Meanwhile, I would go over to pick up my friend John Jaeger for an early Sunday-morning ride and he would get all dressed up and hit the starter button on his BMW R90S (a famous charging system underachiever) and his starter would go, "DIT DIT . . . dit . . . dit" like a faint telegraph message. So we'd put his bike on the charger and go play guitar and swill coffee. Fun, but no ride. Sometimes we'd jump it from his car and make big sparks. A kickstarter would have been easier.

I don't miss kickstarters much on well-tuned modern bikes, and yet . . . every bike I've ever had without one always ends up needing one, usually more than once. There's always bump-starting, but this can be tricky business with a larger, heavier bike, especially if you're alone. But there's more to it than just the convenience of emergency starting.

There is, I think, a real satisfaction to having an engine bark to life with a lunge of the foot rather than a press of the button, as most dirt riders will tell you. To have *felt* that piston through the arch of your boot as it hits compression and fires up a big streetbike is one of those distinctly twentieth-century tactile pleasures that is drifting away from us, like hitting a well-oiled typewriter key or pulling through the wooden Sensenich prop on a Piper Cub.

Seems worth doing, even if we have to utter the occasional dark oath and boil cork now and then. It's these many small rituals, in the end, that make motorcycling something more than just steering.

April 1999

FOREVER YOUNG

While driving through a light snowstorm to see my dad at the nursing home this weekend, I happened to be listening to *A Prairie Home Companion* with Garrison Keillor on the radio.

For those of you who are unfamiliar with this program, it's a variety show broadcast live from St. Paul on National Public Radio, generally highlighting humorists and musicians whose work is not tedious enough to land them a slot on Easy Listening stations. It often features blues, Cajun, bluegrass, folk, and genuine country music. My kind of stuff: Hard Listening.

Anyway, at one point in the show, host Keillor sang one of the great old Bob Dylan songs, "Forever Young." He sang it with a clear, moving simplicity that made it sound almost like a traditional church hymn.

Which I guess it would be natural to do. It's written almost as a psalm or a prayer anyway, each verse ending with the wish, "May you stay forever young . . . "

I have to admit, it made me feel pretty sad. I was going to visit my father, who remains cheerful with a sharp sense of humor, but cannot remember being in the Navy during WWII, nor where his children now live. He can't remember owning his 1966 Mustang, either.

He's forever young in some ways—mostly in his easy wit and our family's recollections—but not in other ways. Time marches on. Even Bob Dylan himself is not looking like a kid these days. It's mostly his music that keeps him fixed in time.

Later that same evening I found myself out in the garage tinkering with the Vincent, doing a mid-winter oil and filter change (why not?). When I stood up, my back was in partial spasm. "Jeez," I muttered, stretching and twisting to take the kinks out, "this bike's in better shape than I am."

And, of course, it is. Laughably so. We are close to the same age—the bike was built in 1950 and I was manufactured two years earlier—but the Shadow was fully restored a couple of years ago and I was not.

Nor is it likely I will be. (For sale: one 1948 Caucasian Male; still able to feed self, but needs full restoration . . . ") Yet the bike looks like it came off the assembly line only about an hour ago. With proper care, it might even be immortal.

I sat down and gazed upon the Vincent for a while, sipping some post-oil-change anti-freeze (otherwise known as a Jim Beam Old Fashioned) with subzero winds rattling dry snow against the windows outside, and wondered who the original owner of my bike might have been.

Who brought it home in early 1951—when the bike was actually sold—and sat in his or her garage (we'll assume *his*, with this kickstart ratio) and did exactly what I was doing now?

It was probably not bought by a teenager. Vincents were not normally a beginner's bike, so if we assume the owner had a real job and was, say, 21 years old, that would make him 69 today. If the first owner were 35, he'd be my dad's age, 83. And if that mystery purchaser were the same age as I was when I bought the bike last fall (God forbid), he would now be 99.

In other words, it's unlikely the first owner of the bike is still riding, and it's entirely possible this same person, without a modicum of good luck and sound genetic heritage, has gone to that great café-racer hangout in the sky. Some hale and hearty people are still riding at 69, but many are not.

Still, the Vincent endures, looking to be in the prime of life.

This phenomenon of the ageless machine was first pointed out to me about 20 years ago in an essay by aviation writer Richard Bach. He noted that old machines—antique aircraft like his 1929 Detroit-Parks biplane, for instance—keep getting rebuilt and rejuvenated, while their pilots slowly turn gray, ultimately to hand over their aircraft to a new generation of pilots.

Which may, of course, be one of the very reasons we like to restore these things.

Everybody wants to be remembered for something, and most of us have devised some small strategy for leaving behind a moderate legacy, whether it's in the green eyes of our children, a house well-built, contagious kindness, oak trees planted along the driveway, or just a perpetual trust fund for disadvantaged motojournalists. Along those same lines, motorcycle preservation is not such a bad way of projecting ourselves forward in time, and it seems more worthwhile with each passing year.

After all, these are good bikes we've got on our hands. I don't know if craftsmanship and clarity of vision will ever again intersect with the same mood of hope, innocence, and sincerity that created our best twentieth-century motorcycles. Motorcycles will definitely continue to improve (almost weekly), but I'm not sure they'll ever become more beautiful or more important to history—or to their owners—than the bikes we saw last year at the Guggenheim.

In other words, those old Triumphs, Ducati Singles, Super Hawks, and Knuckleheads in our garages are probably at least as wonderful as we always suspected they were, well worth caring for and passing along. These bikes are talismans of a lucky accident—the overlapping of our short lives with an era that produced an unusual and exquisite craft.

It's become fairly common these days to note that we are just transient "curators" of the worthwhile things around us, but not too long ago my friend Greg Rammel put a more original spin on it, I think, at least for our own closely focused purposes.

When he and a bunch of riding buddies were standing around in his motorcycle shop near Detroit one evening, tipping beers and talking about the relative costs of classic old bikes, Greg shrugged and said, "It doesn't matter. We don't own these things, anyway. We just rent them."

Greg should know. He's had many years of motorcycles and customers pass through his shop, and he's seen more than a couple of leases expire. Usually on bikes that look better than ever.

September 2000

CAFÉ AMERICANO

There are, as far as I can tell, only two fixed rules in the universe: One is that pouring milk on your cereal will make the phone ring, and the other is that making any major purchase will trigger the immediate availability of something else you've always wanted.

Make a down payment on a home in the morning, and that afternoon you'll see a local ad that says, "For Sale: Brough Superior SS100 once owned by Lawrence of Arabia, minor front end damage; $3,000 firm, or will trade for lawnmower."

Pull into the driveway with a new car, and your next-door neighbor will wander over and ask if you are still interested in his Velocette Thruxton. Timing is everything.

My own recent plight was not quite that dramatic, but almost.

Last month, I took delivery of a new Honda CBR600F4, and the very next morning a 1977 Harley XLCR Café Racer showed up in the want ads. "6,000 miles, all original," it said.

Naturally, I've wanted one of these bikes for years—almost bought one new—but those I've seen for sale have always been in Texas or South Carolina, while I live in Wisconsin.

The committed buyer, of course, would go to Texas or South Carolina for a good bike, but I had never ridden an XLCR and wanted to try one before making that kind of pilgrimage. My strategy, then, was to wait for a bike to turn up in my own backyard. And here it was.

I went to look at the Harley on Saturday morning. A nice runner, well maintained, but also well used, with its share of nicks and scratches, priced near the upper end of the spectrum.

I rode the XLCR and found it surprisingly more comfortable and pleasant than legend had intimated, with wonderful gobs of midrange torque and locomotive-like clout in fourth (top) gear. Still, the owner was asking a fair amount of money for a bike needing cosmetic work. And tires. I told him I would have to think about it for a day.

Returning home, I opened up the morning paper and there was a second 1977 XLCR in the paper. This one had 10,000 miles on the clock, but was priced $2,000 cheaper. It had been stored for the winter at a motorcycle repair shop belonging to my friend Bill Whisenant, and Bill said he'd done some light restoration work on it. A very nice example, he said, "if you like noisy iron-barreled 1,000cc Sportster motors." Luckily, and irrationally, I do. Operationally, they fall under the heading "crude but exciting," and I like the way they look, so I went to see the bike.

A beautiful example indeed, cosmetically restored to almost showroom perfection. Nice paint, new brake lines and hydraulics, NOS shocks, redone wrinkle powdercoat on the cases, fresh Metzelers and drive chain. Dual and solo saddles. Original take-off Goodyear tires, shop manuals, etc. The whole kit.

I took it for a short ride into the hills north of Madison and everything worked perfectly (okay, the steering-head bearings were a tad loose). Steering was stable and neutral through fast sweepers, turn-in effortless. Seat and bars were perfect for my long reach. Great exhaust note from the siamesed pipes. By the time I got back I was a goner. "This bike is me," I mumbled, "apparently obtuse, yet clandestinely subtle. Only more so!"

I went straight to the bank, emptied out the dismal remains of my Perpetual Motorcycle Savings Account (est. 1963), and took a check to the owner, a very pleasant and knowledgeable fellow who produced $3,500 worth of refurbishment receipts for the Harley.

"On to my next project," he said. And then, upon signing over the title, wistfully reflected, "I wish, just once, I could buy a motorcycle from myself."

I knew exactly what he meant. It's rare to find a bike owned by someone who's done everything you yourself would automatically do to fix it up. Sometimes we get lucky.

Since buying the black Café Racer, I've done three or four all-afternoon backroad rides and put about 1,400 miles on it, having already changed its 60-weight oil once (no filter!). That heavy, blackstrap oil is somehow symbolic of the whole bike which, while relatively light (515 pounds wet) and very narrow, has a dense, heavy-duty mechanical feel. If the XLCR were a handgun, it would be a 1911 Colt .45 Automatic.

In any case, I enjoy riding the XLCR, and it has become my current daily rider.

One bonus aspect of the bike, I've discovered, is that everyone likes it. Sportbike riders, Harley guys, kids who have never seen one before. Another now-appreciated machine, like the 400F Honda, that sold poorly when it was new.

In 1977, the XLCR—whose design came from the pen and back-shop labors of Willie G. Davidson himself—was hailed as a beautiful design and an instant collector bike, but hardly anyone bought one. The XLCR was built only in 1977 and 1978, and only 3,123 copies were made (mine is #59).

Harley buyers went for the more traditional and useable Super Glide, while café-racer types found faster and more sophisticated fare in bikes such as the BMW R90S, Kawasaki Z-1, Guzzi V7 Sport, or Ducati 900SS. Solo seating didn't help sell the XLCR, either, though Harley came out with an optional dual saddle and axle-mounted passenger pegs in 1978.

Strangely, none of this seems to matter now as much as it did then. If the Harley Café Racer was a little elemental and old-fashioned in 1977, its shortcomings gradually seem less important with the passage of time.

No one buys an XLCR these days as an only, all-purpose motorcycle. If we really want to go somewhere two-up, or to race the backroads solo, there are legions of newer bikes that are far better than any of the XLCR's competition from 1977.

Take away those period comparisons, and all you have left is a charismatic vintage bike that is beautiful to look at and exciting to ride, even now.

Willie G's Café Racer may have finally reached that magical age where a bike no longer needs to be better than some other venerable thing to justify itself. It only has to move the soul.

February 2001

A TOWN TOO FAR

When I rode into town about two hours before sunset, it occurred to me that Jackson, Wyoming, had everything a touring rider could want at the end of a long, hot day.

Motels, movie theaters, Mexican restaurants, invitingly cool bars with invitingly cool drinks, camping and fishing stores to browse in, bookshops full of books on Western history, and a large number of mixed tourists to gaze upon while eating an ice cream cone on a park bench. The place was jumping.

Not that I'm normally drawn to places with hordes of tourists, but it is nice to be able to walk around town at night and get some exercise without being followed by the police car because you're the only guy who isn't home.

I cruised the entire length of Jackson to scope out the motels, riding all the way to the western city limits and noting that several inns still had VACANCY signs burning. I pulled into a parking space and looked at my watch. It was only about 6:30 P.M. and a little too early to stop, but I had been riding my old R100RS Beemer for about 10 hours and was feeling a little buzzed.

The best way to gauge your touring-fatigue level, I've found, is to get off your bike for a minute and shut it off. If your head is humming like a tuning fork and you can't put change in a parking meter, it's probably time to stop. Dropped gloves are a bad sign, too. The brain is switching over to its menu-contemplation mode (appetizer and beer list phase) and doesn't want to be bothered with basic motor skills.

I should have turned around right then and gone back into town. But I didn't. After all, there were nearly two hours of good riding light left. I looked at my watch and uttered those terrible words, "One more town."

Seemed like a good decision at the time. The ride out of Jackson was stunning. I swung up through the southern end of the Teton range on Highway 22 toward Teton Pass (8,429 ft.), a curving mountain two-lane with only moderate traffic. Pulling off at a scenic overlook, I flipped up my faceshield and looked at the map on my tankbag for a minute.

Hmmm. Not many big towns out there. If the motels were full in the tiny villages of Wilson or Victor or Swan Valley, my next sure bet for a hot meal and a bed would be Idaho Falls. About 85 miles away. The cars were already turning their headlights on, and in the dark shadows of the mountains my faceshield was beginning to shimmer with the halos of many departed bugs. Road signs warned of deer and elk. Maybe I should go back.

Yeah, that was the ticket. Mexican dinner, movie, walk. Buy a book. Have a margarita nightcap. Stop a little early for once and live like a human instead of a forward-progress machine. I turned around and rode back to Jackson, now more glittering than ever in the warm dusk.

Trouble was, much of the glitter came from newly lighted neon that said NO in front of the former VACANCY signs.

I cruised all the way back to the other end of town before I saw one lone vacancy sign, in front of a nice log-cabin-style lodge. But when I walked into the lobby I heard the desk clerk say to a family of four, "Sorry, we just gave away our last room. And absolutely everything in town is full. I've been calling around for the past half-hour, and there's nothing."

The family looked hollow-eyed and tired. So did I, one would suppose.

I had ridden right through town during that critical window of time another motorcycle journalist long ago (I can't remember who) referred to as "the witching hour." It's that fleeting period every evening when motels suddenly fill up, restaurants begin to run out of their prime rib special, and movies start. If you don't stop then, you will probably be out of luck. An hour later, you've missed the boat. One more town is a town too far.

I have ridden through the witching hour and aced myself out of a perfectly idyllic stopping place so many times I hesitate to admit it. I generally ride through some scenic little town that's so perfect Walt Disney might have designed it, and end up sleeping at some bleak motel out on the highway with a diesel idling outside my window, and dining on the last piece of fried chicken from a convenience store where they are just mopping up and their last customer looks like he's waiting for me to leave so he can rob the place.

I should make a little sign and put it on the inside of my fairing that reads, "On the other side of Paradise is a great abyss."

It was almost dark when I headed for Idaho Falls, and I made it a few hours later.

Luckily, Idaho Falls is anything but a great abyss. It's a lovely little city right on the Snake River, with a nice park right around a real set of waterfalls (hence the name, I suppose). Unfortunately, all the motels were full.

Well, not quite. A helpful clerk at a big chain motel called all over town and found one room left, a cancellation at a remarkably inexpensive place across the river. "You'd better head over there right now," he said. "This is, literally, the last room in town."

"Tell them to hold it for me," I said, slamming on my helmet without bothering to fasten the chin strap. It was starting to rain when I found the motel.

Seldom have I been so glad to see a flat bed, a roof, and four walls.

I ate that night at a nearby restaurant that was just closing but let me in anyway, then had a beer at a brew pub that was also just closing but let me in anyway.

Perfect timing, once again. Another big victory for intrepidness and the Western concept of linear progress.

And nothing so warms the heart of the weary, wayward traveler as the sight of chairs stacked upside-down on tables, the quiet clack of salt shakers being refilled by a tired waitress, the reassuring sound of the night manager locking doors from the inside, and the shriek of a vacuum cleaner picking up bread crumbs left by customers who dined much, much earlier.

July 2001

THE WORLD'S MOST FAMOUS BIKE?

During the Geology 101 course I took at the University of Wisconsin, I was always a bit disconcerted by the similarity between the shape of the last great North American glacier and the big blue peninsula of cold temperatures depicted on the Midwestern weather map during the winter months. It looked like a perfect overlay, as if winter were just practicing for the next Ice Age.

And never more than this past winter. It was pretty severe here in the heartland, causing a pandemic of cabin fever. So when my wife Barbara had spring break from the school where she works as a physical therapist, we decided to head south.

The airlines, of course, were overbooked to all the really hot places on Earth, but we found a couple of tickets on a flight to San Antonio, Texas. Home of the Alamo, the River Walk, Tex-Mex food, etc. Not Cozumel, exactly, but warmer than Wisconsin, so off we went.

Nice city, San Antonio. We stayed, literally, right across the street from the Alamo at the famous old Menger Hotel (where Teddy Roosevelt once recruited his Rough Riders), took in the River Walk sights, drank margaritas, heard some live jazz at the Landing, and ate well.

But as any sensible person will tell you, this kind of lightweight fun is good for about two days of diversion, and then you have to See Some Bikes. Or ride. Or something. To the mechanically minded soul, a hardware-free vacation is something of an oxymoron. Rub shoulders for a few days with throngs of non-riding tourists and you begin to feel like a timber wolf at the zoo. Too much zoo, not enough timber.

Luckily, I had an ace up my sleeve. Our friends Herb and Karen Harris had invited us to drive our rental car up to Austin and stay overnight.

Herb is a Vincent collector extraordinaire. I can hardly open a classic motorcycle magazine these days without seeing an article about one of his bikes or projects. He has a large collection of Vincent memorabilia and has gradually assembled what is doubtless the world's best collection of famous racing Vincents.

I flew down to Austin three years ago to do a story on one of his daily riders, a 1951 Series C Black Shadow, and ended up selling virtually all the vehicles I owned to buy the bike—which I later sold to pay off our house loan.

Now I have a piece of paper called a deed and no Vincent. Real smart. But, despite my faulty thinking, Herb and I have stayed friends ever since.

A few changes have been made since my last visit. In 1998, Herb had five or six bikes parked in his spacious living room, with a couple of daily riders out in the attached garage. Now he has a new addition to the house that includes a large motorcycle display room and a guest apartment upstairs. The display room has the aura of a men's club in London, with dark wainscoting, polished wood floors, and a bar along one wall.

I pointed out to Herb that the bar was sorely in need of a Guinness tapper, but he just smiled and said, "Everyone has a different idea of what kind of drinks should be served in here."

Still, Guinness is fundamental. It's the Black Shadow of dark, heavy stouts. I'm not even sure Vincents make any sense unless you've got one in your hand. No doubt Herb will come around and do the right thing.

In any case, this is the display room we all dream of. And there were a few new bikes. Herb has built himself a beautiful hot-rod Shadow with straight pipes, Lightning cams, high-compression pistons, and modern electronic ignition, and he has also acquired the famous Marty Dickerson 1948 Rapide "Blue Bike" speed-record holder.

Nearby stands the Reg Dearden supercharged Black Lightning, a factory supported land-speed effort that went unfulfilled when Vincent stopped production in 1955. He's also got beautiful Series A and B Rapides, a BSA Gold Star, and a nice 1965 Bonneville. New acquisitions out in the "regular" garage are a Ducati 996 S ("The world's greatest half-hour bike," Herb says), a lime-green Triumph Speed Triple, and a BMW R1100RT.

But the centerpiece of the collection, to me, is still the Rollie Free "Bathing Suit" bike, the Bonneville record-setter from 1948, on which Free became the first man to ride an unsupercharged motorcycle at 150 miles per hour, while stripped down to swim trunks and bathing cap and lying flat on the rear fender to cut drag. There have been many other celebrated Vincents—George Brown's *Gunga Din*, *Nero,* and *Super Nero* and so on—but the Rollie Free bike is still The One. For me, at least.

After a nice dinner with Herb and Karen, Barb and I walked through the bike gallery on our way to the guest apartment and I stopped to look at the Rollie Free record bike for a few minutes before turning out the lights.

There it was, menacing and many-jointed as a black widow spider, still with no seat and that Mobilgas Flying Red Horse emblem on the tank. Just like the *Life* magazine photos taken the year I was born.

I've got pictures of this bike in at least 12 Vincent books on my shelf, and in piles of magazines collected over the years. There's a poster of it on my garage wall.

In this quiet moment of bike contemplation, I had to ask myself, *Is this the most famous motorcycle on Earth?*

Arguably, it is. What other bikes are in the same league?

Any of T. E. Lawrence's Brough Superiors, perhaps. Particularly the one on which he was killed. The Hailwood Isle of Man Ducati, certainly, though there seems to be an ongoing dispute over which one was the real TT bike. In the "Life Imitates Art" Department, I suppose the Captain America and Billy Bike choppers from *Easy Rider* are in this category, though both of those were stolen and parted out long ago.

But in the mythology of motorcycling, there aren't many bikes that cast a larger—if you'll excuse me—shadow than the 1948 Bonneville bike.

Before I left the room and went to bed, I rested my right hand for a moment on the twistgrip. But I didn't twist it. Some things you just don't mess with. You could be struck by lightning.

Or haunted by the ghost of Phil Vincent himself. Which, in a house like the Harris's, can easily happen. And does.

January 2002

SO MANY BIKES, SO LITTLE PROGRESS

A few weeks ago, in a sudden fit of energy, I decided to clean my office. This is something I do occasionally to avoid real work, as it provides the illusion of progress when, in fact, nothing is happening. Can't just stare into space, or sit on the porch and drink coffee. People would think I was useless.

So there I was, whistling and cleaning and unearthing mail I should have answered during the first Bush administration, when I accidentally tipped over my large cardboard box of random old photos. My wife Barbara actually organizes pictures chronologically into a photo album, but I throw snapshots into a box. The plan is, someday when it's snowing and there's nothing else to do that day, like open a Guinness and watch *V Four Victory* again, I'll organize them into albums. I'm sure this will happen. Meanwhile, there were pictures all over the floor and I had to scoop them up and put them away. As I grabbed a big handful, I happened to notice one very old picture in particular. It was a snapshot someone had taken in 1975 showing me standing in front of my workbench at Foreign Car Specialists in Madison, Wisconsin, where I worked as a mechanic for six years.

Good times. When I got out of Journalism School at the University of Wisconsin, I couldn't find a writing job, so I went to work as a foreign car mechanic, specializing mostly in British sports cars—MGs, Triumphs, Jaguars, etc. Truth be told, I didn't look very hard for a writing job, because I wanted to race, and this was a shop where nearly everyone raced. We'd work on customers' cars all day, then push our race cars in at night and work on them. It was here, also, that I later started racing motorcycles, with a Honda 400F.

This photo must have been taken on a weekend, because it's daylight and my work area has two racing cars in it, both painted British Racing Green. One was the Lola 204 Formula Ford I'd just bought, and the other was my H-Production Austin-Healey Bugeye Sprite, which I had just sold to pay for the Lola. The new owner hadn't picked it up yet.

And, parked next to the two cars, we have my two motorcycles of the era. One is a brand-new black-and-gold Norton 850 Interstate and the other is my dark-green 1973 Honda CB350G, which I was just about to sell to help pay for the Norton. I'm standing nearby with an untrimmed beard and the usual bushel basket of hair from the era. I look like a cross between Grizzly Adams and Doug Clifford from Credence Clearwater Revival. And if you know who those guys are, you're probably as old as I am.

It's a changing-of-the-guard picture; two of my favorite vehicles are being sold to make room—and money—for two more. These were the early days of my lifelong Transportation illness. In 1975 I was a mere lad of 27 and had owned, at that point, only 11 cars and 6 motorcycles. Such simple times, like the Dawn of Man.

Yes, the Lola was my 11th car (if you count three derelict parts cars) and the Norton was my 6th bike. There have been a few more since then.

One a recent cross-country trip with my friend Tom Cotter, we sat in a bar one night in Frisco, Colorado, and counted up all the vehicles we've owned, writing them down on napkins. I came up with a lifetime count of 42 cars (including vans) and 44 motorcycles. Tom was low on bikes, but was able to tabulate something like 78 cars. Always refreshing to have a few beers with someone who makes you look almost sane.

But back to the snapshot.

I stared at that photo for a while and realized that I now have two of those same vehicles in my garage, after all this time. I have a nice clean green 1973 CB350G, as mentioned here recently, and last spring I bought a basketcase Lola 204, which is this coming winter's restoration project. Don't have a Norton Commando at the moment, but I will almost certainly get another one eventually. Can't help myself. The Austin-Healey Sprite?

My old race car—the one in the photo—is at this minute sitting on an open trailer next to a house about 25 miles from here. The owner has left it outside in the weather for at least 10 years, and I have tried a couple of times to buy it back from him. Unfortunately, we differ on our perceptions of the car's value, so it continues to sit. Maybe I'll talk him out of it eventually, and have a kind of ersatz reunion of the Class of 1975 in my garage. All I'll need is another Norton.

So, if this little time capsule of bikes and cars is still so desirable, why on earth have I spent the past 26 years buying, selling, restoring, fixing, and trading an additional 31 cars and 38 motorcycles? What was it all about, Alfie?

Well, it was about adventure and experimentation. It was about riding in the dirt, crossing continents, experiencing new technology, hearing exotic and different sounds from the tips of mufflers, going faster, racing, doing track days, restoring beautiful old things that needed to be saved, and just exercising my God-given right as an American to be curious and restless.

Still, after all this time, the picture makes me smile just a bit at my own self-delusion. Looking at it now, a couple of things occur to me:

First, if I'd been forced at gunpoint or by some crazy law to keep that 1975 collection forever, I would hardly have experienced any hardship at all during the intervening years. Okay, I might have needed a more reliable two-up touring bike than the Norton, but aesthetically and emotively there was nothing missing. This was a great little group of cars and bikes, and I'd be perfectly happy to have them all right now. In fact, I almost do.

Second, there's the money. Since then, I've had cheap bikes and I've had expensive bikes, but I've never found the slightest relationship between the cost of a motorcycle and the amount of pleasure it afforded me. None.

Yet, even now, this hard-won wisdom doesn't stop me from looking at bikes in all price ranges, from virtually free to ruinously expensive, without prejudice. In fact, I see there's a Honda CBX in the paper today. Never had one of those…

As Tom Petty says, might as well go down swinging.

INDEX